A BROAD AND LIVING WAY

A BROAD AND LIVING WAY

Church and State
A Continuing Establishment

JOHN MOSES

The Canterbury Press
Norwich

© John Moses 1995

First published 1995 by The Canterbury Press Norwich
(a publishing imprint of Hymns Ancient & Modern Limited,
a registered charity)
St Mary's Works, St Mary's Plain,
Norwich, Norfolk, NR3 3BH

British Library Cataloguing in Publication Data

A catalogue record for this book is available
from the British Library

ISBN 1–85311–112–0

*Typeset by Waveney Studios
Diss, Norfolk
and printed in Great Britain by
St Edmundsbury Press Limited
Bury St Edmunds, Suffolk*

'... an Establishment
that has a broad and
living way open to it,
into the hearts of the
people ...'

W. E. GLADSTONE
A Chapter of Autobiography (1868)

Contents

Acknowledgements   *page* viii

Preface   ix

PART I: ON BEING THE CHURCH   1
1 On Being the Church   3
2 The First Five Centuries   15
3 Theories of Church and State   33
4 The Roman Imperium   49

PART II: THE ENGLISH EXPERIENCE   65
5 The English Church   67
6 The English Tradition   84
7 The English Experience   106

PART III: PATTERNS OF ENGAGEMENT   131
8 Patterns of Engagement   133
9 The Law of Liberty   143
10 Indentity and Continuity   156
11 Critical Encounter   174

PART IV: A CONTINUING ESTABLISHMENT   191
12 A Continuing Establishment   193
13 A Contemporary Critique   206
14 A Broad and Living Way   218

Bibliography   249

Index   257

ACKNOWLEDGEMENTS

The writing of this book has been greatly assisted by the Ministry Bursary Award provided by the Ecclesiastical Insurance Group, which enabled me to spend a short period of sabbatical study leave at the Anglican Centre in Rome in the early months of 1994.

It has also been helpful to stay for very brief periods from time to time during the last two years at the St Julian's Community in West Sussex while some of the writing has been done.

I am glad to acknowledge my gratitude to the Director of the Anglican Centre in Rome and to the Warden of the St Julian's Community in West Sussex, together with their colleagues.

It has been helpful in the writing of Chapter 11 to draw upon the thesis submitted by the Revd Patrick Benson to the Open University for the degree of Master of Philosophy, regarding the causes and the effects of the church's confrontation with the state in Kenya during the last decade or so.

Little could have been attempted, however, without the support of my wife and colleagues and friends who have encouraged me in the writing of this book; but most especially I would want to acknowledge how much I owe to Mrs Anity Butt, who has worked strenuously and cheerfully to ensure that this book is prepared for publication.

Preface

This Worlde's Joie by William Matthias speaks of the season's of the year and the span of human life – Spring (Youth), Summer (Maturity), Autumn (Decline), Winter (Death) – and then of a transfigured Spring and re-birth. The spirit of this musical composition is conveyed by the final sentence of the Composer's note: '*This Worlde's Joie* makes no separation between the sacred and the secular; it is, throughout, an act of celebration'.

It is the relation of the sacred and the secular that lies at the heart of all discussion concerning church and state. The church is called to be a sign of the kingdom of God; and there has been from the earliest times an ambivalence in the thinking of Christian people concerning their relationship to the things of this world. But the church is also called to be a community of faith in the world; and the ordering of its affairs will inevitably reflect something of the structures, the culture and the expectations of the situation in which it finds itself. The historic expressions of the church-state relationship in Europe since the time of Constantine have been serious attempts to give practical and public expression to the relation of Christianity to the whole of life.

Every age is a time of transition, but the circumstances in which the church finds itself in Western Europe at the end of the second millenium suggest a period in which the church – all churches – will be greatly tested. The secularism of contemporary life calls in question the idea that the Christian faith has a comprehensive and compelling vision which enables men and women to make sense of their world. The vulnerability of all institutions leaves wide open significant questions concerning the ways in which people, living together in community, will actually move forward and make connections between the past, the present and the future.

The formal relationship of church and state is not one that easily commends itself, and it has therefore seemed right to provide in the first instance some account of the ways in which the alignment of church and state has taken place. It is easy for institutions to forget their past, but some understanding of the story is necessary if the bonds of unity – in church and state – are to be strengthened and renewed.

Patterns of engagement are bound to vary a great deal, and it is instructive to see the church responding at different times both in the light of its theology and of the actual historical circumstances in which it is placed. The church lives in an open relationship with society, but the nature of its association will be determined in part by its own self-awareness and self-definition. The corporate life of the church has been expressed in many ways – experience, movement, sect, institution and empire. These ways of being the church have influenced the church's response to the realities of secular life and temporal power.

Church and state are institutions whose ultimate purposes, although distinct, are not necessarily irreconcilable. It is in the English experience of the establishment of religion that so many of the historic interconnections between church and state have been embodied and brought forward. This book is, therefore, concerned to look from the inside at the Church of England – its story, its tradition, its experience. A wholehearted commitment to ecumenism must not be allowed to diminish the claims that might properly be made by all churches where their distinctive traditions and styles of ministry are concerned.

The identity and and integrity of the Church of England stand or fall not by its position in law as the established church, but by its continuing commitment to the principles of catholicism and reformation. The establishment of the Church of England, which is one of the peculiarities of English life, continues to represent something that is important in the life of both church and nation. But the process of progressive disengagement will undoubtedly continue, and questions about the meaning and the content and the appropriateness of establishment are bound to become increasingly pertinent.

The prospect of disestablishment is one for which there is no great enthusiasm in church or state, but there seems to be an inevitability about the process that must lead the Church of England eventually to establish a new concordat. The important questions appear, therefore, to be: What are the dominant characteristics of the church's relationship with the state throughout history? What are the principles that have been enshrined in the Anglican experience of establishment that might be judged to be fundamental to the life of both church and state? What is the theology that must inform the church's understanding of itself and of its relationship with society?

It has been helpful in attempting this task to draw upon the thinking of many observers of the English scene in successive generations. This book is concerned to argue unashamedly for a continuing establishment of religion in England. The separation of the sacred and the secular is not a notion that commends itself to this writer – either in theology or in the practical experience of ministry as a priest in the Church of England.

The bedrock of the church's life is to be found in the dynamic of scripture, tradition and reason. But there is within the experience of the Church of England a tradition of comprehension and liberality which, if it can be rediscovered, may yet serve the church as it attempts to pursue 'a broad and living way ... into the hearts of the people'.

Chelmsford   JOHN MOSES
February 1995

PART 1

ON BEING THE CHURCH

Chapter 1

On Being The Church

The church is called to be a sign of the kingdom of God. It is a community of faith in which God's purposes are perceived and acknowledged and proclaimed. Its original and distinguishing feature is the conviction that in Jesus 'the fullness of God was pleased to dwell, and through Him to reconcile all things, whether on earth or in heaven, making peace by the blood of His cross'.[1]

The scriptures, the sacraments, the creeds, the forms of ministry, the traditions of worship and prayer give shape and definition to the church's life. They provide the parameters within which the church can speak both of the personal call to holiness and of the public call to the transformation of the existing world order.

It is an inevitable consequence of being in the world that the church will take to itself the structures that are appropriate for the ordering of its life and work. These structures reflect not merely the church's self-understanding, but also the culture, the traditions and the expectations of the environment in which it finds itself. The apostolic and prophetic task of the church is contained within the framework of a community, a society, an institution.

There is, however, a culture of indifference, of cynicism, of despair which surrounds so many institutions at the present time. Institutions – like individuals – can be self-regarding and self-serving. They are vulnerable to complacency, manipulation, corruption and decay. There is inevitably a disparity between the ideal that they represent and the experience of what they are and what they do as they go about their work.

3

The church is no exception to this general rule. Moreover, the church will always carry within itself something of the ambivalence that is bound to determine its relationship to the things of this world. Jesus bore passionate witness to the sovereignty of God's kingdom. The church is required to wrestle with what it means to be a community of faith in the world.

The church cannot live its life in isolation from the world. It is mindful of its place within the divine economy; but it is required, nonetheless, to live in an open relationship with the wider community in which it is set. The priority of mission has led the church down the centuries to engage with the world.

The story of church and state might appear at first sight to isolate one aspect of the church's life; but the changing patterns of engagement between church and state represent serious attempts to give practical and public expression to the relation of Christianity to the whole of life.

Every church must regularise its relationship with the state. The observer of the European scene, looking back over the last sixteen hundred years, might assume that the establishment of religion in one form or another is the norm of church life. The conversion of Constantine and his public recognition of the church initiated the church's formal association with the state. But preceding any legal or constitutional alignment lay many generations in which the church had been required to engage with the world and to accommodate itself in one way or another to the realities of life.

The story of church-state relations has been determined by the church's theology and by the hard facts of history. There is an interplay between the church's perception of its task and the actual circumstances in which the church is placed at any time. It is impossible to achieve any understanding of the nature and the purpose of institutions unless something is known of their story: their origins, their development and the influences that have directed their course at any time. It is the lack of an historical perspective that impoverishes the church

– and not only the church – in so many areas of contemporary concern.

All students of the sociology of religion have been greatly influenced by the distinction between a sect and a church that has been made by Max Weber[2] and Ernst Troeltsch[3]. This fundamental distinction has been taken up and endorsed by Richard Niebuhr,[4] and he has gone further and addressed the wider but related question of how the church engages with contemporary culture.[5] The distinction between sect and church is important, but Troeltsch was also concerned to acknowledge that these types can be present at one and the same time. 'For Troeltsch, the individual mystic, the exclusive sect and the inclusive church are all endemic features of Christianity, even in its earliest phase.'[6]

Troeltsch's identification of the mystic as an experiential type of Christianity which might properly stand alongside the sect and the church acknowledges that the story of the church cannot necessarily be considered simply on the basis of either the sect-type or the church-type. It may, therefore, be helpful to trace as many as five phases in the life of the church: *experience, movement, sect, institution and empire.*

These phases go beyond the primary distinction between sect and church employed by Weber, Troeltsch and Niebuhr. They attempt to reflect more fully the variations that can be found in the corporate life of the church. They are all ways of *being the church*. They have in each case a theological and a pragmatic basis. They are expressions of the church's self-awareness and of its relationship with the world.

They must not be considered as a chronological progression that can be traced as one phase gives way to another. One phase will often predominate at any time, but the other phases will also be present in a developed or an embryonic form. They can be found in sequence and in parallel with one another. These phases or modes of being are well-established and continuing aspects of the church's life which are always bound to be present and which vie with one another for expression.

It is in the *experience* of redemption through the death and resurrection of Jesus Christ that the first phase of the church's life can be identified. There is a personal dimension. Jesus' proclamation of the kingdom continues to place before people the challenge of a radically new way of living in God and for God. The experience of the early church, illuminated and empowered by the Holy Spirit, is that if anyone is in Christ there is a new creation.[7] But there is also a corporate dimension. The church is a community of faith in which the believers are united in fellowship in Christ,[8] in the Spirit,[9] and with one another.[10] These are the abiding marks of the church in all phases of its development; but, in this first phase, there is an acute awareness of Christ's indwelling,[11] of the Holy Spirit's empowering,[12] and of fellowship and communion with one another.[13] Christ is the Head of the body.[14] The Spirit is the source of the church's life.[15]

The New Testament provides a remarkable insight into this experience of redemption in the primitive church at Jerusalem in the first generation. It is a characteristic of this first phase that there is both a profound intensity and an overwhelming sense of urgency that the good news must be shared. The first apostles spoke freely of all that God had done in Jesus, and called for repentance, confession of faith in His name, and baptism.[16]

There is no initial impetus towards the establishment of any religious association or cult. The life of the church as a sect – let alone as an institution or an empire – lies in the future; but the early and short-lived experiment in communism in the Jerusalem church, which might well be seen as the uncritical expression of the new and abundant life in Christ, is a good instance of attempting to work out corporately the experience of faith.[17] But there are other marks of the church's life which are also present at this stage as the new converts devoted themselves to the apostles' teaching and fellowship, to the breaking of bread and the prayers.[18] Experience within this first phase is not totally open, totally free. There are the first signs of self-awareness and self-definition as a community of faith.

There is an experience of redemption which belongs to the whole church in all phases of its development. This experience is not always easily articulated and will remain for large numbers of people something that is profoundly personal, elusive and unselfconscious; and yet it continues to be the bed-rock of Christian commitment and discipleship. But experience as a self-conscious aspect of the church's life continues to be an important phenomenon and manifests itself repeatedly throughout history.

It is nearly always the case that the church will move rapidly from experience to *movement*. Indeed, these two phases cannot easily be separated. The starting-point will be experience, but in this second phase the compulsion of the gospel and the dynamic of evangelism are paramount. The innate character of movement is expressed by the variety of ways in which the word is used. It is movement outwards. It is movement towards people and towards places. It is movement for a purpose. It is movement towards an end. The activity might be strategic or spontaneous but the church has a gospel to communicate and the urgent desire to do so.

The church has been a missionary church from the beginning – the early preaching of the apostles in Jerusalem;[19] the movement outwards prompted by the martyrdom of Stephen;[20] the missionary journeys of Paul.[21] It is clear that the newly established churches displayed great differences both in outward appearance and in their inner life. These differences were determined both by the tradition they had received from their respective founders and by the situation in which they were actually placed. Paul's letters to the church at Corinth amply demonstrate the intensity, the variety and the confusion of church life; but there is evidence that alongside these things there were also to be found the rudimentary forms of oversight, discipline, instruction in the faith, and pastoral ministry.

The strengths and the weaknesses of this phase of the church's life are best captured by words like strategy and spontaneity. There is an important sense in which these characteristics continue to mark subsequent movements in the history of the church. But the more developed phases of church life – sect and institution and empire – presuppose a high degree of self-consciousness and organisation. It is inevitable in these changed circumstances that movements will tend to be movements within the church rather than without.

The third phase of the church's life – the *sect* – takes us beyond experience and movement, although it represents a reversion to a primitive form of Christianity, based upon certain elements in what is believed to be the New Testament ideal. The sect is essentially a voluntary association. It places great importance upon the priesthood of all believers, the fellowship of the elect, and the autonomy of the local congregation. There is a clear distinction between those who belong and those who do not belong. Church membership is a matter of individual choice, and there is customarily a strong tendency towards adult baptism.

The sect will frequently reject authorised and ordained clergy. Belief is relatively clear-cut and a rigid orthodoxy is usually upheld. Much emphasis is placed upon the sovereignty of the bible and upon the responsibility of the congregation for the government of the church under the guidance of the Holy Spirit. The sacraments are often experienced as symbols of fellowship. There will frequently be found a rigorous interpretation of the ethical demands of the gospel.

The sect is a minority group. It is an exclusive community and the distinguishing mark of this aspect of the church's life is its separation from the world. Its fundamental stance towards the state and secular authority will be one of tolerance or indifference or hostility. It is separatist, even ascetic, in its attitude to the world. There is no desire to bring the wider community within its reach except on its own terms. There is always a tendency to reject secular life, to confront the world in a prophetic spirit of judgement, and to look for a new social order which is built upon its interpretation of the principles of the gospel.

There is one other thing that should properly be said. A sect defines itself by its separation from the world; but it can also be argued that a sect is an identifiable group from which assent is withheld, either by the prevailing secular authority and culture or by the prevailing dominant church. The Christian church could not be anything other than a sect while it battled for recognition in the early centuries. When the church became an institution, mindful of its dignity and the comprehensive nature of its authority, other groups which emerged within the life of the church were compelled to adopt the status of sects because their special requirements or characteristics or aspirations did not correspond with the uniformity which the institution was now imposing upon the life of the church.

It is the drawing of the line between inclusive and exclusive, between what can be permitted and what cannot be permitted, which is so significant where the church's awareness of itself as an institution or as a sect is concerned. It is unquestionably the case that the *institution* is essentially inclusive. This fourth aspect of the church's life requires a degree of self-confidence which has not been present in earlier phases. The church in this phase of its development is a comprehensive, all-embracing institution. Indeed, it has been likened to a social group analogous to the family or the nation.[22] Individuals are required to join a sect, whereas they are born into the church. 'Churches are inclusive institutions, frequently national in scope, and emphasising the universality of the gospel'.[23]

The institution is mindful of its identity, its integrity, its authority. It attaches great importance to the *depositum fidei* – the scriptures, the creeds, the sacraments, the orders of ministry. Its teaching function is exercised in large measure by a regular ministry that is both authorised and authoritative. It attempts to secure a fair degree of conformity in thought and practice. It does not live comfortably with the manifestations of church life that are abnormal, idiosyncratic, eccentric. It holds on tenaciously to the ideal of uniformity. It seeks to maintain control; but there is always implicit in its pastoral strategy a strong sense of the incarnation, because the institution is rooted in the life of the world and attempts to encompass within the wide embrace of its ministry all things earthly and heavenly.

It is important to insist that the institution, by contrast with the sect, is universal: that is to say, it is concerned with the whole life of humanity. It possesses the necessary degree of self-awareness and self-confidence to take its place in the world and to stand alongside other institutions. The dividing-line between church and state, church and community, is not always clearly drawn. Ecclesiastical authority and civic authority are two aspects of one society; and the institution is able to accept the existing social order and to accommodate the existing authorities in the political sphere.

The institution understands the complexities of life and the ambiguities of discipleship. Its engagement with the world will invariably involve the institution in compromise. Indeed, it will often be allied with – or be reckoned to be allied with – the political, economic and cultural interests of a nation or of the dominant class within society. But the church as an institution embraces, or attempts to embrace, everyone and everything. The institution becomes, therefore, an integral part of the social order and thus becomes an element of stability and continuity within it.

It would be inappropriate to assume that this fourth phase can only be discerned in later centuries when the early church had secured full recognition within the Roman Empire. One of the characteristics of the institution is that it has a philosophy of history. This philosophy will not usually receive formal expression in credal statements, liturgies, articles of religion or canon law; but it will be found in the writings of its most creative theologians. It is in this sense that Paul's theological interpretation of history, in asserting the universality of the gospel as he thought his way beyond the constraints of Judaism, can be seen to be so significant for the ages when experience and movement and sect had given way to institution and empire. Full account must always be taken of the modifications or variations, even at times the contradictions, that are to be found in each phase of the church's life; but the evidence of the early centuries suggests that the church moved forwards and backwards between sect and institution with even the first stirrings of imperial ambition.

A pattern emerges in all these phases in which the church first functions as a sect or an institution or an *empire* internally – that is to say, within the life of the church – before it functions in such a way externally in relation to the world. There is a line of succession in the early centuries which moves logically from authoritative statements concerning the monarchical episcopate[24] to the authority of the church[25] to the primacy of the Roman see.[26] But it is not only in the papal monarchy of the later middle ages that this fifth phase in the life of the church is to be found. It is there in a modified form in some of the churches of the reformation which, while they jettisoned the claims of the papacy, carried forward into the post-renaissance and post-reformation world the medieval concept of a unity of church and state within a Christian commonwealth in which the privileged position of the established church was enforced by penal legislation.

There are many parallels that can be drawn between institution and empire, but the all-important difference is essentially to do with the absolute nature of the claims that are made. It means in practice that the church, having stood alongside secular authorities and powers, is now concerned to contain and subdue them within the sovereignty and the unity it has finally secured. Proceeding from the premise that the natural is subordinate to the supernatural, the temporal to the spiritual, it is now the task of empire to insist that 'the state must be baptised, disciplined, directed and formed by the supernatural society of the church'.[27]

The universal claims of the church as an empire are in their most developed form unavoidably totalitarian in character. It is the custodian and the guardian of absolute truth which it defines and interprets. It assigns to its hierarchy juridical powers which cut across the legitimate responsibilities of others. It subsumes within its own life interests and activities that belong to the wider community. It shares with the church as an institution a philosophy of history, but it then imposes its theological and ecclesiological interpretation upon the world. There is a theological basis, and it can be found in the conviction that the church's mission is nothing less than the conversion of the world as a preliminary step towards the fullness of its redemption in Christ and its transformation in the power of the Holy Spirit. But any theological rationale that might be advanced must also acknowledge the exigencies of actual historical situations, the corruption of power, and the ambition to which individuals and institutions are vulnerable.

These five phases have been called aspects of the church's life, ways of being the church. They are broad categories, and they defy all attempts to apply them uncritically as the church's engagement with the world is explored at each stage of its development. There are too many qualifications that must be made, too many discrepancies and divergencies of which account must be taken.

There is, for example, the continuity of primary characteristics which enables the church to pass from one phase or mode of being to another. There can be no vitality in the sect, the institution or the empire if the experience of redemption is not renewed, if the gospel imperative of mission which lies at the heart of movement is not to be found. Nor will the phases of experience and movement make any abiding contribution unless they are able to respect the integrity of the church's faith and the authority of its ministry.

There is also the fact that these phases live in a series of open relationships with each other. The church is able to move forwards and backwards as one phase gives way to another, even though times of transition will often be marked by tension, divided loyalties, conflict. The sect can become an institution if it has the theology, the vision, the self-confidence and the desire to do so. The institution can contain within itself individuals and groups and congregations who behave in such a way as to suggest that the church is nothing more than a sect. The institution and the empire will have within their boundaries from time to time dramatic instances of experience and movement which they will learn from and accommodate, or contain with some misgiving, or seek to deny and suppress.

These broad categories remain, however, as being sufficiently firm, sufficiently definitive, to be helpful. The phases interconnect with one another at so many points. It is as though they represent five magnetic points in the church's life. Experience, movement, sect, institution and empire are the directions in which the church might be drawn at any time as pressures from without or within determine the ways in which it moves forward.

The church is a community of faith whose origins and whose developing life lie hidden in the purposes of God. But in its engagement with the world it is a society that is seen to be both natural and supernatural, temporal and spiritual. The story of the church is a tapestry in which the warp of faith is crossed time and again with the weft of event and personality and opportunity and situation. The interconnections lead inevitably to the realities of experience, movement, sect, institution and empire.

NOTES
1 Colossians i. 19–20.
2 Max Weber, *The Sociology of Religion*, Trans. by E. Fischoff, London 1965.
3 Ernst Troeltsch, *The Social Teaching of the Christian Churches*, Trans. by Olive Wyon, 2 vols. George Allen & Unwin 1931.
4 H. Richard Niebuhr, *The Social Sources of Denominationalism*, Meridan Books: The World Publishing Company 1971.
5 H. Richard Niebuhr. *Christ and Culture*, Faber and Faber 1952.
6 Robin Gill, *Prophecy and Praxis*, Marshall Morgan and Scott 1981.
7 2 Corinthians v 17.
8 1 Corinthians i 9.
9 Romans viii 14–17.
10 Ephesians iv 25.
11 Ephesians iii 17.
12 Acts i 8.
13 1 John i 7.
14 Colossians i 18.
15 Acts ii 1–4; Ephesians iv 1–5.
16 Acts ii 38.
17 Acts iv 32.

18 Acts ii 42.
19 Acts ii 14–40; iii 12–26; iv 8–12.
20 Acts viii 1.
21 Acts xiii i–xx 38.
22 H. Richard Niebuhr, *The Social Sources of Denominationalism*, Meridian Books: The World Publishing Company 1971, p. 17.
23 Ibid.
24 Clement of Rome, *Epistle to the Corinthians*.
25 Cyprian, *The Unity of the Catholic Church*.
26 Pope Innocent I, *Ep. 25.* to Decentius, Bishop of Eugubium.
27 Frank Gavin, *Seven Centuries of the Problem of Church and State*, Princeton University Press 1938.

Chapter 2

The First Five Centuries

It is in the first five centuries of the Christian era that shape and definition were given to the church's life. The seventeenth century tag employed by Anglican theologians – 'one canon, two testaments, three creeds, four councils, five centuries'[1] – bears witness to the conviction that these centuries were determinative for the fundamentals of faith and order, the all-important threads of continuity. But these centuries are important also in so far as they demonstrate the church's growing self-understanding and the changing patterns of its engagement with secular authority. It is possible to discern even in this earliest period of the church's life the phases of experience, movement, sect, institution and empire.

It is in the events of death and resurrection, transformed by the power of the Holy Spirit, that the Christian church finds its origins and raison d'etre. The infant church bore all the marks of first-century Palestinian Judaism. Indeed, it was generally judged at the outset to be a new movement within Judaism. Its first place of assembly for worship for the Christian converts in Jerusalem was the temple. Its scriptures were the Jewish scriptures. Its gospel or good news told of God's dramatic intervention in the death and resurrection of Jesus in fulfilment of His promises to Israel. Its earliest teachings were influenced by the traditions and disciplines of Judaism. Its earliest dilemmas were determined by the need to extricate itself from the requirements of the Jewish law.

The missionary work of the Jerusalem church appears to have been confined at the beginning to Jewish Palestine. But the Hellenists who fled, following upon the martyrdom of

15

Stephen, took the work forward in new areas; and it was among the young churches of the diaspora that the idea of a mission to the Gentile world was conceived and acted upon. Paul became the leader of the Gentile mission and he, together with Barnabas, secured at the Council of Jerusalem the recognition they sought for Gentile converts and for their freedom from the more rigorous demands of the Jewish law.

The church moved out of Palestine into Asia Minor and Greece, spreading rapidly throughout the Mediterranean world. It invariably put down roots in the first place in the cities and large towns, spreading slowly to the villages, and finally into the countryside. The early churches displayed great differences, but the Pauline letters suggest not merely a growing self-awareness but also developing patterns of worship and ministry and discipline and pastoral oversight.

The insecurities of church life were compounded by the lack of a developed tradition; by a vulnerability to spirit-inspired interpretations of the gospel; by the habits of sexual promiscuity within the prevailing culture; by the potential for deep division through heresy and schism; by the exclusiveness of the Christian body; by the hostility of the Jews; by spasmodic outbreaks of mob violence and, in due course, by periods of systematic persecution. But the limited evidence provided by the New Testament suggests that the infant church – in these early phases of experience, movement and sect – possessed the energy and spontaneity and incoherence that invariably mark a new and significant development in the religious story of humankind.

The liberation of the church from the constraints of Juadism prepared the way for its expansion throughout the Mediterranean world. The transition from experience to movement to sect was already taking place; but it was the internal needs of the church which required it to order its life in such a way that, sooner rather than later, it might appear throughout the Roman Empire as an institution which had identity, authority and cohesion.

The picture is necessarily obscure, but three circumstances can be identified which undoubtedly shaped the pattern of the church's response: the abandonment of the early expectation of Christ's second coming; the death of the apostles; and the early struggles against heresy. There was an urgent need to make long term arrangements for the maintenance and the development of its life and work.

It was in the evolution of the office of the bishop, in the provision of an authoritative tradition in the canon of scripture, and in the formulation of credal statements that the church fashioned for itself what have become the elements of continuity, the guarantees of order and unity.

The Pauline letters and the Didache[2] have much to tell us about the development of leadership and the differentiation of responsibility within the church. The apostles, prophets and teachers were of primary importance and continued to be significant until the beginning of the second century. There were clearly many places at this stage where bishops and deacons merely took their place among various forms of ministry in the service of the local church. The picture is uncertain and confused. There is no uniformity of practice or development. But the demise of the prophetic ministry and the need to give some wider frame of reference to the exercise of authority in the local church clearly counted for something; and it must also have been the case that in difficult times, and especially when the faith was under attack from gnostic influences, it was through the concentration of authority in a single person that the church was best able to maintain the integrity of its faith and witness.

It is in the writings of Clement of Rome,[3] of Ignatius of Antioch,[4] of Irenaeus of Lyons,[5] and of Cyprian of Carthage[6] that the developments can be most easily traced in the understanding of the office of the bishop as a focus of unity, as the custodian of the church's disciplinary powers, as the guarantee of continuity in apostolic faith.

It is Cyprian, writing in the middle years of the third century, who asserts that, 'It is impossible to have God as Father without having the Church as Mother'.[7] The unity of the church finds expression in the apostolic office of the bishop, and those who separate themselves from the bishop separate themselves from the church and, therefore, from the truth and from salvation. Cyprian's understanding of the church, which is inseparable from his understanding of the episcopal office, provided the church with one of the theological stepping stones which eventually enabled it to move forward from sect and institution to empire.

What had begun as a pastoral office within a small local community, possessing in many places in the first instance an inferior status and a subordinate authority, became one of the vital threads of continuity in the church, and the way was therefore prepared for its development as a public office in the wider world. But before the church and its bishops assumed their wider responsibilities in the late Roman Empire, the church was becoming 'a unity although it was embodied in thousands of churches and hundreds of bishops'.[8]

The apostolic office of the bishop was required to serve as the custodian and the guarantee of the tradition; but it was in the canon of the New Testament that the tradition finally took shape. There was a practical necessity to put in written form the earliest traditions concerning the words of the Lord and the writings of the apostles so that they might be available at all times and in all places – for instruction in the faith, for interpretation and exposition, and for the defence of the tradition.

It is yet again the apostles who were judged to be the authoritative bearers of the tradition. The need to defend the tradition against writings which were influenced by a gnostic spirit meant that recognition and authority were normally confined to what was believed to be the teaching of the apostles. The Pauline writings constituted the main body of the apostolic letters; and although the four gospels did not all claim apostolic authorship it was assumed that their integrity had been established by the working of the Holy Spirit in the church. It was only in the latter half of the second century that the canon of the New Testament took shape, eventually standing alongside the writings of the Old Testament and bringing their witness to completion.

The evolution of the episcopal office is parallelled in the emergence of the canon of the New Testament and in the formulation of credal statements. The free interpretations of the prophetic spirit were no longer trustworthy, and especially in the face of heresy. It was the apostles alone who could be acknowledged as 'the only unconditionally legitimate vehicles of the Spirit'.[9]

The earliest confession of the primitive church that 'Jesus is Lord' was the starting-point for the evolution of every credal statement, but there was from the beginning a great variety of expressions of faith which undoubtedly put us in touch with the teaching and the liturgy of the early church. The articles of faith to be found in the Apostles' Creed appear from about the end of the first century in the church's formularies; and the three-fold confession of faith in the Father, the Son and the Holy Spirit, which appears in the concluding greeting of St Paul's Second Letter to the Corinthians and in the baptismal formula at the end of St Matthew's Gospel, gave rise to a great multiplicity of Trinitarian creeds. The most important confessional statements concerning the nature and the work of Christ are found in the earliest surviving eucharistic prayer in the liturgy of Hippolytus.[10]

It is probably difficult to exaggerate the importance of the connection between credal statements, instruction in the faith, and public liturgy. Mention has already been made of the significance of spirit-inspired expositions and interpretations in worship until in the second century the responsibility for ordering worship passed in large measure to the bishop and the presbyter. But alongside the picture of early Christian worship provided by Paul in his First Letter to the Corinthians – speaking in tongues, prophetic interpretations, addresses, prayers, singing, the breaking of bread – there is evidence of the formulation at an early stage of Christian psalms or doctrinal hymns of praise. What is to be found here is all of a piece with the evolution of the episcopal office and the formulation of the New Testament canon. It was necessary for the church – for the sake of its own interior life and good order and development – to provide formularies of

faith which might both articulate the tradition and be appropriate vehicles for instruction and for employment in the
offering of worship.

It is nonetheless true that doctrinal statements maintained
throughout this period a fair degree of openness and flexibil-
ity. The creeds might properly be regarded as summaries of
the faith of the church, but they were also part of the liturgy
of the church and shared in the freedom of what can only
be called a living liturgy. There is an unfamiliar dimension
of vitality and spontaneity in the conclusion that 'in the
whole of the ancient church there are not two writers who
quote one and the same creed, and even one and the same
church father formulates his 'creed' differently on different
occasions'.[11]

The historic creeds of the early church have become for
later centuries one of the authentic marks of the church's self-
definition as a community of faith. But in their developing
forms – and in their contexts – they provide echoes of the
tradition which found expression in instruction for the cate-
chumenate, in the rite of baptism, in the proclamation of the
gospel, and in the celebration of the eucharistic liturgy.

Implicit in all these things – the evolution of the episcopal
office, the emergence of the canon of scripture, and the
formulation of credal statements – is the development of a
theological tradition which constitutes also one of the vital
threads of continuity and which speaks eloquently both of
the church's self-awareness and of its desire to engage intellectually and critically with the world.

Irenaeus has been regarded by many as the father of
Christian orthodoxy. He was mindful of the roots of the
Christian tradition and he drew freely upon Pauline thought.
His first concern was to defend the tradition against sectar-
ian and heretical movements, and his major work *Adversus
Haereses* was directed against the teaching of the gnostics.
Irenaeus belongs to a theological tradition which stands
unashamedly within the life of the church, and which draws
together the authentic elements in the apostolic tradition in
its exposition of the integrity of the gospel.

It is, however, in the writings of the Apologists[12] that a significant development can be discerned. Their work dates from the middle years of the second century. They were concerned, like Irenaeus, to propose a rational or philosophical account of the world in its relation to God. They covered common ground – the unity and the transcendence of God, the doctrine of creation, the idea of the logos, the problem of evil. But their distinctive contribution was to offer a reasoned defence of the Christian faith and to commend it to men of education. Their writings do not belong to a single literary type, but they have a common concern in the relation of Christian faith to the pagan world. They stood by and large within the mainstream of Christian orthodoxy, but they were concerned to write on the boundaries of intellectual thought and philosophical enquiry.

It is this tradition of writing, reconciling the claims of faith and reason, which demonstrated more than anything else the church's self-confidence and its willingness to engage in public dialogue. The Mediterranean world possessed a common intellectual culture, and in the writings of the Apologists the dialogue with the presuppositions of pagan philosophy became conscious and explicit. But it was Origen[13] who, belonging to a slightly later period, built upon the work of the Apologists in his desire to show that the principles of the Christian religion could be reconciled with the thought of the Greek philosophers. He attempted to provide a systematic theology which brought together the Christian understanding of God and the world and man in a way that corresponded with the ideas and values that constituted the Hellenistic world-picture.

The evolution of Christianity as a Gentile rather than a Jewish religion by the end of the third century was due in part to the development of a rational theology in the Greek tradition. The dialogue with the culture of the Mediterranean world preceded the advent of Christianity. The Jews of the dispersion had long since translated the law and the prophets into the Greek tongue. The interpretation of the Hebrew scriptures had inevitably drawn upon Greek thought. Greek philosophy had, therefore, provided ideas and forms of language which are to be found in Christian writings of the first and second centuries. But the significance of the Apologists cannot be exaggerated. It was they who took 'the final and crucial step towards the conquest of the world by Christianity: they won the spirit of Greek science for the message of the church'.[14]

The emergence of a theological tradition – rational, systematic and apologetic – marked one more important step along the way as the church took its place as a public institution with a world-view which dared to make comprehensive claims to faith and obedience.

The evolution of a robust theological tradition coincided with the church's emergence throughout the Mediterranean world as the possessor of a large constituency of support. The church had become by the end of the third century a sizeable and influential minority throughout the empire and beyond. There had undoubtedly been great fluctuations in the fortunes of the churches, but the church had continued to grow through a process of individual conversions. The church cut across the requirements of the Roman Empire that any particular religious faith should be confined to its respective national community. The church had no such community to which it could be confined. Its claims were universal. It drew into itself all the peoples of the empire. The church had been a *religio illicita* – a prohibited faith – throughout the periods of persecution from the time of Nero[15] until the Edict of Milan in 313. But during these early centuries there had been intervals of relative quiet in which the church attempted to establish a *modus vivendi* with the wider community.

There is ample evidence of the desire of Christian people to share fully in the life of the secular world. Tertullian, writing at the beginning of the third century and drawing presumably upon his experience of the church in North Africa, maintains that 'in living in this world, we make use of your forum, your meat market, your baths, shops and workshops, your inns and weekly markets, and whatever else belongs to your economic life. We go with you by sea. We are soldiers or farmers. We exchange goods with you, and whatever we make as a work of art or for use serves your purposes.'[16]

The same theme is taken up at a similar period by the unknown writer of the Epistle to Diognetus: 'The distinction between Christians and other men is neither in country nor language nor customs. For they do not dwell in cities in some place of their own, nor do they use any strange variety of dialect, nor practise any extraordinary kind of life. (They follow) the local custom both in clothing and food and in the rest of life'.[17]

The church was learning as it moved from one phase or mode of being to another to accommodate the world and to accommodate itself to the world. Several professions had been judged from the begining to be irreconcilable with Christian discipleship, but by the beginning of the second century the absolute prohibition on Christians serving in the imperial armies was being abandoned. And yet the church continued to make comprehensive claims upon its members. The picture of church life provided by *The Apostolic Tradition* of Hippolytus portrays the church as 'an omni-competent social organism, exercising a stringent moral authority over all its members ... from the cradle to the grave. Worship, edification, social life, benevolence and phil-anthropy are all included in the scope of the Christian community's consciousness'.[18]

The church continued to grow in prestige and self-confi-dence, surviving successive outbreaks of persecution, and holding now in high regard the large numbers of martyrs who had died for the faith. The number of believers increased not only among the population at large, but among the educated classes. Christians had been inhibited in earlier times from holding public office in the government of the city or the state, because it was believed that the worship of pagan gods, the offering of worship to the emperor, and the power of the sword were all inseparable from such office. By the early years of the third century, Christians were often released from the obligation to offer sacrifices, and there is evidence of Christians taking their place in the administrative life of the empire. By the middle of the third century the right of the church to own property was recognised. New and larger churches were being built, and it is probable that there were more than forty churches in Rome by the beginning of the fourth century. Christianity had entered the bloodstream of the Mediterranean world.

Eusebius, writing at the beginning of the fourth century immediately prior to the final and most terrible outbreak of persecution, tells that 'Christians were to be found at court and in the army, and might freely confess their faith; the bishops enjoyed respect in their contact with the provincial governors and, indeed, occasionally Christians reached the highest posts in the administration'.[19]

And yet, there has been from the beginning an inherent ambiguity in the relation of Christian people to the world. The writer of the Epistle to Diognetus comments upon 'the wonderful and confessedly strange character of their own citizenship ... They dwell in their own fatherlands as if sojourners in them, they share all things as strangers. Every foreign country is their fatherland and every fatherland is a foreign country'.[20]

It is exactly here that we are brought to the rub of the church's relation with the Roman Empire. The experience of the church went beyond ambiguity. Tertullian, while emphasising the solidarity of Christian people with the normal life of the community, was at pains to insist that 'we do not join in your festivals to the gods, we do not press wreaths upon our heads, we do not go to plays, and we buy no incense from you'.[21]

The chief complaint against the church lay in the fact that Christians constituted an identifiable group within society whose supernatural loyalty compelled them to refuse to offer worship to the emperor. Christianity was unacceptable largely because its adherents would not acknowledge the divinity of the emperor. But it was precisely the worship of the emperor that gave to the Roman Empire whatever cohesion it possessed. It was the bond of unity. It is the measure of the church's progress through the various phases of experience, movement, sect and institution that, 'In a comparatively short time the Christian church became an enclave within the Roman Empire, a kind of *imperium in imperio*'.[22]

The church was judged to be hostile, or potentially hostile, to the established order. The prevailing climate was not infrequently one of insecurity. Local outbreaks of mob violence gave way to periods of persecution which varied in their severity, and which in turn gave way to periods of toleration and peace. There is some evidence of defection at times of persecution; but there was never any lack of strong-willed bishops who urged the church to withstand all forms of oppression; and Tertullian's dictum for the church under persecution – that the blood of the martyrs is the seed of the church – remains as a testimony to the sacrifice of the martyrs.

It was in the decade immediately prior to the conversion of Constantine and the Edict of Milan that the church suffered one of the most thoroughgoing periods of persecution. Christians were deprived of the legal protection which the state gave to its citizens. The court and the army were purged. Privileges were removed from all members of the upper classes who professed the Christian faith. Churches were destroyed; sacred books were burnt; clergy were arrested and imprisoned, and every attempt was made to compel them to recant. This final and grievous onslaught against the church had scarcely run its course when another event, the conversion of Constantine, provided an entirely different way of coping with the strength of the church and initiated a new and decisive phase in the history of church and state.

The conversion of Constantine represented an important break with the earlier pattern of relationships. The publication of the Edict of Milan in 313 was a recognition of the church's legitimacy and of its right to exist. The church gained freedom for worship and equality with all other religions. Buildings and lands that had been confiscated were returned and financial privileges were granted to the clergy as the church began to enjoy the advantages of imperial favour. The process of disintegration within the Roman Empire had gathered pace since the middle years of the third century. Constantine's overriding concern was the unity of the empire. It was almost as though he was concerned to found the Roman Empire afresh and to do so on the basis of the Christian religion. Constantine did not make Christianity the official or established religion of the empire; but he was concerned to take the vitality of the Christian church and to weave it into the fabric of the empire as a bond of unity.

The long process initiated by Constantine continued throughout the fourth century. Constantine was active in building new churches, and surviving fragments of his legislation suggest a variety of areas in which Christian thought influenced law-making. But Constantine was prepared to move cautiously in the work of Christianising the empire, whereas his sons[23] moved far more speedily, and it was they who ordered the closure of pagan temples and forbade the offering of sacrifices to the pagan gods.

There was a brief period of relapse during the reign of the Emperor Julian (361–363) who, taking seriously his role as *pontifex maximus* of the empire, believed that he was called to restore the ancient cults of the gods. But the final victory of the church was within reach and, with the restoration of the church to favour following upon his death, the legal status that had previously been granted to the church and to the clergy was restored, together with the sources of income and the privileges they had enjoyed. Pagan sacrifices were forbidden; all ancient customs regarding the pagan religions were discontinued; and with the repeal of the edict of tolerance by Gratian in 379 every form of worship outside the catholic church was prohibited.

It was with the edict of Theodosius I and Gratian and Valentinian in 380 that Christianity became the official religion of the Roman Empire, but it was 'the religion taught by St Peter to the Romans' that was enjoined upon all peoples in the empire.[24] Great emphasis was placed upon doctrinal orthodoxy: bishops were required to hold the faith of the Council of Nicaea(325), and subsequent laws underscored the validity that the emperors gave to the doctrinal formulae published by the Council of Constantinople(381). The emperors were acting in concert to promote the privileges of the church; and with the decree of May 383, prohibiting the renunciation of the Christian faith, the final significant step was taken along the road of securing for the Christian faith the privileged position of absolute primacy and pre-eminence as the established religion of the Roman Empire.

The significance of these years lies in developments of far greater importance than the demise of the pagan gods and the eventual triumph of the Christian church. Constantine made no concessions in asserting the comprehensive responsibilities of his imperial office. He was persuaded that he had been entrusted by God with 'the rule of the whole world ... in order that I should watch over it'.[25] His address to the bishops at the Council of Nicaea reminded them that, 'You have been installed bishops for the inner affairs of the church, and I have been installed by God for its outer affairs'.[26] But there were no hard and fast lines of demarcation in Constantine's mind between inner and outer affairs.

It was the empire's need for unity which encouraged Constantine to intervene in the affairs of the church. The point had been reached when the unity of the empire and the unity of the church could not be considered in isolation from each other. Divisions within the church – Donatism[27] in North Africa and Arianism[28] in the East – were threatening the unity of the empire. Troublesome bishops were removed from their sees in the interest of uniting the empire through the church, but the significant step forward lay in the calling of the first ecumenical council of the church, the Council of Nicaea in 325, in order to address questions of faith and order.

It is difficult to exaggerate the importance that the church has attached down the centuries to the four great ecumenical councils – Nicaea(325), Constantinople(381), Ephesus(431) and Chalcedon(451). In every case they were summoned by the emperor to address questions and controversies that were

dividing the church through heretical teaching. Their significance lies not merely in any doctrinal synthesis or resolution
that was achieved, but in the greater unity they secured and
in the movement towards a greater centralisation of authority within the church.

Constantine was undoubtedly moved by political considerations when he called the Council of Nicaea. His presence
at the council throughout its discussions and his response in
publishing the conclusions of the council as imperial edicts
testify to the importance he attached to its work. But it is
doubtful if the church could have called such a council into
being at that time; and certainly there was no consensus
within the church which would have taken it unaided down
the path of greater coherence, greater agreement in fundamental matters of doctrine, greater unity – and all on the
basis of a greater centralisation of authority.

The second development of great significance in the fourth
century concerns the authority of the bishop of Rome. There
is no doubt that the roots of the Roman primacy go down
deep into the early story of the church. It was, perhaps,
inevitable that Rome, imperial Rome, should attempt to
assume the primacy of honour and jurisdiction. Rome was
the only church in the west which could trace its list of
bishops back to the apostolic age; and Rome became, therefore, the apostolic authority of the church in the west at an
early date. By the middle years of the second century the
leadership of the Roman church had become monarchical
rather than collegiate in character.

Repeated attempts were made to assert the Roman
primacy, but these attempts were not readily and universally
conceded. Claims to pre-eminence were resisted, and especially by the churches of the east, and most notably by
Cyprian for whom the unity of the church was a mystical
reality, which was demonstrated visibly in the unanimous co-
operation of the bishops. Peter's call to primacy was for
Cyprian a symbol – no less and no more – of the unity of the
apostolic office. There was a single church which was incar-
nated in several individual churches; and, in exactly the same

way, there was a single episcopal office which was embodied in its individual holders.[29]

There was a notable increase in the claims of the Roman see during the latter half of the fourth century, and these were frequently supported by imperial decrees and, if occasion required, by the use of force. It was the catholic orthodoxy of the bishop of Rome and of the emperor that was acknowledged by the edict of Theodosius I in 380. But the all-important development in the west lay in the dualism that emerged with the episcopal authority exercised by the papacy alongside the political authority exercised by the emperor. Pope Gelasius I, writing to the Emperor Anastatius I in 494, set out the position with great simplicity: 'The world is chiefly governed by these two – the sacred authority of bishops and the royal power'.[30]

It was this understanding of church-state relations in the west that was endorsed by Augustine, writing in the early years of the fifth century, with his model of a continuing dialogue and tension between the two cities, heavenly and earthly. But it was the strength of the papacy that ensured the survival of a dual authority in the west, at least until such a time as the papacy had extended the scope of its authority and jurisdiction to the point where it could make claims that were unashamedly imperial as the sole arbiter of all things in heaven and on earth.

It would not have been possible to foresee the decisive shift in church-state relations, in both the east and the west, that would be brought about in the course of the fourth century. The earlier cycle of ridicule, toleration and persecution had given way to one of recognition, active endorsement and establishment. By the end of the fourth century the extent of the church's expansion was plain for all to see. Many large churches were becoming substantial landowners. The bishops were required to represent the secular needs and interests of their people over and above their spiritual functions. There is clear evidence that Christian thought influenced imperial legislation in matters relating to personal and family relationships, the ownership of property and usury. The underlying structure of society remained in place – private property, slavery, finance, trade, military power – but the church would wrestle over the centuries with questions concerning the ways in which it might best use the advantages and the opportunities it now possessed. A Christian influence extended itself gradually, and not least of all in education, in literature and in art, even though the traditional models of Greece and Rome continued to exercise a pervasive influence.

The conversion of Constantine had led inexorably to the association, if not actually the incorporation, of church and state in each other. In the east, the process of Christianising the empire reached its culmination in the Emperor Justinian[31] in the sixth century, who presided over a church-state in his roles as *imperator* and *pontifex maximus*. Taking the model provided by Constantine, and building on the foundations laid by Constantine and his successors, Justinian developed the caesaro-papism which shaped the pattern of church-state relations in the east. In the west, the dual authority of the papacy and the empire held sway, albeit at times in an uneasy tension, but church and state were so closely associated that the interests of both often appeared to be identical. In the east and in the west, the church had become a vital element in the fabric of society. Beyond the early phases of experience and movement and sect, there lay for the church the realities of institutional life and the beckoning prospects of imperial power.

There has been an ambivalence in the western church from time to time about all that is represented by the conversion of Constantine and by this thoroughgoing association and identification of church and state. But the point had long since been reached in the numerical growth of the church when the unity of church and state were interconnected and could not be easily disentangled from each other. The pattern of church-state relations which had now evolved was to determine in large measure the history of Europe – in the east and in the west – and still informs so many of the underlying presuppositions which influence the life of church and state.

NOTES

1 Cited by H.R. MacAdoo, *The Spirit of Anglicanism*, A. & C. Black 1965. p. 320.
2 The *Didache*. An early Christian manual on morals and church practice. 1st or 2nd century.
3 Clement, Bishop of Rome, c.96.
4 Ignatius, Bishop of Antioch, c.35–c.107.
5 Irenaeus, Bishop of Lyons, c.130–c.200.
6 Cyprian, Bishop of Carthage, d.258.
7 Cyprian, *The Unity of the Early Church*. Cited by Hans Lietzmann, *A History of the Early Church*, Trans. by Bertram Lee Wolf, Vol. II, *The Founding of the Church Universal*, Lutterworth Press 1960, p. 231.
8 Hans Lietzmann, *op.cit.*, p. 68.
9 Ibid., p. 97.
10 *The Apostolic Tradition* of Hippolytus. c.225.
11 Hans Lietzmann, *op.cit.*, p. 115.
12 The Apologists. Christian writers (c.120–220) who include Aristides, Justin Martyr, Tatian, Athenagoras, Theophilus, Minucius, Felix and Tertullian.
13 Origen, c.185–c.254.
14 Hans Lietzmann, *op.cit.*, p. 177.
15 Claudius Nero, Roman Emperor. 37–68.
16 Cited by Hans Lietzmann, *op.cit.*, Vol. II, pp. 153–4.
17 Epistle to Diognetus 5.
18 Frank Gavin, *op.cit.*, p. 11.
19 Hans Lietzmann, *op.cit.*, Vol. III, p. 58.
20 Epistle to Diognetus 5.
21 Tertullian, *Apologeticum*, 42.
22 Frank Gavin, *op.cit.*, p. 11.
23 Constantine II, 317–340. Constantius II, 317–361. Constans, c.323–350.
24 Cited by Cyril Garbett, *Church and State in England*, Hodder and Stoughton 1950, p. 14.
25 Cited by Hans Lietzmann, *op.cit.*, Vol. III, p. 153.
26 Ibid., p. 159.
27 Donatism: A schismatic tradition within the African Church which owed its origin early in the fourth century to opposition to Christians, and especially bishops, who had surrendered the scriptures during the persecution of Diocletian. The Donatists refused to recognise the validity of the sacraments administered by such bishops and clergy.
28 Arianism: A heretical body of teaching which, taking its name from Arius, denied the divinity of Jesus. The teaching of Arius was condemned by the Council of Nicaea in 325, which used the term *homoousios* to express the consubstantiality of the Father and the Son. But the influence of Arianism persisted throughout the middle years of the fourth century until the orthodoxy of the catholic faith as expressed in the Nicene Creed was finally endorsed at the Council of Constantinople in 381.

29 Cited by Hans Lietzmann, *op.cit.*, Vol. II. p. 255.
30 Cited by Adrian Hastings, *Church and State: The English Experience*, University of Exeter Press 1991, p. 9.
31 Justinian I, Roman Emperor, 483–565.

Chapter 3

Theories of Church and State

It is one of the marks of the church's growing self-awareness that there should have been in these later generations in the early history of the church some serious attempts to address questions concerning the relations of church and state. It is misleading to speak of *theories* of church and state; but the assertions that are made from the time of Ambrose,[1] while they might lack the completeness of fully developed theories, represent firm, comprehensive and dogmatic attempts to define the sources and the boundaries of authority.

There is a conviction to be found throughout the New Testament that all power belongs to God;[2] but the nature of church life in the first generation did not require that any thought should be given to the practical working out of wider questions. The picture of Jesus presented in the gospels suggests a pattern of engagement and confrontation; but the eschatological hope of the early church determined the thrust of apostolic preaching and pointed beyond the things of this world to the judgement that the Father had committed to the Son.

It was, perhaps, inevitable that some interpreters in later ages should have seized upon a handful of verses in the New Testament to justify specific ways of addressing or resolving the questions concerning church and state. But there is nothing in the New Testament to justify such a use of scripture, and the few references that can be found concerning the behaviour of Christian people in relation to secular authority do not provide any theological basis for patterns of relationship that properly belong to later centuries.

Three passages have been improperly cited as the foundation of a New Testament understanding of church and state: Jesus' saying concerning the payment of tribute to Caesar;[3] Paul's remarks concerning submission to the governing authorities;[4] and the admonition in the First Letter of St Peter to be subject to every human institution.[5]

It may well be that Jesus' saying concerning the payment of tribute to Caesar was preserved and employed to defend Christians against false charges of disloyalty to the emperor;[6] but there is no enunciation in this passage of any principle concerning church and state, or of their respective spheres of responsibility. Jesus does not deny the authority of Caesar; but He does urge all who will listen to look beyond their immediate concerns and to acknowledge the claims of God.

Paul's remarks in his Letter to the Romans constitute a strong statement concerning the duty of Christian obedience; but they bear no relation to the main thrust of Paul's theology which is concerned with the person and the work of Christ. It may be that Paul was concerned in this passage to bring early enthusiasts back to the practicalities of living in the world. What can be stated is that these seven verses do not provide an adequate basis for any theory concerning the nature and the limits of Christian obedience to the state. There are unhappy instances that can be cited throughout history of submission by the church to the predominant power of the state; but these verses cannot be used to justify compliance or collusion.

The admonition in the First Letter of St Peter to be subject to every human institution for the Lord's sake serves as an introduction to a longer section in which the subordination of the Christian is held up as an ideal. The disciple is urged to engage in all the relationships of life in a spirit of self-giving according to the example of Christ.

There is, nonetheless, implicit in these passages a recognition of secular power as one of the realities of life. This basic awareness, coupled with the injunction in the First Letter to

Timothy to pray for those in authority,[7] suggests that the state is an instrument that may be used by God. Its primary function is the maintenance of good order and the punishment of wrongdoing. The authority of its officers is exercised within the permissive and moral will of God.

The modern distinction between the church and the wider community had no meaning in the ancient world. The city-state of Greece and the pagan empire of Rome, together with the theocratic state of Israel, all spoke of a fundamental unity of life. Moreover, the evolution of the church – through its various phases of experience, movement, sect and institution – coincided with significant developments throughout the Roman world. The expansion of the empire, the mingling of the races, the proliferation of various cults and mystery religions had all prepared the way for the worship of the emperor as the bond of unity. 'A congeries of peoples and tribes and cities, lacking any such strong tie as the modern sentiment of nationality, could find no other bond of union except a common religion.'[8]

But the church's response has never been one of unqualified acquiescence. The pattern of Jesus' public ministry speaks powerfully of the ambivalence that will inevitably determine the church's relationship to the things of this world. He bears a passionate witness to the sovereignty of God's kingdom. He makes absolute demands upon those who would find the new life to which He calls. But this ambivalance is to be found also in some of the early expositions of the meaning of the gospel. Alongside all that has been said about the explicit references to secular power in the New Testament, there must be set some acknowledgement of the theological convictions – that Christ's redemption has brought deliverance from bondage to the elemental spirits of the universe;[9] that the mortal combat in which Christians are engaged is with the principalities and powers, with the world rulers of this present darkness;[10] and that the world, the present order, is passing away.[11]

The rejection of the world, which is never allowed to stand without qualification in the New Testament, is reflected in some of the non-canonical Christian writings of the first and second centuries. The Epistle of Barnabas urges its readers to 'loathe the error of the present time, that we may be loved for that which is to come'.[12] The First Epistle of Clement of Rome speaks of the church as 'the special portion of a Holy God'.[13] The Didache begins with its distinction between the ways of life and the ways of death, and its insistence that 'there is a great difference between the two ways'.[14] The Shepherd of Hermas introduces his series of Visions, Mandates and Parables with the picture of God's holy church transcending the whole created order, so that God for the sake of 'His elect ... may fulfil to them the promise which He promised with great glory and rejoicing, if so be that they shall keep the ordinances of God, which they received with great faith'.[15]

But the ambivalance that is to be found in the church's teaching in these early generations should not be pressed too far. The theological statements and the pastoral judgements did not relate to constitutional or juridical questions concerning the spheres of authority that properly belong to church and state. They were concerned to address the prior question of what it means to be a community of faith in the world. It is only in this context that early expressions of acknowledgement, acquiescence, renunciation or hostility can be properly understood. But the prior question is important; and the response of the church to constitutional questions in later ages would be shaped, at least in part, by implicit judgements about the world and its relation to God and the nature of secular power.

The church continued to grow, leaving behind the early phases of experience and movement, learning to cross the boundary between sect and institution. But the church's growth – numerical, doctrinal and administrative – did not alter the fact that there were considerable variations at any time as communities of believers found themselves at different stages of development, wrestling with the problems posed by their own situations.

The emergence of three movements in the early history of

the church – mysticism, Montanism and monasticism – threw into sharp relief the questions concerning the church's engagement with the world. These movements, which have continued to appear in a variety of forms in later centuries, were characterised in some instances by a tendency to separate themselves from the church's institutional and organisational life and to stand in judgement over against the church and the world.

Mysticism is a universal phenomenon that is to be found in all religions. It appeared early in the story of the Christian church. Its primary emphasis is upon the knowledge of God – direct, personal and inward – which can be attained in this life; and evidence of mystical experience is certainly to be found in many of the church's most profound and sophisticated minds. But mysticism can also degenerate into a spirit-religion, characterised by the enthusiastic possession and exercise of the Spirit's more dramatic gifts, rejecting the established forms of religious life, and with a tendency to create spiritual ghettoes in which the mysteries of salvation can be appropriated by those who have been initiated.

Montanism was an apocalyptic movement that appeared in the second half of the second century. It lived in expectation of the imminent outpouring of the Holy Spirit on the church, of which it saw the first signs in its own prophets. The movement soon developed ascetic traits and it was noted, especially in North Africa, for its rigorous ethical teaching and discipline. Enthusiasm and prophecy were the two dominant characteristics of Montanism. The movement had its parallels in the earliest years and has been seen by some as a reversion to the early fervour of the primitive church in the face of the church's growing confidence as an institution in the wider life of the empire.

One early and enduring attempt to secure the ideal of a purified and thoroughgoing Christian profession and Christian community is to be found in the monastic movement. The solitary life of the desert fathers was primarily an affirmation of living with and for God. Behind the developed forms of monasticism in later centuries lay the primary

emphasis upon the call to holiness and the corporate life
which is embodied in the rules that order the community and
determine the practical behaviour of its members to one
another.

It is one of the paradoxes of church history that a movement which had its origins and the mainspring of its inspira-
tion in these things should have become one of the
foundation stones of Christian civilisation. The monasteries
of medieval Europe made a massive contribution to agricul-
ture, architecture, scholarship, government and community
life. They became the custodians and the transmitters of the
culture of the western world. But the starting-point had been
the prior question about what it means to make a Christian
profession and to be a community of faith in the world. It is
as though monasticism was required to carry on behalf of the
whole church this primary call to holiness, thus setting the
institutional church free to engage on its own terms with the
world in which it was set.

It is possible to trace in all these things a continuing
emphasis upon the prophetic tradition of a righteous remnant. It is undoubtedly there in these various movements; but
it is also to be found in the story of the early church as a
whole. The Christian church, although it was woven into the
fabric of society through the activity of its members, came to
have an independent existence. A young missionary church,
which had grown beyond the constraints of Judaism, was
necessarily required to explore the ways in which it could
relate as a community of believers to the wider community to
which it belonged. The response, in so far as general judgements can be permitted and sustained, appears to have been
increasingly one of participation with a fair degree of spiritual detachment.

It may well be that Augustine,[16] writing at a far later time,
nevertheless succeeded in capturing something of the spirit of
such a response, when he wrote of the heavenly city living in
the earthly city as 'a captive in its pilgrimage'.[17] The promise
of redemption and the gift of the Spirit have already been
received, but the heavenly city 'does not hesitate to conform

to the laws of the earthly city whereby are administered the things suited to the maintenance of mortal life'.[18] There was for the Christian a double loyalty previously unknown in the ancient world. The church, which evolved as sect and institution, taking its place eventually alongside the state, came therefore to represent 'the final breakdown of the old imperial idea and the starting-point of a radically new development'.[19]

It was inevitable that the growing significance of the church as an institution throughout the empire should raise critical questions regarding the nature of its relationship with the state. The building-blocks of the church's institutional life had long since been put in place: the episcopal office, the canon of scripture, the credal statements, the theological tradition. In the course of the fourth and fifth centuries, following upon the conversion of Constantine and the establishment of the Christian religion, the ecumenical councils secured for the church both a wider measure of agreement in doctrine and a greater centralisation of authority. The establishment of the church was a public recognition of the fact that the unity of the church and the unity of the empire were inseparable from each other.

The church took its place in the course of this long process of evolution as an institution with its own autonomy and authority in areas outside the jurisdiction of the state. The relationship of church and state was one that the ancient world had not been required to address. The uniqueness of the church's position lay in the affirmation of the dual nature – and, therefore, of the dual loyalties – that Christian disciples as individuals and the Christian church as an institution were required to carry and sustain.

There is a paradox at the heart of the dualism that now informs the church's response to the questions raised by its increasingly deep involvement in the affairs of state. But paradox had been present from the beginning in the church's understanding and presentation of the gospel – law and grace, the wrath of God and the divine compassion, faith and works. Paradox had been present also in the ambivalence

which dominated the church's teaching in the apostolic and
sub-apostolic ages as it addressed the perennial question of
being in but not of the world. Dualism represented a practical working out of the paradoxes that are implicit in the faith
and life of the church. It was concerned to hold together in
tension things which can easily be distinguished but
which might also be complementary and necessary to each
other.

The church depended, especially during the early years of
toleration and establishment, upon the continuing goodwill
and active support of the emperor. The position that was
now taken by the church, and especially by its bishops, in
public affairs meant that points of conflict were bound to
arise. Church and state had come to represent institutions
whose ultimate purposes, although distinct, were not necessarily irreconcilable. Dualism provided important boundary
markers; and yet, although serious attempts were made to
define and determine the areas of jurisdiction, there was a
strong sense of the complementarity of the responsibilities to
be carried by church and state. It is this understanding of the
complementarity of civil and ecclesiastical power that is so
important. What was being rediscovered through these definitions of authority was something that approximated to the
ancient concept of the unity of life – in government, in
community, and in citizenship.

It is in the writings and work of Ambrose, Augustine,
Gelasius,[20] and Justinian that there can be traced the earliest
approaches to theories of church and state. They did not
provide coherent philosophies of church-state relations. They
understood the realities of power. They were mindful of
the dignity of the church and its apostolic calling. They were
concerned to address practical questions and they were
required to do so at a formative period. Their writings,
their sermons, their political judgements and interventions
greatly influenced Christian thought over the centuries to
come.

The first significant assertion of the integrity and the
autonomy of the church was made by Ambrose. He was well

placed as the confidant of three emperors to experience at
first hand the presenting problems; and it was through a
succession of incidents in the course of his episcopate that he
emphasised the rights of the church. His understanding of
the appropriate relation between state and church can be
inferred from his intervention in the debate concerning the
removal of the pagan altar of victory from the senate house;
in his refusal to make churches available to the Arians at the
request of the dowager empress; in his protest against the
order of the Emperor Theodosius to rebuild the synagogue at
Callinicum; and in his excommunication of Theodosius for
the massacre of the people of Thessalonika following upon
rioting against the local governor.

Ambrose was a mighty champion of Christian orthodoxy,
an administrator, a pastor, a preacher. He brought to his
involvement in the politics of his day his understanding of
the scriptures and of the dignity and authority of the church.
State and church – or, to be more precise, the state in the
person of the emperor and the church in the person of its
bishops – had their specific areas of responsibility and jurisdiction. The state had full responsibility for the work of
government, including the maintenance of public order; but
it was the duty of the church to act as the guardian of the
state's conscience. The church had full responsibility for
resolving all matters of faith and discipline; but it was the
duty of the state to see that the church was able to reach such
decisions in the councils of the church and to ensure that they
were enforced.

But there is in Ambrose's understanding of these things an
important dimension which derives from the fact that a
Christian emperor must inevitably have a different kind of
relationship from his pagan predecessors with the church
and its bishops, with its teaching office, and with the exercise
of its discipline. It is this awareness that is to be found in
Ambrose's assertion that 'the emperor is *within* the church,
not *over* the church'.[21] It is this conviction which makes
it possible for Ambrose to insist that 'in a cause of faith,
bishops are wont to judge Christian emperors, not emperors

to judge bishops'.[22] It is this all-important dimension which led Ambrose to state without any qualification that the emperor had no rights over sacred things: 'To the emperor belong the palaces; to the bishops the churches. To the emperor is committed jurisdiction over public buildings but not over sacred ones'.[23]

State and church are no longer to be regarded as mutually exclusive spheres of activity. They do not exist in isolation, and their different responsibilities should only be exercised if full account is taken of the needs of each other. What is, therefore, being required is an inter-penetration of state and church. But there is a significant shift of emphasis. The state is not to be identified with the church, but the ultimate authority – because the emperor is a *Christian* emperor – lies within the church and its jurisdiction.

It is unquestionably Augustine, whose conversion to the Christian faith owed much to Ambrose, who exercised the greatest influence upon the thought of later ages, and not least of all in the understanding of church-state relations. Augustine – like Ambrose – was caught up in the turmoil of his day, and his theological writings must be seen in the context of all that was happening in church and state. His theology was formulated and expressed as he confronted the Manichaean heresy, the Pelagian movement, and the Donatist controversy which inflicted deep division upon the church in North Africa. But it was the sack of Rome by the barbarian invaders in 410 which made such a profound impression upon contemporary observers; and it was against the background of this event and the questions that it raised in men's minds that Augustine sought to write about the relation of human history to the purposes of God.

Augustine's writing was always theological and apologetic in character, and the *De Civitate Dei* is no exception. He brought to this work his awareness of the divine purpose and his strong sense of the majesty and the triumph of the catholic church. He contrasted earthly polities which rise and fall with the city of God which, although manifested in the world, remains eternal. He attempted to show how the earthly and the heavenly cities interconnect, even though they remain fundamentally different in their essential nature. The two cities, the earthly and the heavenly, are not to be understood as the state and the church under other names. They are not two societies standing alongside each other with their own structures and spheres of responsibility. They are, rather, two principles, embodying respectively love of self and love of God.

The state was for Augustine – as it had been for Ambrose – a part of the natural order and, therefore, a divine necessity. The church – the church that is visible and militant here on earth – is not to be identified with the *civitas dei*, but it is – at least in part – a symbolic, albeit inadequate, representation of the *civitas dei*. Augustine does not suggest that the secular and the ecclesiastical authorities are two complementary and interdependent powers.

Augustine did not attempt to provide a developed theory of state and church; but he did bequeath to later centuries the idea of a Christian commonwealth, together with a philosophy of history which sees such a commonwealth as the crown and climax of God's purposes and of man's spiritual development. It is undoubtedly the case that much of the influence of *De Civitate Dei* in the middle ages was based on a misunderstanding of its true meaning. The empire and the papacy were both to use Augustine to justify their claims to pre-eminence. The chief significance of Augustine's writing lies in the fact that it encouraged an attitude of mind which could see the *civitas dei* as a church-state built upon the foundations of catholic Christendom, and which led – directly or indirectly – to an understanding of the church's task and role which was unashamedly imperial.

It is the writings of Pope Gelasius I which appear on first sight to define most clearly the complementary powers of state and church; although a closer reading – as with Ambrose and Augustine – suggests at the very least a primacy of honour and probably something approaching a pre-eminence of jurisdiction for the church.

Gelasius' brief but important pontificate was something of

a landmark in the development of the papacy. He was tenacious and zealous in upholding the primacy and jurisdiction of the Roman see, and especially in regard to the claims of Constantinople. He was inevitably caught up in the controversies, the dissensions and the practical questions that arose out of Arianism, Pelagianism[24] and Manichaeism[25]. His understanding of state-church relations can be traced in the letters written to the Emperor Zeno in 489 and to the Emperor Anastasius I in 494, and in the so-called fourth *tractate*, generally known as the Tome of Gelasius.

The relationship of the emperor to the church is determined in large measure by the fact that he is a *Christian* emperor. Gelasius' letter to the Emperor Zeno is remarkably reminiscent of Ambrose's enunciation of the relationship that must subsist between the Christian emperor and the Christian bishop. It is the emperor's duty 'to learn what is the content of religion, not to teach it. He has received the privileges of his power in civil affairs from God ... It is God's purpose that the bishops should be responsible for the administration of the church, not the secular powers; the latter, if they are Christian, according to His will ought to be subject to the church and to the bishops'.[26]

It is in the letter to the Emperor Anastasius I that the classical statement regarding state and church as Two Powers or Two Swords receives its fullest definition. Gelasius compared and contrasted secular and spiritual powers, discriminating clearly between what is imperial and what is episcopal. This idea of the Two Powers influenced the thinking of state and church throughout the medieval period, but Gelasius was not concerned to provide some permanent resolution of state-church relations, but to establish a rational ground for the conviction that the church's authority in spiritual matters is pre-eminent. His injunction to the emperor is plain, 'that though in your office you preside over the human race, yet you bow your head in devout humility before those who govern the things of God and await from them the means of your salvation'.[27]

The theological basis of Gelasius' thinking is enlarged

upon in the fourth *Tractate* in which both *sacerdotium* and *regnum* are derived from Christ, the one true Priest-King, who distinguishes 'the respective duties of each power by its appropriate functions and distinctive office'.[28] The jurisdictions of church and state – of bishop and emperor – are to remain distinct and separate, bound by the mutual regard that they have for each other. 'Thus it was provided that Christian emperors would be in need of bishops for the sake of eternal life, and bishops for the sake of the good order of this temporal world would observe imperial ordinances.'[29]

The writings of Ambrose, Augustine and Gelasius have much to say – implicitly or explicitly – about the Christian church as the basis of unity within the empire, about the scriptural conviction that all authorities and powers are ordained by God, about the interdependence of secular and spiritual power and the appropriate relationships of emperor and bishop, about the idea – tentative but potentially significant – of a Christian commonwealth. It is, however, in the eastern empire and the eastern church through the work of the Emperor Justinian I that these foundation principles of church and state were taken to a logical conclusion.

Justinian was the most energetic of the early Byzantine emperors. He was concerned to establish the political and religious unity of the empire in the east and in the west, and he provided a sound juridical basis for the empire in his legal code. He was resolute and vigorous in his defence of Christian orthodoxy, in his persecution of heresy, and in the work of conversion. He has been called 'the most conspicuous theologian of the sixth century'.[30] His influence has determined the pattern of church-state relations in eastern and orthodox Christianity, but it has also informed developments in the western world in the medieval period and at the time of the reformation in the sixteenth century.

Justinian's work has four important features: the unity of church and state; the role of the emperor; the tradition of law; and the necessity of enforcement. Justinian made no distinction between the secular and the sacred. The temporal and the eternal, the material and the spiritual, find their origin in God. Society is a unity; and it is, therefore, called to be both state and church. It is only on the basis of these principles that the emperor can exercise his proper role as *imperator* and *pontifex maximus*. He has received his imperial power from God and implicit in this responsibility is an active and influential oversight of the church. It was, therefore, a matter of principle for Justinian that he should be deeply involved in the appointment of bishops, the enforcement of doctrine, and the general ordering of church life. But he was no less concerned to ensure that the bishops were invested with civil authority and played a full part in the general life of the empire.

The authority that Justinian exercised in relation to the church derived from the power of universal visitation which is built into his legal code.[31] Justinian's revision of the Code of Theodosius was supplemented by further constitutions and digests, and these together formed the *corpus juris civilis* which became the authoritative statement of Roman law. The Code of Justinian brought the Roman tradition of law within the bounds of the Christian tradition, providing the foundation document for the civil law of society and for the canon law of the church. But alongside the tradition of law lay the necessity of enforcement, and Justinian – in his relation to the church-state over which he presided – wrote into his legislation the use of force against pagans, heretics, schismatics, Jews and unbelievers. The will of the emperor, zealous for the unity of church and state, gave a legitimacy to the high degree of state absolutism in ecclesiastical affairs which has characterised the Byzantine tradition of church life down the centuries.

There is much here that picks up and interprets in a new way the traditions of the ancient world concerning the unity of life and of human society. Justinian's influence has been discerned not only in the eastern church, but in Charlemagne's vision of the Holy Roman Empire and in the distinctive characteristics of the English reformation, which placed such strong emphasis upon the unity of church and state, the role of the sovereign, the tradition of law, and – for several centuries – the necessity of penal legislation.

Justinian represents one model of church-state relations in which the empire becomes a spiritual reality, taking to itself the traditions and purposes of the church, but in return for which the church loses something of its independence and autonomy. In the west – influenced in large measures by Ambrose, Augustine and Gelasius in the earlier centuries – there is some continuing awareness of the duality and complementarity of secular and spiritual powers; although there is also to be found a gradual movement towards a society that is both theocratic and hierarchical and in which the church moves inexorably beyond experience, movement, sect and institution to the age of empire.

NOTES

1 Ambrose, Bishop of Milan, c.339–397.
2 St John xix 11; Romans xiii 1; Hebrews i 3; Revelation ii 26.
3 St Matthew xxii 15–22; St Mark xii 13–17; St Luke xx 19–26.
4 Romans xiii 1–7.
5 1 Peter ii 13–17.
6 D.E. Nineham, *The Gospel of St Mark*, Penguin Books 1963. p. 314.
7 1 Timothy ii 1–2.
8 George H. Sabine, *A History of Political Theory*, George G. Harrap 1957. p. 165.
9 Galatians iv 3.
10 Ephesians vi 12.
11 1 John ii 17.
12 Epistle to Barnabas, c.70–c.100. Epistle to Barnabas, para. iv. J.B. Lightfoot, *The Apostolic Fathers*, Macmillan, 1926. p. 271.
13 First Epistle of Clement of Rome, c.96, para. xxx. J.B. Lightfoot. *Ibid*. p. 69.
14 The Didache, 1st or 2nd century. The Didache, para i. J.B. Lightfoot, *Ibid*. p. 229.
15 The Shepherd of Hermas, c.140–c.155. The Shepherd of Hermas, Vision I, para. iii. J.B. Lightfoot, *Ibid*. p. 407.
16 Augustine, Bishop of Hippo, 354–430.
17 Augustine, *De Civitate Dei*, xix 17.
18 Ibid.
19 George H. Sabine, *Ibid*, p. 165.
20 Gelasius, Bishop of Rome. d.496.
21 Ambrose, *Against Auxentius on the Giving up the Basilicas*, para 36.

22 Ambrose, *Letter* 21, para 4.

23 Ambrose, *Letter* 20, para 19.

24 Pelagianism: A theological tradition, deriving from the teaching of Pelagius early in the fifth century, which taught that the first steps towards salvation are taken by a person's own efforts rather than by the supernatural assistance of divine grace.

25 Manichaeism: The teaching of Manes or Manichaeus in the third century, which combined a cosmic dualism – a primaeval conflict between light and darkness – with a severe asceticism. It was influential in the African Church in the fourth century.

26 Cited by T.G. Jalland, *The Church and the Papacy*, SPCK 1944. p. 326.

27 Ibid.

28 Ibd., pp. 328–9.

29 Ibid., p. 329.

30 Frank Gavin, *op.cit.*, p. 7.

31 R.W. Chuch, *On the Relations Between Church and State*, Macmillan & Co. 1899. p. 19. (An article reprinted from the Christian Remembrancer. April 1850).

Chapter 4

The Roman Imperium

The early church, influenced profoundly by the traditions of the Roman Empire, bequeathed to the medieval world the ideal of a universal society. The full realisation of this ideal was to be found in the western world and in the western church only in the later centuries of the middle ages.

The centuries that followed immediately upon the sack of Rome in 410 were dominated by the invasion of the Barbarians, the migration of peoples, the dismemberment of the empire as a political reality, the settlement of new peoples in what had previously been the western provinces of the empire, the establishment of the early kingdoms, and the formation of alliances by which state and church attempted to secure their positions.

Even as late as the end of the sixth century the empire was still the only significant political reality, providing some sense of continuity with the ancient world. But between the sixth and the ninth centuries, Western Europe became increasingly self-contained as the responsibility for its political fortunes passed inexorably into the hands of the invaders, the new settlements and the early kingdoms, who had finally broken the structure of imperial administration.

From the time of Constantine the unity of state and church had been interconnected in the minds of emperors and bishops alike, but the unity and well-being of the church depended in part upon the power of enforcement and coercion. The political unity within which an enlarged Christendom had been set was fast being eroded and by 700 three of the five ancient patriarchal churches had disappeared as

Christendom lost North Africa, Syria and Palestine to Islam.

The expansion of the church continued throughout this period in the western world as it had done from the fourth century through the conversion and baptism of whole communities, either in response to the example of their leaders or as a consequence of a policy of coercion. It was in large measure in this way that the Christian church extended its influence in Western and Northern Europe. The papacy continued to assert its claims to pre-eminence, assisted by the vacancy created in Rome itself as the balance of political power moved to Constantinople and the Byzantine emperors proved to be incapable of defending Rome. Pope Gregory II's firm response to the Eastern Emperor in 729 indicated the emerging constituency where papal claims to oversight and jurisdiction would not be lightly gainsaid. 'The whole west has its eyes on us ... It relies on us and on St Peter ... whom all the kingdoms of the west honour as if he were God Himself.' [1]

It was in the Holy Roman Empire, established by the coronation of Charlemagne as Emperor of the West by Pope Leo III in 800, that the ideal of the universal Christian society was briefly realised. It has long since been suggested that Charlemagne's empire was built upon the foundations of Augustine's *De Civitate Dei*.[2] It was to be a Christian commonwealth, the City of God on earth. But it is no less apparent that the Holy Roman Empire – and the role of the emperor within it – owed much to the theology and work of Justinian. Charlemagne established a secular theocracy which was reminiscent of the caesaro-papism associated with Justinian and the Byzantine Emperors.

The Frankish kings had embraced catholic Christianity, and this was to be the common denominator – spiritually and culturally – of Charlemagne's empire. Christendom had lost by the end of the eighth century whatever political unity it had previously enjoyed, and Charlemagne held out the prospect of a new unity in which the catholic faith was to be the integrating force. But the unity that Charlemagne required could only be achieved if evangelization and civilization went forward together. The church had maintained its pattern of organisation and its tradition of scholarship. Its missionary work now had aspects that were unashamedly political and educational: it was concerned to unify and to civilize.

For Charlemagne, as for Justinian in the sixth century, the Christian Prince is the one in whom *imperium* and *sacerdotium* are brought together. There is an acknowledgement of the spiritual independence of the church and of the unique prerogative of the papacy, but Charlemagne took from the ideal of a Christian empire the rights and responsibilities of imperial oversight. The independence of the church and the prerogative of the papacy can only be exercised within the unity of the empire and the sovereignty of its emperor.

The Frankish kings legislated on religious matters by means of general enactments called *capitularia*. These are a miscellaneous collection of laws, edicts, canons and injunctions drawn from a variety of sources. They constitute a *corpus* of legislation for a Christian society. They speak of a thoroughgoing interest in the welfare of the church. Charlemagne's authority over and within the church extended to doctrinal matters, liturgical reform, the nomination to bishoprics, the conversion of heretics, the education of the clergy, the disciplining of clergy for ecclesiastical offences, and political and religious reforms.

Within the newly established framework of absolute government in Western Europe, the church strengthened its position in society and secured significant advantages. It was the achievement of the Frankish kings and emperors to lay the foundations of the church's power in the centuries to come – through the appropriation of glebe land to the church; through the payment of tithes; through the extended jurisdiction of the clergy; and through the increased power of the clergy in relation to questions of marriages and wills.

The promise held out by Charlemagne was not fulfilled. The empire disintegrated after his death, and barbarian raids to the north and to the east in the tenth and the eleventh centuries inflicted a new age of disruption and anarchy upon the western world. But the ideal of the Holy Roman Empire was never abandoned and it found expression – politically and ecclesiastically – throughout European history over a period of a thousand years. State-church relations revolved in large measure around attempts either to separate or to hold together *imperium* and *sacerdotium*. There is an abiding conviction implicit in the Holy Roman Empire, which has never been entirely lost, that 'it is the Christian world as a whole ... that is the entire church, and makes up the entire commonwealth'.[3]

The church had been since the fall of Rome the main custodian of the ancient traditions of public authority and civil order. In the period of disorder that followed upon the break-up of the Frankish empire large units of administration with a strong centralised authority could not be sustained. The organisation of society and of government was required to be essentially local. Land was the basis of wealth, and its significance within the life of the local community was underscored by the Germanic tradition of law, which placed great emphasis upon the relation of law and custom to the locality or territory of the people whom it supported.

It was precisely in a situation in which land and law had become the basis of relationships that feudalism emerged as the organising principle of the mutual obligations which serviced and sustained the life of the local community. Feudalism developed in many different ways, but it provided a network of relationships – personal and public, legal and moral, economic and social – which dominated the eleventh and the twelfth centuries. It was related to people and property. It gave public expression to the obligations of the lord and his vassals. It had important consequences for the traditional bases of power – the army, the revenues, and the administration of justice. It provided a structure within which the hereditary principle could take root both in land and in public office.

Feudalism strengthened the determination and the ability of secular authorities to intervene in matters that touched directly upon the life of the church and the exercise of its spiritual authority. In the early middle ages the papacy had attempted to support the independence of bishops in the newly established kingdoms and to strengthen their line of accountability to Rome. But feudalism represented a comprehensive pattern of organisation that was essentially local. It embodied a cluster of interests – land, property, law, custom, relationships, obligations – and it was inevitable that kings and great magnates and the lords of estates should attempt to maintain and to extend their own authority within their areas of jurisdiction.

The interests of state and church had long since been judged on both sides to be interdependent. The church had asserted its claim to spiritual autonomy, but it had also welcomed and worked hard to secure over more than half a millenium a tradition of deep involvement on the part of the state in ecclesiastical affairs. This tradition of engagement and involvement had touched every aspect of the church's life. Emperors had summoned councils of the church and had been encouraged to enforce doctrinal orthodoxy, to persecute heretics, and to assist the conversion of pagans. Kings and magantes had founded bishoprics and monastic houses. Landowners had been encouraged to build churches on their estates and to make provision for the maintenance of the priest. Glebe land had been given to the church. The tithe had been established. The clergy had been given jurisdiction in many areas of life.

No one doubted that temporal power was of divine origin. What was believed to be the Augustinian tradition spoke of an all-embracing Christian commonwealth which brought temporal power into the service of the church. Charlemagne's Holy Roman Empire had given expression to this ideal. The Gelasian theory of the Two Powers or the Two Swords continued to be influential. Power was exercised within one society, a Christian society, but in practice the emperor and the pope represented the two principles of authority, secular and spiritual, which had their origin in the natural and the divine law.

The unity of the western church was centred on Rome and was identified increasingly throughout the middle ages with the papacy; but the degree of local episcopal autonomy and, indeed, of lay involvement was significant in a feudal society. Secular influence had frequently been exercised in the appointment of bishops and abbots, and differences of opinion at the time of episcopal elections presented opportunities for intervention by the papcy or by the emperor or king. The problem presented by a feudal society related to the custom of the temporal power, the emperor or other lay princes, investing the newly elected bishop or abbot with the ring and the crozier as the symbols of their authority and jurisdiction, and also receiving homage prior to consecration. The custom was closely linked to the whole question of lay patronage. It was an assertion of the overall authority and jurisdiction of the temporal power.

The practice was condemned by Pope Nicholas II in 1059 and all lay investiture was expressly forbidden by Pope Gregory VII in 1075. Fifty years were to pass before the matter was finally resolved by the Concordat of Worms in 1122 and the Second Lateran Council in 1123. The emperor finally gave up the right to invest with the ring and the crozier, although he continued to bestow the temporalities. The controversy raised large questions, political and theological. It was concerned with the boundaries of secular and ecclesiastical authority. It reflected the growing tension between interests that were really local or national and universal. But it demonstrated also the church's growing self-consciousness and its determination to redefine the balance of power as the papal monarchy established its claim to a predominant and universal jurisdiction and laid down the ground rules of a new Roman imperium.

It was inevitable that the papacy should engage with the empire in this controversy if the church was to become anything more than a vassal church in a feudal state. Emperors from Otto I to Henry III, following upon the pattern of Charlemagne, had imposed measures of reform upon the church at a time when the papacy had degenerated. The

Gelasian theory continued to receive formal acknowledgement, and the Emperor Otto III and Pope Sylvester II had
written to each other around 1000, 'Nostrum, nostrum est
imperium Romanum'.[4] But the struggle for predominance
between the empire and the papacy dealt a death blow to the
notion of the Two Powers or the Two Swords. The unitary
authority of the empire was superseded by the unitary
authority of the papal monarchy. It was the imperium of the
Roman see that undergirded the reconstruction of society in
the middle ages and gave to these later centuries whatever
measure of unity they possessed.

Supervision and intervention are the words that best
capture the spirit in which the papacy ordered its relations
with the temporal power. It was as though the papacy had
turned on its head the visitatorial powers that Constantine
and Justinian and Charlemagne had claimed for the emperor
in relation to the church. What was established was a new
imperium – theocratic, hierarchical, absolutist – in which the
church, and in particular the papacy, was to be the only legitimate repository of authority. The papacy enjoyed a supra-
national position and the jurisdiction that was claimed by the
Roman see was used by a succession of popes against a
succession of emperors and kings from the eleventh to the
fourteenth centuries: Pope Paschal II against the Emperor
Henry V; Pope Alexander III against the Emperor Frederick
Barbarossa; Pope Innocent III against the Emperor Otto IV
and against King John of England; Pope Innocent IV against
the Emperor Frederick II; Pope Boniface VIII against King
Philip the Fair of France; Pope John XXII against King Louis
of Bavaria.

The Roman see had been concerned from the earliest
centuries to establish its primacy within the church. A variety
of circumstances and influences now ensured that the papacy
was well-placed to assert its primacy within the empire. The
eleventh century witnessed a desire for reform within the
church and a determination to secure independence in relation to the temporal power. Subsequent centuries were to see
an assertion of the claims that had been implicit from the

middle years of the eleventh century – namely, the primacy and the pre-eminence of the papacy in all matters relating to temporal or ecclesiastical power.

The monastic reforms associated with Cluny had led to the revival of an ascetic idealism; and this had influenced the vigour with which Pope Gregory VII pursued policies determined to establish clerical celibacy and to root out simony from the life of the church. The investiture controversy had focussed attention upon the question of lay patronage and of lay intervention in the election and confirmation of bishops and abbots. But there were simultaneously other developments in the state-church relation which indicated the direction in which affairs would move forward – the centralisation of papal authority and organisation; the encouragement of bishops to appeal to Rome in the event of disputes; the emphasis upon the church's need to hold and to administer ecclesiastical property without constraint; and the revival of canon law which provided the foundation and the framework within which the papacy could exercise a universal jurisdiction.

Pope Gregory VII had maintained his concern to protect the independence of the church within the system contemplated by the Gelasian theory; but, in struggling to set the church free from some of the constraints and corruptions of feudal society, Gregory had created a feudal church. What was established was a papal monarchy in the Roman imperial tradition, so that Gregory combined for all practical purposes within the Roman curia 'the political power of the Holy Roman Empire with the ecclesiastical authority of the Holy Roman Church'.[5]

The church's jurisdiction in matters of personal and public morality had been acknowledged over many centuries, but Gregory went beyond the church's authority in these spheres and spoke of the duty of the spiritual power to exercise moral discipline over every person within a Christian society. What such an assertion of ecclesiastical authority meant in practice was that the legitimacy of government resided ultimately in the papacy. Certainly Gregory's address to the

council at Rome in 1080 left little doubt about the part that
the church was called to play in his understanding of church-
state relations. 'So act, I beg you, holy fathers and princes,
that all the world may know that, if you have power to bind
and loose in heaven, you have power on earth to take away
or to grant empires, kingdoms, principalities, dukedoms,
marches, counties, and the possessions of all men according
to their merits ... Let kings and all the princes of the world
learn how great you are and what power you have and let the
small men fear to disobey the command of your church.'[6]

Papal power grew in part because it was able to meet the
needs of the ecclesiastical hierarchy that was established
throughout the western world. Religious communities
played an important part in this process in the eleventh and
the twelfth centuries by turning to the Roman see to safeguard their interests against both temporal and ecclesiastical
authorities, kings and bishops. The secular clergy were also
glad to look to Rome so that their freedom from secular
courts and from secular taxation might be established, their
property secured, and their disputes settled.

Canon law had previously related in large measure to the
sacraments of the church. It was an extension of the privileges conferred by the sacrament of ordination that enabled
a revised and expanded canon law to provide the theoretical
basis for the jurisdiction of the church. The Roman curia
emerged from the middle years of the twelfth century as a
universal court of justice in a vast area of legislation. Of the
seventy-seven surviving papal letters to England in the first
half of 1244, about one-third are papal directives in ecclesiastical law suits; about one-third convey papal judgements in
matters concerning ecclesiastical law; and the remainder
consist of confirmations, licences, and exhortations of various kinds.[7]

The subordination of the temporal to the spiritual power
was a theme taken up by ecclesiastical writers in the twelfth,
the thirteenth and the fourteenth centuries. John of
Salisbury[8] wrote of 'the inherent superiority of the spiritual
power', insisting that the Two Swords belonged to the

church, and that it was entirely within the competence of the
church to confer the power of coercion upon the prince.[9]
Aquinas[10] was concerned to construct a rational scheme
which comprehended God and nature and man; and it was
he who brought into the debate the Aristotelian principle
that the lower exists for, and is governed by, the higher. It
was this principle that was used so rigorously by Egidius
Colonna,[11] who defined the *plenitudo potestatis* of the
papacy as an independent or self-motivating power. Standing
unashamedly in a theocratic and imperial tradition, he introduced the concept of *dominium* which, although it included
all forms of temporal and political power, required the sanc-
tification of the church in order that it might be exercised
justly and lawfully.

A succession of lawyer-popes in the twelfth, the thirteenth
and the fourteenth centuries – Alexander III, Innocent III,
Gregory IX, Innocent IV and Boniface VIII – secured for the
papacy a pre-eminent sovereignty and jurisdiction. 'The
development of the *corpus juris canonici* ... merely meant the
taking over from the *corpus juris civilis* of the concep-
tion of the sovereign power of the emperor, and its transfer-
ence to the pope. The doctrine of the *plenitudo potestatis* ...
is purely the Roman theory of sovereignty vested in the
pope'.[12]

The papal claims to sovereignty were buttressed by a
succession of documents – the Donation of Constantine, the
False Decretals, and the *Decretum Gratiani*. The Donation
of Constantine is a document which probably dates from the
period of the Frankish empire in the eighth and ninth
centuries. Its purpose was to strengthen the power of the
church, and especially of the Roman see. The document was
embodied in the False Decretals which were first used from
the middle years of the eleventh century. Their concern was
to strengthen the authority of the bishop as the primary unit
of church government and to support his direct line of
responsibility to the pope. The *Decretum Gratiani*, dating
from the mid-twelfth century, brings together a large collection of patristic texts, conciliar decrees and papal pronounce-

ments; but its primary purpose is to justify the subordination of civil to ecclesiastical authority.

These documents undoubtedly served their purpose as items of propaganda in the saga of state-church relations; but it was, perhaps, in the adoption of the title *Vicar of Christ* from around the middle years of the twelfth century, superseding the older title of *Vicar of St Peter*, that the claim to universal sovereignty and jurisdiction received full and formal expression.

The papal claim to *plenitudo potestatis* had been advanced by Pope Innocent III[13]. Persuaded that 'the Holy See ... is set in the midst, below God but above man',[14] Innocent claimed for the papacy a unique power in church and state which was both superior to and fundamentally different in kind from that exercised by any other authority. It was basically a theory of feudal over-lordship which he put forward to justify universal powers of intervention and arbitration, including in the bull *Venerabilem* in 1202 the right to adjudicate in imperial elections.

Pope Innocent IV[15] developed this understanding of papal power, going beyond all categories of feudal relationship, and basing it entirely upon his position as the Vicar of Christ. 'Jesus Christ Himself made Peter and Peter's successors His vicars when He gave them the keys of the heavenly kingdom and said, Feed my sheep. Though there are many offices and governments in the world, there can always be an appeal to the pope when necessary, whether the need arises from the law, because the judge is uncertain what decision he ought legally to give, or from fact, because there is no higher judge, or because inferior judges cannot execute their judgement, or are not willing to do justice as they ought.'[16] The theory amounted to nothing less than the assertion of a universal sovereignty which designated the pope the source of all power and the court of final authority and appeal.

The most blatant demonstration of the papacy's imperial claims was made in 1300 when Pope Boniface VIII[17] declared to the crowds who had come to Rome for the papal jubilee, 'I am Caesar. I am Emperor'.[18] Boniface enunciated the theory of papal sovereignty over princes and kingdoms in the bull *Ausculta Fili* in 1301, and this was followed in the following year by the bull *Unam Sanctam* in which he defended the jurisdiction of the papacy over all creatures. The Gelasian theory had been finally abandoned. The two swords belong to the church. The pope is supreme in the church. Submission to the papacy is required as a condition of salvation.

Boniface's proud statement of the imperial pretensions of the papacy failed to take account of the political realities of the world with which he wrestled day by day. There had been throughout the thirteenth century a growing sense of national identity and national feeling. The wealth, the self-confidence and the assertiveness of secular princes were increasing. An articulate lay voice was becoming critical of the hierarchical structure and the autocracy of the Roman imperium. The bonds of unity were strong – a common culture, a common ritual, a common theology – but the fabric of the medieval world was to be torn apart as political and economic interests liberated themselves from the all-embracing and oppressive control of the church.

The ecclesiastical system that had been developed between the eleventh and the fourteenth centuries was powerful and effective, but it required the concurrence of the secular powers if it was to be sustained. The struggles of Pope Boniface VIII with Philip the Fair and of Pope John XII with Louis of Bavaria illustrate the inability of the papacy either to understand or to contain all that was happening. These controversies were significant in two respects. They demonstrated the significance of national sentiment and required that alongside the *imperium* of the empire and the *sacerdotium* of the papacy there should now stand the kingdom of a people with a growing sense of national identity. They led also to a repudiation of the papacy's assumed powers of intervention and arbitration.

The meaning of this redefinition of the balance of power was a theme explored by a number of ecclesiastical writers. The twelfth century English document known as the *York*

Anonymous represented an early dissenting voice where something approaching the sacredness of the secular and the sacredness of nationality could be found. The claims of Pope Gregory VII, especially in regard to lay investiture, were judged to have no legitimate foundation. There was to be found instead a high doctrine of the monarch and of his position in church and state.

A succession of writers early in the fourteenth century – John of Paris,[19] Dante,[20] Marsilio of Padua[21] and William of Ockham[22] – wrote in such a way as to suggest that the theory of the Two Powers or the Two Swords continued to be valid and that the competence of the Roman see should be confined to matters spiritual and pastoral. John of Paris, protesting against the sovereign power with which the papacy had been invested, argued the case for the independence of the French monarch. Marsilio of Padua, drawing upon the ideal of the Italian city-state, maintained that the state is the unifying power to which the church must be subordinated.

It was not merely the powers of the papacy but the institution itself, its integrity and credibility, that was called into question in the course of the fourteenth and fifteenth centuries. The Babylonish Captivity of the church when the papal seat was removed to Avignon, following upon the conflict with the French monarch, led to a long period in which French interests determined papal policy. The division of the church in the Great Schism when rival popes at Avignon and Rome competed with each other was exploited by secular rulers who attempted to extricate themselves from the oppressive burdens of papal taxation and papal jurisdiction. The secular pretensions of successive papal families, the luxury of the papal court, and the venality of papal government became the ground of cynical and trenchant criticism.

It was the Great Schism that led to the demand for reform from within the church associated with the conciliar movement, and especially with the Councils of Constance[23] and Basel.[24] The fundamental principle of the conciliar theory was that the church – like the emerging nation states – was a community of people, that power was vested in the body as a whole, and that it had the inherent authority for self-government. The movement attempted to achieve wholesale and effective reform, and although the Council of Constance played a decisive part in bringing the Great Schism to an end, it failed both to reform the church and to change its form of government.

The Roman imperium had dominated the later middle ages, but the impotence of the papacy in responding to the changing dynamics of secular power and its failure to put its own house in order and bring the Great Schism to an end were unmistakable signs that the old order was passing. Church and society had been inextricably bound up with each other throughout this period. Western Europe had been a unified Christian community and the medieval church was distinguished by its identification with every aspect of organised society. Full rights of citizenship had belonged, at least in theory, to those who professed the Christian faith. Catholic Europe had possessed a geographical compactness within with the structures of ecclesiastical and civil authority could operate; but this too was passing as the explorers of the fifteenth and the sixteenth centuries opened the eyes of Europe to new continents.

There is truth in Thomas Hobbes's[25] mischievous comment that the papacy was the ghost of the deceased Roman empire sitting crowned on the grave thereof. The spirit of the Roman imperium survived long after the substance of temporal power had been lost. There is a logical line of development from Gregory VII, Innocent III, Innocent IV and Boniface VIII which leads to the Council of Trent,[26] to the First Vatican Council,[27] and ultimately to the *Codex Juris Canonici* of 1918 in which faith and morals are brought fully within the jurisdiction of the pope, and dogma as a whole becomes part of the papal *potestas jurisdictionis*.

There is a sense in which the Roman imperium of the middle ages signified the extent of the church's achievement. Experience, movement, sect and institution had given way to a world order in which the unifying principle was the Christian church. Its triumph had been the establishment of a 'single word-wide society (which) may be called with only a difference of emphasis either a commonwealth or a church'.[28] The imperial model would continue to inform church polity in both the Roman Catholic communion and in some of the churches of the reformation. The idea and the ideal of a whole society as a *corpus Christianum* was one that would continue to commend itself to church and state.

NOTES

1 Cited by R.W. Southern, *Western Society and the Church in the Middle Ages*, Penguin Books 1988, p. 59.
2 James Bryce, *The Holy Roman Empire*, Macmillan & Co. 1928, p. 93.
3 J.N. Figgis, *The Political Aspects of St Augustine's 'City of God'*, Longmans, Green & Co. 1921, p. 86.
4 Ibid., p. 87.
5 H. Richard, Niebuhr, *The Social Sources of Denominationalism*, Meridian Books: The World Publishing company 1971, p. 118.
6 Cited by R.W. and A.J. Carlyle, *A History of Medieval Political Theory in the West*, 6 vols. New York and London, 1903–1936, Vol IV. p. 201.
7 R.W. Southern, *op. cit.*, p. 124.
8 John of Salisbury, Bishop of Chartres, c.1115–1180.
9 George H. Sabine, *op.cit.*, p. 208.
10 Thomas Aquinas, c.1225–1274.
11 Egidius Colonna, author of *De Ecclesiastica Potestata*, written c.1302.
12 J.N. Figgis, *Churches in the Modern State*, Longmans, Green & Co. 1914, pp. 135–6.
13 Pope Innocent III, 1160–1216.
14 Cited by Sidney Z. Ehler, *Twenty Centuries of Church and State*, The Newman Press 1957, p. 38.
15 Pope Innocent IV, d.1254.
16 Cited by R.W. and A.J. Carlyle, *op.cit.*, vol. v. p. 323. note 1.
17 Pope Boniface VIII, c.1234–1303.
18 Cited by Cyril Garbett, *Church and State in England*, Hodder and Stoughton 1950, p. 17.
19 John of Paris. See especially *De Potestate regia et Papali*, c.1302–1303.
20 Dante, 1265–1351. See especially *De Monarchia* c.1313.
21 Marsilio of Padua, c.1275–1342. See especially *Defensor Pacis*. c.1324.
22 William of Ockham, c.1300–1349. See especially *Dialogus super Dignitate Papali et Regia*. c.1338–1342.
23 Council of Constance, 1414–1418.
24 Council of Basel, 1431–1449.

25 Thomas Hobbes, 1588–1679.
26 Council of Trent, 1545–1563.
27 First Vatican Council, 1869–1870.
28 George H. Sabine, *op.cit.*, p. 228.

PART II

THE ENGLISH EXPERIENCE

Chapter 5

The English Church

The inter-relationship of church and state in England was first given its classic expression in the opening words of the Preface of Bede's *Ecclesiastical History – Historiam Gentis Anglorum Ecclesiasticum*. It was through the Angles, following upon Augustine's mission at the behest of Pope Gregory the Great in 597, that the Christian faith had been restored to the land that had previously been known as Britannia. Bede brought to his telling of the story a strong sense of God's purposes in history, and his *Ecclesiastical History* has been compared with the historical books of the Old Testament in giving shape and definition to the sense of national identity and national destiny. There was at an early stage an awareness of England and of the English which is without parallel in other parts of western Europe.

The English nation was the child of the church.[2] Since the conversion of the first Anglo-Saxon Kings, there had been an intimate relationship between church and state. The church gave its authority and sanction to kingship, to law, and to the unity of the nation. The church provided the king's chief advisers and, as the machinery of government developed, what was for all practical purposes the civil service, undergirded by a network of parochial clergy who were, in effect, 'a civilising and a governmental agency'.[3] The favour of the state was shown in the privileges granted to the clergy, and in the protection by law of gifts of land and money to the church. 'The unity of the church in England was the pattern of the unity of the state; the cohesion of the church was for ages the substitute for the cohesion which the divided nation

67

was unable otherwise to realise ... It was to an extraordinary degree a national church; national in its comprehensiveness as well as in its exclusiveness'.[4]

It was not easy in Anglo-Saxon England to distinguish between the sacred and the secular, between church and state. There was a strong tradition of ecclesiastical independence; and yet for a succession of English kings in the tenth and eleventh centuries the king was 'Christ's Vicegerent'[5] or 'the Vicar of the most High King',[6] and it was by one authority that laws were enacted, both ecclesiastical and secular. There was an alignment of interests and powers, although the burden of responsibility had passed, at least in theory, to the king in whom could now be seen the first signs of what would become over the generations an unacceptable supremacy. 'The king is the overseer, the chief minister and the spokesman of the body; he orders justice to be done, whether in church or state, and sees that it is done.'[7]

Lying outside the boundaries of the Holy Roman Empire – both in the time of Charlemagne and in later centuries – England became 'the most compact and self-conscious state of western Europe'.[8] The Norman Conquest ensured that England was inevitably drawn into the wider unity of Europe and of the papacy; and 'the *ecclesia Anglicana* was conscious of being that part of the western church which the Most High had planted in England'.[9] The Conqueror was determined to provide a strong administration in state and church centred upon the authority of the crown; but papal authority and jurisdiction could not be disregarded, and over the next three centuries the church found itself hard pressed to maintain its independence in the face of the demands – and frequently the conflicting demands – of king and pope.

Anselm[10] fought valiantly to maintain the spiritual independence of the church and gave strong support also to those who pleaded for the maintenance of traditional local practices.[11] The brave assertion of Magna Carta in a later generation – *ut ecclesia Anglicana libera sit* – was bound to be qualified for a church whose integrity was inescapably bound up with the tension of being either a vassal church in a feudal state or a vassal church in a feudal papacy.

Controversy between the English monarchy and the papacy concerned the extent and the limits of their respective authorities. There was the familiar catalogue of complaints against papal taxation, papal 'provisions', papal interference in episcopal appointments, papal jurisdiction; but the struggles were not only between state and church against the papacy, but also between state and church within the nation.

The growing awareness of national identity and sentiment in France and Germany and Spain, coupled with the increasing self-confidence of their rulers, led to the emergence of a formula in the course of the fourteenth century which insisted that the king had the same power in his kingdom as the emperor has in the empire.[12] This formula signified a new phase in church-state relations, following upon the earlier disputes between the papacy and French and German kings, in which the over-arching authority and jurisdiction of the emperor and the papacy would be exercised increasingly by the king within his realm.

English kings were not slow to assert their claims to sovereignty and, as a precursor to the reformation statutes of the 1530s, the Statute of Praemuneri of 1393, although subsequently withdrawn under pain of excommunication, stated unequivocally what might be judged to be the historical understanding of the authority of the crown within the realm. '(That) the crown of England, which has always been so free and independent, as not to have any earthly sovereign, but to be immediately subject to God in all things touching the prerogatives of royalty of the said crown, should be made subject to the pope, and the laws and statutes of the realm defeated and set aside by him at pleasure, to the utter destruction of the sovereignty of our Lord the king, his crown and royalty, and his whole kingdom ... God forbid'.[13]

The complementarity of the Two Powers or the Two Swords, represented by the *imperium* of the empire and the *sacerdotium* of the papacy had long since been superseded.

The claims to a universal jurisdiction advanced by the papacy could no longer be sustained. The balance of power was changing and relationships between the monarchies and the papacy were being re-negotiated in France, in Germany and in Spain in the course of the fifteenth and the early sixteenth centuries.

The theory and the practice of papal absolutism gave way throughout Europe to the theory and the practice of royal absolutism. It was the crown – in France, in England, in Spain – which was establishing strong central governments around which the unity of the nation could be built. The new wealth of the nation states, and especially of the emerging middle class, required strong government and the stability which only the crown might secure. The failure of the church to reform itself and to address the abuses of power had led to a rejection of clerical control over secular government. A growing sense of national consciousness had been encouraged by learning, by literature, by the renaissance spirit of enquiry and expression. A new awareness of national independence and national unity was matched by the self-confidence and the self-assertiveness of the temporal princes.

It is one of the ironies of the sixteenth century that the reformation extended and consolidated the power of the monarchy. The Lutheran movement led inevitably to the destruction of Christendom, even in western Europe, as a single polity. Luther's break with Rome removed unwittingly the check upon the secular power that the church had possessed in the middle ages. But the early reformers did not abandon the idea of a church that would be co-extensive with the state. The medieval ideal, the imperial ideal, of the church-state was retained.

Lutheranism rested ultimately upon the conviction that the church is the assembly of all believers in Christ upon earth. It appealed to the authority of scripture, to justification by faith, to private prayer, to the role of the laity. But Luther took full account of the political realities of his day and sought full integration with the life of the state. Calvin, by contrast with Luther, asserted the supremacy of the spiritual authority, although he took for granted the acquiescence and the concurrence of the temporal power. But Luther, Zwingli and Calvin were all concerned to establish inclusive churches and to secure their support with the authority of the civil power. In Lutheran thought the interests of church and state were inter-connected, and it followed – in a world where the authority of the prince was believed to be of divine origin – that a reformed church polity would inevitably see the prerogatives of spiritual and secular power pass in large measure to the prince.

It was within the nation state – and no more so than in England – that the imperial idea of a church-state was to be realised anew, albeit in a modified form. The Church *in* England was re-shaped and re-formed as the Church *of* England in the upheavals of the sixteenth century. The English reformation was at least in part a protestant reformation. It was concerned with the purifying of religion. It reconciled catholic order and reformed doctrine. But it was also intimately bound up with questions of national identity, and it cannot be fully understood without reference to the renaissance and reformation politics of which it formed a part.

The occasion of the Tudor Reformation was 'the king's matter' – the desire of King Henry VIII to obtain a divorce from Queen Katherine of Aragon, and the failure of the papacy, inhibited by the Emperor Charles V, to address and to resolve the issue in the way that was required by the king. But the matter raised far wider questions concerning the extent of papal involvement in English life, the relation of the papacy to the crown, and the meaning of sovereignty in a nation state.

A strong monarchy in an increasingly centralised national state would need to establish sooner or later a new *modus vivendi* with the church. The power and wealth of the church meant that it had become, in effect, an *imperium in imperio*. It has been reckoned that at the time of the reformation one-fifth to one-third of all land in England was held by the church.[14] The Statutes of Provisions and Praemunire had attempted from the middle years of the fourteenth century to restrain the demands of the papacy and to protect the rights of the crown; and a growing tradition of anti-clericalism fastened upon the immunities enjoyed by the church, the wealth of the monasteries, the alleged avarice and corruption of the clerical and the religious life, the abuses of ecclesiastical courts.

One of the problems posed by papal claims to a universal jurisdiction lay in the fact that in most countries in Western Europe the affairs of church and state could not be easily distinguished. Civil and ecclesiastical persons, administrations and courts were inextricably bound up with each other. A succession of legal writers in England in the fifteenth and the early sixteenth centuries had attacked the church courts on the grounds that they had blurred the distinction between civil and spiritual authority, and that they had in consequence denied to the king the right to administer justice to all his subjects.

It was a relatively conservative reformation that was carried through in England in so far as the fundamentals of faith and order were concerned. Henry VIII had taken pride in the title of 'Defender of the Faith' bestowed upon him by Pope Clement VII; but the renaissance had given rise to a new humanism which demanded freedom of enquiry. It challenged established authorities and corrupt practices within the life of the church.

Wycliffe's[15] trenchant criticism of abuses in the church in the fourteenth century and his appeal to scripture as the sole authority for Christian faith and conduct had been taken up in England by his Poor Preachers and later by the Lollards. The scholasticism and quiet scepticism of Erasmus[16] inhibited him from being the most significant figure in the reformation controversies, but his edition of the Greek New Testament in 1516 greatly influenced theological studies, and his critical satires of monasteries and of the prevalent corruptions of the church prepared the way for the reformation in Europe. It was, however, Luther's[17] passionate espousal of all these concerns – his denial of the primacy of the Roman see and of the infallibilty of General Councils; his objection to the sacrifice of the mass and of the doctrine of transubstanti-ation; his opposition to the religious orders, to the celibacy of the clergy, to the sale of indulgences – that led to his public confrontation with Rome; while his translation of the bible made it a formative influence in the development of the German language and of German religion.

The significance of Wycliffe, Erasmus and Luther for the English reformation does not lie in any direct influence they exercised upon new doctrinal formulae. Theological minds in England were alert to all that was being said, but the influ-ence – although discernible – was discreet and limited. One of the intriguing questions concerns the extent to which the thoroughgoing protestantism of the reformers was shaped by the spirit of the age. One judgement is that Luther's emphatic assertion, 'Here I stand!', spoke for those who were deter-mined to establish their autonomy not only theologically, but also politically, economically, intellectually.[18]

The independence that the reformers claimed on the basis of scriptural authority was set within the context of the sovereignty of God. The dissolution of feudal society; the long-standing disputes concerning spiritual and temporal power; the emergence of questions concerning national sovereignty, independent jurisdiction and law provided something of the backcloth to the unequivocal emphasis of the protestant reformers upon the absolute sovereignty of God in whose will all law finds its origin.

The English reformation was a protracted process and recent studies[19] suggest that it owed much, at least at the time of the Henrician reformation in the 1530s, to a handful of determined ministers within the king's council, led on by the competence and determination of Thomas Cromwell.[20] The limited evidence does not permit final judgements, but there is sufficient reason to suggest that the reformation of the 1530s was imposed upon a nation that was not looking for fundamental changes in religion.

The experience of thirty years – from Henry VIII's sum-moning of the reformation parliament in November 1529 to

the passing of the Acts of Uniformity and Supremacy by
Elizabeth I's parliament in April 1559 – has much to say
about human vanity, ambition, and the corruptions of
power; about constitutional uncertainty, political determination, the fluctuations of policy, the exercise of state-craft, and
demonstrations of gross political ineptitude; about innate
conservatism and radical disdain; about theological conviction and doctrinal relativity; about moral courage, persecution, expedient withdrawal and martyrdom.

It has to be asked, however, if this process is fundamentally
different from the way in which significant changes have
always occurred throughout history in the life of church and
state. It was certainly in the whole complex of circumstances
and personalities, of events and interests and influences, that
the papal monarchy had evolved – albeit over a far longer
period – in the medieval world. It is relatively easy for a
church which is determined to be a sect to stand within the
securities of its own internal life; but a church which has
been drawn inexorably down the road of being either an
institution or an empire, in which the Christian commonwealth comprehends both church and state, cannot so easily
escape the interplay of forces, spiritual and temporal, which
determine the way in which its life is taken forward.

The sixteenth century received from the middle ages an
understanding of church-state relations which gave 'a
supremely important place to the rule of law and the due
processes of its execution expressed in terms of jurisdiction'.[21] The English reformation statutes were Acts of Parliament,[22] and its was therefore by the authority of the crown in
parliament that the new ecclesiastical settlement came into
being. The church was no longer a separate *regnum*. It was
that part of the body politic which is called the spirituality.
The reformation of the Church in England was caught up in
the discovery of what it means to be a nation state with its
own independent sovereignty and jurisdiction. The new
ecclesiastical settlement was part of a far wider constitutional settlement – 'this realm of England is an Empire'.[23]

The constitutional building-blocks of the English Refor-

mation – over and above the repudiation of the papacy –
were an appeal to ancient custom, an assertion of national
sovereignty and jurisdiction, and an affirmation of the royal
supremacy. These things were brought together in the desig-
nation of the sovereign in the reign of Henry VIII as 'the only
supreme head in earth of the Church of England',[24] and in
the reign of Elizabeth I as 'the only Supreme governor of this
realm ... as well in all spiritual or ecclesiastical things or
causes as temporal'.[25]

It would be inaccurate to caricature the assertion of the
royal supremacy as a mere Erastianism, a subordination of
the church to the state. There had been a theological debate
which went back over more than four centuries about the
sovereignty of secular rulers. University faculties of divinity
in the early years of the sixteenth century had been caught up
in the scholarly controversy about the nature of the church
and its relation to the civil power. John Fisher,[26] Thomas
More[27], Stephen Gardiner[28] and Reginald Pole[29] – stern critics of the English reformation – all took seriously the argument about the different spheres of the sacred and the
secular, and the rights of the temporal prince within his own
dominions, even in ecclesiastical matters.

It is necessary to emphasise that within the unfolding story
of church-state relations what is often referred to as the state
or the secular power was, in fact, a *person* – 'a person,
having a conscience, owning personal responsibility, and one
with (the church) in faith, in practice, in sentiment, in
purpose, acknowledging (its) laws, sympathising with (its)
objects'.[30] Constantine, Justinian and Charlemagne serve as
powerful reminders of the visitatorial powers which had
been conceded gladly by the church to the Christian prince as
being 'by divine right, and as of divine origin; not as a delegated but an independent authority, inherent in the royal
function and office'.[31] But it was implicit in this dependent
relationship that the prince would be a godly prince – able
and willing to befriend and protect the church, and determined to ensure that the laws and canons of the church
would be the basis of government.[32] It is one of the unhappy

distortions of this ancient tradition, imposed by the drift across Europe towards royal absolutism, that the sixteenth century should have inculcated the idea 'that to be a true man it was sufficient to be a true subject, obedient to one's lawful prince'.[33]

The English reformation statutes gave to the crown supreme authority in ecclesiastical affairs in so far as legislative, administrative and judicial matters were concerned. But it is necessary to distinguish between those things that came within the prerogative of the crown by virtue of the supreme headship or governship and those things that remained within the competence of the church. The Thirty-Nine Articles of Religion, which were finally published with the authority of the crown and of parliament in 1571, provided a succinct summary of the reformed faith of the church and of the dogmatic position adopted by the Church of England in relation to questions raised by the sixteenth century. Article 37 concerning the Civil Magistrates is clear in its assertion that 'we give not to our Princes the ministering either of God's Word, or of the Sacraments ...but that only prerogative, which we see to have been given always to all godly Princes in holy Scriptures, by God Himself; that is, that they should rule all estates and degrees committed to their charge by God, whether they be Ecclesiastical or Temporal'.

The distinction employed by Stephen Gardiner as early as 1535 between *potestas ordinis* and *potestas jurisdictionis* was fully recognised in the reformation settlement. It was a mixed economy that was established, but one in which the forms of law and precedent were scrupulously observed. Three examples must suffice. The king did not consecrate bishops; but he chose those who should be consecrated, and he required that they should be elected by the dean and chapter of the cathedral, and he received their homage prior to consecration. The king did not sit in church courts; but he acted through those who were learned in ecclesiastical law. The king did not draft new canons; but the convocations, in whom the responsibility was vested, could meet only with his consent, and they were required to seek the royal assent before the canons could be published and enforced by law.

The English reformation took up and adapted in a distinctive way aspects of the church-state relation which had been present since the time of Constantine: the inter-dependence of church and state; the role of the Christian prince; the Christian faith as the bond of unity. The sixteenth century could not comfortably envisage two co-equal jurisdictions in one state. The powers that had previously been claimed by the papacy were taken in large measure by the crown so that the church in England might henceforward be within the state and not above it. There was actually little in the crown's day by day relation with the Church of England – save for the total repudiation of the papacy – which was fundamentally at variance with the relation of the French and Spanish monarchies with the church in their realms. The one additional distinguishing feature of the English reformation was, of course, the relation between crown and parliament in accomplishing the reformation. The assertion of national sovereignty and jurisdiction, the establishment of a Christian commonwealth in which church and state were intimately inter-locked with each other: these things were the work of the crown in parliament.

The period of the reformation presents a variety of conflicting evidence concerning the causes, the development, the meaning and the consequences of all that had taken place. It was unquestionably a long and complex process, and the significance of what had been accomplished – as with so many developments in the life of the church – could not be seen for many generations. The English people were undoubtedly divided by all that happened over a period of thirty years and more. There is evidence at different times of discontent on both sides – catholic and reformed – in all parts of the country. Some have observed 'the general acquiescence' with which the Henrician reformation was received.[34] Some have argued that 'on the whole English men and women did not want the reformation'.[35] Some emphasised the popular and the authentically religious character of the English reformation.[36]

It is certainly possible to discern a strong determination in

the 1530s to achieve a reformation settlement that was
scripturally based and a laity that was scripturally
educated.[37] The Injunctions of 1536 and 1538 required
clergy to teach the Lord's Prayer, the Articles of Faith, the
Ten Commandments, and to examine parishioners in these
things. They required the preaching of a quarterly sermon by
licensed preachers based upon scriptural faith. They encouraged wealthy clergy to support scholars at the grammar
schools and at the universities. They encouraged non-resi-
dent clergy to make financial provision for the payment of
assistant curates, the maintenance of the chancel of the
parish church, and the relief of the poor. These were modest
developments, but they signified the beginnings of a long
process by which some of the anomalies and abuses of
church life could be addressed.

The protestant reformers were concerned to recover the
primary authority of scripture in the faith and teaching of the
church; and it was the placing of the English bible in every
parish church in the land that constituted in the long term
the most significant step forward in these early years. This
development was underscored by the reading of the English
bible in pubic worship and by the introduction in due course
of the English Prayer Books. But it is the symbolism of the
English bible in the parish church that has represented for
many the authentic mark of renaissance and reformation in
English life. The bible was to become not merely the basis of
the church's liturgy and the touchstone of its doctrine, but
also the firm foundation of private devotion and personal
piety. The bible was to enter the consciousness – and the
unconsciousness – of the English people, influencing and
shaping their language, their literature, their religious
aspirations, their personal and public values.

But public opinion is not shaped – at least in the short term
– by legislation. The fluctuations of religious policy undoubtedly left a nation that was bemused, tormented, divided. The
legislative reforms of Henry VIII were coupled with the
innate conservatism of the king in doctrinal matters and the
desire on the part of the reformers to push on with the

religious changes that the new settlement made possible. The thoroughgoing protestant reforms attempted during the protectorates of Somerset and Northumberland in the reign of Edward VI gave way to the oppressive backlash of catholic reaction under Mary Tudor.

A mere summary of these things – in general or in detail – cannot convey, however, what the reformation meant to people in the parishes. The shameless suppression of the monasteries; the dissolution of the chantries; the destruction of images; the removal of altars; the transformation in the appearance of the churches – these things would have been visible to all. The abolition of the Latin Mass; the introduction of the English bible; the authorisation in quick succession of new Prayer Books; the simplification of ceremonies; the abolition of clerical celibacy – these things, too, would have impinged upon the habits, the perceptions, the expectations of people. The ejection of clergy from their livings; the restoration of old statutes against heresy; the arrest, the examination and the execution of catholics and protestants alike – these things could not fail to be observed.

And yet too little is known about popular opinion to say with any confidence what meaning was given to these upheavals. It may well be that 'a substantial body of lay opinion still preferred the old ways'.[38] It is doubtful – given the innate conservatism of religious faith and the habits and traditions of generations – if protestant doctrine really entered into the minds and hearts of people in these years. But there is evidence of hostility to the old order in some parts of the country, even if there was no great enthusiasm for protestantism. But times change and if it was true that 'the English Reformation was still external to most of the people' at the accession of Mary Tudor,[39] it was no less the case that the new settlement of 1559 brought to an end this period of change in which the foundation documents of a reformed order in church and state were established.

It may well be right to conclude that it was 'the courage of the martyrs ... the steadfastness of the victims ... in the Marian persecutions that baptised the English Reformation in blood and drove into English minds the fateful association of eccleisiastical tyranny with the see of Rome'.[40] But it would be folly to infer that the process of reformation was concluded by the passing of the Acts of Uniformity and Supremacy in 1559. There is good reason to suggest that even as late as 1570 'the result was still unsettled and the theological positions not yet sharply and irrevocably defined'.[41] The full meaning of what had been accomplished – the English tradition and the English experience of a reformed Christian polity – had yet to be realised.

There is no unanimity of opinion among historians, but two observations should be allowed to stand alongside one another, each testifying to aspects of the traumas of reformation which are not exclusive, but which require continuing reflection as the story of the English Church unfolds. The first proposes that, in so far as any unifying theme might be found in the conflicting currents of reformation and counter-reformation in England, it lies in 'a change of view point concerning the nature and function of religion, both in the individual and in society'.[42] The second, which is based in part upon a detailed analysis of church wardens' accounts throughout the period, suggests that 'the English reformation has been treated too much as a confessional struggle and not sufficiently as an episode in the history of secular British polity'.[43]

The point is made with more than a touch of irony that, 'The association had been there from the beginning, for Christianity was after all imposed in these islands by a series of royal decisions. In this sense the protestant reformation was indeed a harking back to the primitive church, though not in the way that the reformers intended'.[44] The 'nature and function of religion' and the 'secular British polity' were matters that would both become increasingly important over the centuries as the reformed *ecclesia Anglicana* explored its vocation of being the church in and for the nation.

The churches of the reformation in central and northern Europe endorsed and embodied the principle of nationality. They continued to hold the traditional model of a church-state polity in which the church was co-extensive with the nation, and church and state represented the two aspects of a single commonwealth. It might well be argued that in this respect, as in so many others, the churches of the reformation retained and carried forward an important aspect of catholicism.[45] The whole tradition of catholic faith and order as it had been established in England was drastically and dramatically revised. The essential features of catholicism were retained, but what were judged to be the medieval distortions – in doctrine, in order and in discipline – were discarded. But the Church of England had separated itself not merely from the papacy but from the wider communion of faith in Western Europe. It would prove well able to hold its own in a divided Christendom, but it would remain to some extent an insular church – governmentally and spiritually – until in an entirely different age the pressures of an international world order and of a re-kindled ecumenism exposed all churches to wider influences.

There was a significant shift in church-state relations throughout Europe in the course of the sixteenth century in both catholic and protestant countries. The relationship between the ecclesiastical and the secular powers, albeit within one society, was being renegotiated to the advantage of the secular or temporal power. But the question for the Church of England did not merely concern its relations to the Roman see but to 'the aspirations of national life'.[46] The English tradition was to receive its most comprehensive exposition in the course of the next generation in Hooker's *Laws of Ecclesiastical Polity*. It was fundamental to Hooker's understanding of what had been achieved that 'there is not any man of the Church of England but the same man is also a member of the commonwealth; nor any man a member of the commonwealth, which is not also of the Church of England'.[47] Catholic recusancy and puritanism were both to call in question the extent to which this ideal could ever be sustained; but the reformation had carried forward into a new age the tradition of inter-dependence between the spiritual and the temporal that had been one of

the most enduring characteristics of the church as institution
or empire over more than a thousand years.

NOTES

1 Patrick Wormald, *The Venerable Bede and the 'Church of the English'*. Essay in *The English Religious Tradition and the Genius of Anglicanism*, Edited by Geoffrey Rowell, Ikon 1992, pp. 23–4.

2 See J.R. Green, *The Making of England*, Macmillan & Co, 1881, p. 334.
  'If England could not find its national life in the supremacy of Northumbria or Mercia, it found it in the church; and amidst the wreck of kingdoms the power of the church grew steadily greater, because the church alone expressed the national consciousness of the English people'.

3 Leslie Hunter (Editor), *The English Church: A New Look*, Penguin Books 1966. p. 59.

4 William Stubbs, *The Constitutional History of England*, 3 vols, Oxford 1874. Vol. I. p. 266.

5 Ethelred, King of England, c.968–1016. Cited by R.W. Church, *op.cit.*, p.39.

6 Canute, King of Denmark, England and Norway, d.1035. Cited by R.W. Church. Ibid. p. 37.

7 R.W. Church. Ibid. p. 38.

8 Adrian Hastings, *op.cit.*, p. 10.

9 Z.N. Brooke, *The English Church and the Papacy*, Cambridge 1952. p. 21.

10 Anselm, Archbishop of Canterbury, c.1033–1109.

11 Richard Southern. *Anselm and the English Religious Tradition*. Essay in *The English Religious Tradition and the Genius of Anglicanism*. Edited by Geoffrey Rowell, Ikon 1992, pp. 41–2.

12 Rex in regno suo est imperator regni suo est.

13 Statute of Praemunire of 16 Richard II 1393. Cited by R.W. Church, *op.cit.*, p. 44.

14 Owen Chadwick, *The Reformation*, Penguin Books 1972, p. 97.

15 John Wycliffe, c.1329–1384.

16 Desiderius Erasmus, c.1466–1536.

17 MartinLuther, 1483–1546.

18 Erik Erikson, *Young Man Luther*, Faber & Faber 1958. p. 244.

19 G.R. Elton, *Policy and Police*, Cambridge 1972. John Scarisbrick, *The Reformation of the English People*, Oxford 1984. David Starkey, *The Reign of Henry VIII: Personalities and Politics*, 1985. David Starkey (Editor), *The English Court*, 1987. Christopher Haigh (Editor), *The English Reformation Revised*, Cambridge 1987. Eamon Duffy, *The Stripping of the Altars*, Yale University Press 1992. Christopher Haigh, *English Reformations*, Clarendon Press 1993. But see also: A.G. Dickens, *The English Reformation*, B.T. Batsford, 1989.

20 Thomas Cromwell, Earl of Essex. c.1485–1540.
21 R.E. Head, *Royal Supremacy and the Trials of Bishops 1558–1725.* SPCK 1962, p. 1.
22 Act of Annates (1532). Act in Restraint of Appeals (1533). Act of Annates (1534). Act against Papal Dispensations (1534). Act for the Submission of Clergy (1534). Act of Supremacy (1534). Act of Uniformity (1559). Act of Supremacy (1559).
23 Act in Restraint of Appeals (1533). 24 Henry VIII c.12; Statutes of the realm iii 247.
24 Act of Supremacy (1534). 26 Henry VIII, c.1; Statutes of the Realm iii 492.
25 Act of Supremacy (1559). 1 Elizabeth, c.1; Statutes of the Realm iv 350.
26 John Fisher, Bishop of Rochester, 1469–1535.
27 Thomas More, Lord Chancellor of England, 1478–1535.
28 Stephen Gardiner, Bishop of Winchester, c.1490–1555.
29 Reginald Pole, Archbishop of Canterbury, 1500–1558.
30 R.W. Church, *op.cit.*, p. 13.
31 Ibid., p. 16.
32 Ibid., p. 17.
33 Patrick Collinson, *Thomas Cranmer.* Essay in *The English Religious Tradition and the Genius of Anglicanism*, Ed. by Geoffrey Rowell, Ikon 1992, p. 85. See also Jasper Ridley, *Thomas Cranmer*, Oxford 1962, p. 12.
34 F.M. Powicke, *The Reformation in England*, OUP 1941, p. 7.
35 John Scarisbrick, *The Reformation and the English People*, Oxford 1984, p. 1.
36 A.G. Dickens, *The English Reformation*, B.T. Batsford 1965.
37 Ibid., p. 135.
38 Owen Chadwick, *The Reformation*, Penguin Books 1964, p. 136.
39 Ibid., p. 122.
40 Ibid., p. 128.
41 D.M. Palliser, *Popular Reactions to the Reformation During the Years of Uncertainty 1530–1570.* Essay published in Christopher Haigh (Editor), *The English Reformation Revised.* CUP 1987, p. 95.
42 A.G. Dickens, *op.cit.*, p. 325.
43 Ronald Hutton, *The Local Impact of the Tudor Reformations.* Essay published in: Christopher Haigh (Editor), *op.cit.*, p. 138.
44 Ibid.
45 Ernst Troeltsch, *op.cit.*, Vol. I, p. 282.
46 Mandell Creighton, *The Church and the Nation*, Longmans, Green & Co., 1900, p. 11.
47 Richard Hooker, *Of the Laws of Ecclesiastical Polity*, VIII. 1.2.

Chapter 6

The English Tradition

It is, perhaps, characteristic of the English Church that the reformation settlement should have preceded the development of a theological tradition. The controversies of the reformation period provided the context in which the English tradition developed. The Book of Common Prayer,[1] the Ordinal,[2] the Thirty-Nine Articles[3], the Second Book of Homolies,[4] and the 'Canon of Preaching'[5] constituted a *corpus* of texts, doctrinal and liturgical, which gave early definition to the reformed faith, ceremonial and practice of the Church of England.

It is here that there can be found the appeal to scripture and to the early fathers of the church which was characteristic of the English tradition from the beginning. It was this appeal which set the English Church free from the preoccupations of the medieval church. Its tradition had, therefore, at its heart an appeal to the fundamentals of faith that belonged to the first five centuries of the Christian era and which preceded the earliest divisions of the church.

The writings of the early Anglican divines – John Jewel,[6] Matthew Parker,[7] Richard Hooker,[8] John Whitgift,[9] Lancelot Andrewes[10] – emphasised the continuity of the *ecclesia Anglicana* with the early church; and it was Elizabeth I's proud boast to parliament in 1598 that 'the estate and government of this Church of England as now it standeth in this reformation ... both in form and doctrine ... is agreeable with the scriptures, with the most ancient general councils, with the practice of the primitive church, and with the judgement of all the old learned fathers'.[11]

It is John Jewel who has been considered over the centuries as the first apologist of the Elizabethan settlement.[12] He had been throughout his early years one of the leaders of the reforming party, and his consecration as Bishop of Salisbury followed almost immediately upon his return from exile at the time of Elizabeth's accession. He stood firmly behind the reformation settlement in 1559, and he attempted to hold a middle course between Roman Catholicism and Puritanism, taking his authority from the fathers of the early church.

Jewel's famous work – *Apologia Ecclesiae Anglicanae*[13] – was 'the first full-length essay in Anglican self-understanding'.[14] The work was published in 1562, and it is probable that it was commissioned by Elizabeth's ministers as both an explanation and a defence of the position taken by the English Church. The *Apologia* is unashamedly polemical in tone. It endeavoured to prove that a general reformation had been necessary, that the Council of Trent was unable to carry through any comprehensive reform, and that local churches had the right to legislate through provincial synods. Jewel defended the royal supremacy over against the claims of the papacy. He wrote vigorously against the superstitions and corruptions of Rome, and challenged his opponents to demonstrate the truth of their position by reference to the scriptures and to the early fathers.

Jewel pointed to the retention by the Church of England of the historic creeds, of the threefold orders of ministry, and of the sacraments of the gospel as evidence of its continuity with the apostles and the early catholic fathers. 'We have returned to the Apostles and old Catholic fathers. We have planted no new religion but only renewed the old that was undoubtedly founded and used by the Apostles of Christ and other Holy Fathers of the primitive Church'.[15] The *Apologia* and Jewel's subsequent work – *Defence of the Apologie of the Church of England*[16] – were not considered to be private and personal writings. They took their place alongside the English Bible, the Book of Common Prayer, and the Book of Homilies. They were public documents – official statements – of the English church and English state.[17]

It is, however, Hooker's *Laws of Ecclesiastical Polity*[18] which has provided the most comprehensive and enduring exposition of Anglicanism. The immediate background to the work was the controversy between the preaching ministries of Richard Hooker and Walter Travers at the Temple Church. Izaak Walton observed that, 'The forenoon sermon spoke of Canterbury, and the afternoon, Geneva.'[19] The *Polity* has been judged by some to have been 'an officially sponsored collaborative venture';[20] but there is reason to believe that it was entirely Hooker's work, and that it came out of the trauma of his ministry at the Temple.[21]

The *Ecclesiastical Polity* is a massive work of scholarship; and Hooker stands, therefore, as the forerunner of a long line of Anglican clergy who, as incumbents in the Church of England, have contributed significantly by their learning to the intellectual life of the church and of society. Hooker drew upon biblical, patristic and scholastic thought. Biblical theology, philosophy, moral theology and ecclesiology are interwoven with each other. The *Polity* has been compared in its scope with the *Summa Theologica* of Aquinas, and Hooker was undoubtedly influenced by the thinking of Aristotle and Aquinas. It is an extraordinary work of synthesis as it brings into a harmony the ambiguities of the English reformation settlement.

The *Ecclesiastical Polity* was written to defend the Elizabethan settlement against the Puritans, who sought a far more radical break in faith and in church order than had yet been attempted. It set out to refute the seven broad principles of Puritanism; but it provided also a systematic exposition of the English Reformation, giving coherence to its thought and its practical expression. Its achievement was quite simply that it formed 'a continuous and coherent whole presenting a philosophy and theology congenial to the Anglican *Book of Common Prayer* and the traditional aspects of the Elizabethan settlement. In Hooker Anglicanism is no longer merely an apologetic, it has become a coherent theology'.[22]

Any study of the church in the first five centuries is bound to acknowledge the developments that gave to the church its self-awareness and self-definition and its capacity for self-development. The episcopal office, the canon of the New Testament, the historic creeds, the first four ecumenical councils: these have provided the church with the all-important threads of continuity. But there were three other developments which proved also be of great significance in the story of the church. There was the development of a theological tradition – rational, systematic, apologetic – in which faith and reason were concerned to engage critically with the world. There was also the awareness as the church left behind the early phases of experience, movement and sect that the spiritual and the temporal are required to live in relation to each other, that church and state are inter-connected and inter-dependent. There was as a consequence of these things the emergence of a philosophical tradition, even a philosophy of history, which in its changing forms – Paul, Irenaeus, the Apologists, Origen, Augustine – was concerned to relate human history to the purposes of God and to reconcile the church's understanding of God and the world and man.

The English reformation had been concerned to establish within a reformed church polity the primary authority of the scriptures, of the gospel sacraments, of the three-fold orders of ministry, of the historic creeds, of the early ecumenical councils. It was Hooker's achievement to bring all these things within a wide-ranging theological and philosophical system, maintaining the essential continuities with the early and the medieval church, and holding fast to the theory and the practice of a Christian commonwealth in which church and state are one.

The English Church had already demonstrated its commitment to scripture and tradition. Hooker placed reason alongside these two as the primary resources with which Christian theology is required to work. Indeed, it is in the interplay of scripture, tradition and reason that the English theological tradition has evolved. But reason is not self-authenticating. It must be brought into a living relationship with scripture and tradition. It is only then that the validity and the authority of reason can be demonstrated. This is to be seen most clearly in Hooker when he addresses matters of contemporary concern: questions relating to ecclesiastical law, to the sacraments, to episcopacy, to the relation of church and state. The three-fold authority is scrupulously maintained, and reason is exercised in such a way that truth is seen to comprehend in so far as it is able all the differing points of view.

It is not compromise but comprehension that is Hooker's distinctive characteristic. It is exactly here that the abiding usefulness of Hooker is to be found. His significance lies not so much in his teaching as in his method. It is an approach, an attitude of mind. Its discipline is the freedom of reason brought into open dialogue with scripture and tradition. Its fruit is the comprehensiveness – understood in the sense of comprehension – which goes to the heart of the English tradition.

Hooker was clear about the sufficiency of scripture for salvation. He accepted the primacy of scripture, but he went beyond Lutherans and Calvinists in accepting the co-inherence of scripture and the church. Scripture serves special purposes. It has the primary authority in matters of faith and morals, yet the church has the authority to draw out the implications of scripture for each succeeding age. He resisted, therefore, the Puritan conviction that all things can be determined solely by reference to scripture, and he prepared the way for the use of other kinds of knowledge which are presupposed by scripture even though they may not actually be found in scripture.

Hooker set his face against both the fundamentalism of scripture and the fundamentalism of tradition. The scriptures have an absolute claim upon the church's understanding. Tradition has in Hooker's thought a relative value. 'All things cannot be of ancient continuance, which are expedient and needful for the ordering of spiritual affairs: but the Church being a body which dieth not hath always power, as occasion requireth, no less to ordain that which never was, than to ratify what hath been before ... The Church hath authority to establish that for an order at one time, which at

another time it may abolish, and in both may do well.'[23] All
things relating to the ordering of the church's life are capable
of development: 'why should the later ages of the Church be
deprived of the liberty the former had?'[24] But it is through
the guidance of the Spirit that the church is led by the law of
reason to discover those things that are expedient for its life.[25]

Reference has already been made in passing to the freedom, the validity and the authority of reason in Hooker's
thought. *The Ecclesiastical Polity* constitutes a massive
defence of reason. It is in this sense that Hooker's work
might be judged to provide the foundation of a liberal
method. Reason – brought into relation with scripture and
tradition – is well able to address questions concerning
church polity and to be a determining factor in theology.

The *Ecclesiastical Polity* commences with a magisterial
examination of law in the created order, in human society, in
scripture, and in church polity. This emphasis upon law
enables Hooker to refute Puritan claims that the law of God
is to be found only in the scriptures. Law is the basis of
government and of all political and social obligations. A
Christian commonwealth, which finds practical expression
in a church-state polity, cannot therefore be rejected by the
Puritans without their rejecting also the principle of law by
which God has ordered all things. But the importance of the
Polity does not lie merely in the rejection of the Puritan position. Hooker's emphasis upon law is significant in four
respects.

It demonstrates the importance of natural law. Hooker
elaborated a whole theory of law, of which nothing less
could be said than that, 'her seat is the bosom of God, her
voice the harmony of the world'.[26] This natural law, which
governs the universe, is the expression of God's supreme
reason in the light of which all things must be interpreted.
'Laws human must be made according to the general laws of
nature, and without contradiction unto any positive law in
Scripture'.[27]

It underlines the importance of continuity in the Christian
tradition. The ancient world and the middle ages understood

the importance of law. Hooker provided an exposition whereby the earlier traditions which he took up and re-interpreted could be carried forward.

It illuminates the comprehensiveness or comprehension which Hooker was at paints to secure. He explored the interconnections that constitute the ordered universe. 'God hath created no thing simply for itself: but each thing in all things, and of every thing each part in other hath such interest, that in the *whole world* nothing is found whereunto anything created can say, 'I need thee not'.[28]

It provides a theological interpretation of life. What is given in the *Polity* is the foundation of a philosophy of history. Hooker's emphasis upon law, tested by scripture and brought into a developing relationship with scripture and tradition, becomes the rational basis of all human relationships – in church and state, in society, in history.

Hooker moves beyond all these things to locate the central mystery of salvation in the incarnation; and in this respect also he provides what will become one of the abiding concerns of the English tradition. Hooker's Christology, in common with that of all sixteenth century reformers, stands in the mainstream of Christian Chalcedonian orthodoxy: 'there are but four things which concur to make complete the whole state of our Lord Jesus Christ: his Deity, his manhood, the conjunction of both, and the distinction of the one from the other being joined in one'.[29] It is the incarnation that makes possible man's participation in God, but this participation cannot exist apart from the union of God and man in Christ.

The purpose of the incarnation is nothing less than the redemption of the world: 'The world's salvation was without the incarnation of the Son of God a thing impossible'.[30] God and God's redemption of man find full recognition, but there is also in Hooker a strong emphasis upon Christ's redemptive power in society, and upon the church as a redeemed society. It is Hooker's incarnational theology which undergirds his understanding of the church, the sacraments, and the relation of church and state.

It is in the context of participation in Christ that Hooker reflects upon the church. He distinguishes between the visible and the mystical church, although he is at pains to emphasise that 'visible and invisible maketh not two Churches; but the divers estate and condition of the same Church'.[31] Hooker is mindful of the continuity of the church's tradition, but it is in the continuity of faith and order with the early church that the wholeness and the guarantee of catholicity are to be found. The visible church is capable of corruption, and when it is in error there is a responsibility to purge and to reform it.

Hooker's primary concern is to address questions relating to the visible church. The church has a supernatural and sacramental life, but there is a strong emphasis upon the church as 'a visible society of men'.[32] The church is inescapably related to human institutions. Indeed, Hooker prefers to use 'the name of church-Polity ... because it contains both government and also whatever besides belongeth to the ordering of the Church in public'.[33] Nothing can take away the responsibility of making proper provision for 'ordering the public spiritual affairs of the Church of God',[34] but the relation of the church to the world – its historical progression, its institutions, its culture – is given a significance which has been one of the distinguishing marks of the church as institution and empire, and which was to become one of the dominant characteristics of the English tradition.

It is in the fifth book of the *Polity* that Hooker provides a comprehensive exposition of the practice of the English Church. The orders of ministry, public prayer, preaching, the sacraments and the necessity of a godly and learned clergy are all brought within the compass of Hooker's argument. The book serves as a theological commentary upon the English Prayer Book. It is Hooker's rationale, profound and systematic, of the reformed faith and practice.

Hooker's understanding of the church is influenced by his understanding of scripture. His classic interpretation of the tradition of the English church does not derive from the reformation statutes but from an ecclesiology which is rooted in scripture. His assertion of a church polity, of its organs of government, of the role of the prince all proceed from an exposition of scripture and of the traditions of the church. Hooker's starting-point is participation in Christ, the grace of word and sacraments, the mutual fellowship and society of Christian people with one another. But the practical out-working of all these things is to be found in the Christian commonwealth. 'Hooker's ideal is the *Res Publica Christiana* ... the Christian state. In such a state, the head of the state is the head of the church. That is because there is one cultural life, one common good and one governmental mode of expressing that common way of life.'[35]

The prominence that is given by Hooker to his treatment of the relation between church and state reflects the preoccupations of the sixteenth century. It was not the least of his complaints against the Puritans that they regarded church and state as two distinct societies. Hooker judges that such a distinction – and he finds exactly the same distinction for all practical purposes in the Roman Church as well – is a covert way of abrogating to the church a supremacy in relation to the temporal power.

It is here that Hooker's extraordinary capacity for synthesis and comprehension can be seen. He brings together the traditions of the ancient world and of the middle ages, and he holds them in a creative tension with the principle of nationality that belongs to his own age. Hooker is adamant that 'with us one society is both the Church and commonwealth'.[36] His model is the people of Israel in the Old Testament, 'which people was not part of them the commonwealth and part of them the Church of God, but the selfsame people whole and entire were both under one Chief Governor, on whose supreme authority they did all depend'.[37]

It is only in the context of a society in which church and commonwealth are one that Hooker is able to speak about the royal supremacy. But there should be no misunderstanding about the headship of Christ over his church and the headship or governorship which is vested in the crown. 'As the head is the highest part of man; so Christ is the highest in the Church, inseparably knit with it ... The headship which we give unto kings is altogether visibly exercised, and ordereth only the external frame of the Church's affairs here amongst us; so that it plainly differeth from Christ's, even in very nature and kind.'[38]

Hooker draws upon a variety of models, Roman and Byzantine, but his authority is taken from scripture. It is from Christ that kings receive their authority;[39] and the distinction between the headship of Christ and the headship of kings is made abundantly plain. 'Christ is head as being the fountain of life and ghostly nutriment, the well-spring of spiritual blessings poured into the Church; they heads, as being his principal instruments for the Church's outward government: He head, as founder of the house; they as his chiefest overseers.'[40]

There is nothing in the *Polity* which provides a theoretical basis for absolute power. Church and state are two facets of one society. Their unity is to be found in the person of the king. But the authority of the crown is not be confused with that previously exercised by the papacy. Hooker stands firmly against the absolutism of the Roman see and of the temporal monarch. The supreme governor is under God and under the law. The role of the king in relation to the commonwealth – church and state – is determined by the laws of an ecclesiastical polity.

It is because church and state are one that parliament is required to represent both. 'The parliament of England, together with the convocation annexed thereunto, is that whereupon the very essence of all government within this kingdom doth depend'.[41] Hooker undoubtedly drew upon ideas derived from the conciliar movement in the fifteenth century, but he provides a considered exposition of the balance of power in the Tudor constitution. The exercise of headship is to be constitutional and conciliar. It is a remarkable affirmation of the vocation of the state, of the significance of government, of the authority – even the royal priesthood – of the laity. Parliament has 'competent authority' in matters ecclesiastical so that when everything has been done by the church to order its affairs aright, the crown in parliament retains the determining voice because 'it is the general consent of all that giveth them the form and vigour of laws'.[42] Hooker provides a constitutional theory of government in which the crown, the church and the people are a single entity.

Hooker brings to all these things an historical perspective. He rejects the totalitarian claims implicit in the Roman imperium of the papal monarchy. The English reformation had been for him a reformation of the catholic church in England, and he looks back to an earlier age in which church and state had found a common unity in the great ideal of a Christian commonwealth. The ecclesiastical polity which he enunciated owed something to the model associated with Constantine, Justinian and Charlemagne; but it is presented without the imperial overtones of the church-state that had emerged in Western Europe in the late middle ages. It is something more than an institution and something less than an empire that Hooker sets before us.

The comprehension or comprehensiveness associated with Hooker has been caricatured as a theological rationale of the *via media*. There is a measured quality, a reasonableness, about Hooker's writing as he expounds 'the old and the new, and brings both together in one scheme of thought and life'.[43] But Hooker stood in this respect in a tradition that had long since established itself. The English reformation represents a thoroughgoing attempt to be both catholic and reformed.

Cranmer, writing in his Preface to the English Bible of 1540 about the ceremonies of the church, distinguished between those 'so addicted to their old customs (that they) thinke it a great matter of conscience to departe from a peece of the leaste (of them) ... (and those) so new fangle that they woulde innovate all thinge and so doe despyse the olde that nothynge can lyke them, but that is newe'.[44] Cranmer was not concerned to make provision exclusively for either party but to 'profitte them both'.[45]

Cranmer's policy was taken up after Elizabeth's accession

by Matthew Parker. It was he who represented in the early years the reasonableness of the Elizabethan settlement. He took from Aristotle's 'golden mean' an attitude of mind, a basic stance, expressed in the language of his day as 'golden mediocrity', which served to shape the awareness of the *via media* which had been from the beginning a characteristic of the English tradition. But Parker was consistent in this regard with the Queen who desired that 'none should be suffered to decline either on the left or on the right hand from the direct line limited by authority of our sacred laws and Injunctions'.[46]

The *via media* finds expression not only in the constitutional settlement but in the way in which the doctrinal controversies of the reformation period were actually resolved in England. Hooker and the seventeenth century divines who followed in his tradition distinguished between 'things necessary for salvation and things convenient in practice'.[47] Hooker attached great importance to 'the principle of measure' which for him finds its origin in the nature of God.[48] Hooker is entirely consistent with his own principle of comprehension. He attempts to reconcile wherever possible things that might properly be held together within his understanding of God – His nature, His revelation, His purposes, His providence. It is not the least of Hooker's achievements that he has bequeathed to the English tradition a renewed determination to hold together faith and reason, scripture and tradition, nature and grace.

The *via media* undoubtedly owed much to the determination of the reformers to find a way between the claims of Rome and Geneva; but some account must also be taken of 'the love of balance, restraint, moderation, measure, which ... appear to be innate in the English temper'.[49] It is in the seventeenth century, dominated by religious controversy, that the English Church came to occupy the middle ground between the conflicting demands of Rome and Calvinism and Puritanism. Quite apart from doctrinal and political considerations, there was a feeling for the *via media* which expressed itself in the continuing dialogue between scripture,

tradition and reason; in the appeal to the authority of the
early fathers and in an openness to new learning; in a
commitment to the historic continuity of the catholic church
and in the freedom of national churches.

The seventeenth century has been seen by many in retrospect as the golden age of the Church of England. Lancelot
Andrewes, John Donne,[50] George Herbert,[51] Nicholas
Ferrar[52] and Jeremy Taylor[53] speak of a wealth of learning
and piety and practical divinity. Hooker's influence continued to inform theological debate, but there has never been in
the English tradition one theologian to whom subsequent
generations have turned for definitive answers in matters of
faith. It is, rather, the way in which theological questions are
handled that is so important. 'What is distinctively Anglican
is not a theology but a theological method'.[54] And this
method – reasoned, ordered, measured, devout – which first
found expression in Hooker was to be developed fully in the
course of the following century in theological treatises, in
sermons, in devotional literature, in poetry.

The question of authority continued to present itself, but
the seventeenth century divines refused to give infallible
authority to scripture, tradition or reason. It was Andrewes's
emphatic claim that the teaching of the English Church was
quite simply the teaching of scripture, as it had been interpreted by the early church. The appeal to antiquity was a
common theme. It served to substantiate the claim of the
church to be catholic and reformed: 'there is no principal
dogma in which we do not agree with the Fathers and they
with us'.[55] The appeal to antiquity was never allowed to
stand alone and without reference to scripture; but it was the
fathers of the church in the first five centuries who provided
'the assurance and the norm of Catholicity'.[56]

Lancelot Andrewes's reputation as a preacher and a
confessor must stand alongside his work as a theologian and
an exponent of the English tradition. It is Nicholas Llosky
who has best captured something of Andrewes's understanding of theology and of its function within the church.
Theology was not for him 'a system of thought ... but a

progress in the experience of the mystery, the way of *union with God in the communion of the Church*.[57]

The emphasis upon the incarnation which has already characterised the English tradition leads now into a fuller understanding of the sacramental life. There is a meditative quality in Andrewes's theological writing, and the primary points of reference are the Trinity, the incarnation, and *theosis*. It is the Patristic doctrine of *theosis*, the deification of man, which Llosky also brings to our attention in Andrewes's theology. 'Theology then is for the service of the entire man on his way towards union with the personal God, the way of deification. It is the most profound experience of the Church that the theologian expresses in the Church and for the Church'.[58]

A full examination of the religious literature of the period leads to the conclusion that 'what we have to look for ... is not so much finality as direction'.[59] There is a great diversity of opinion to be found, but an underlying coherence is secured by the fundamental commitment to scripture, tradition and reason.

The emphasis upon the great biblical themes of creation and incarnation requires that all fields of knowledge shall lie open to scrutiny and that account must, therefore, be taken of natural theology. The appeal to antiquity carried with it an acknowledgement of the visible church and of the importance of the episcopate as a sign of apostolic continuity. The freedom of reason demanded not liberalism but liberality, an openness of mind and spirit that could live with questions to which answers could not easily be given.

Finality belonged to the fundamentals of faith; freedom could be given to matters that were not essential. 'It was in establishing a certain 'direction', and in avoiding a premature fixation that Anglican theology in its formative period showed at once its character and wisdom and its underlying consistency.'[60]

No account of the English tradition, in so far as it took shape in this period, can fail to take account of public prayer and private devotion. The directions of Archbishop Laud[61]

regarding the dignified ordering of public worship need to be
set alongside the importance of the English bible, the offering
of the English liturgy, and the tradition of preaching in the
English Church. Devotional works for private use – sermons,
meditations, prayer, moral theology – brought before those
who were able to read a rich range of material, scriptural and
sacramental, expressing the learning and the practical divinity of the English tradition. The depth and the discipline of
the spiritual life were reflected in many ways and not least of
all in the *Preces Privatae* of Lancelot Andrewes; in the
preaching and the poetry of John Donne; in the portrait of
the *Country Parson* offered by George Herbert, together
with so much of his poetry; in the community founded at
Little Gidding by Nicholas Ferrar; and in the devotional
writings of Jeremy Taylor.

The tradition that had emerged would be vulnerable to
new influences, but the boundary markers were firmly established and the method and the spirit of theological enquiry
would remain. The over-arching authority of scripture,
tradition and reason was never in dispute, although it was
the claims of reason that were pressed by the Cambridge
Platonists,[62] the Latitudinarians,[63] and the Deists.[64]

The Platonists judged reason to be the proper arbiter of
natural and revealed religion and argued on that basis for
comprehension within the church. The Latitudinarians took
forward this tradition of moderation, arguing – as men of
latitude – for freedom of interpretation in matters of dogma.
The rationality of the Christian revelation and of Christian
morality provided the basis for a practical philanthropy. The
Deists, whose influence in England was relatively slight and
whose work was vigorously refuted by Bishop Butler,[65] represented a type of natural religion which placed the overriding
emphasis upon God as Creator but without the distinctive
elements of the Christian relevation. Their significance lies,
perhaps, in the fact that it is in their work that the first serious questions can be found concerning the authenticity – and
the authority – of scripture.

Recent scholarship[66] has taken us beyond the earlier caricatures of the eighteenth century church with their portrayals of worldiness, complacency and neglect. The ethos of the Georgian church was rational and ethical rather than emotional, dogmatic and mystical. The idea and the ideal of moderation was encouraged and maintained, enabling the church to define itself by contrast with the corruption and the superstitions of catholicism and the enthusiasm of protestantism. But the developing tradition of the church included a continuing emphasis upon education; a recognition of the importance of personal and family devotion; and, in the later years of the eighteenth century, an assertion of the voluntary principle and of the place of the laity through the formation of numerous bodies which were concerned to take forward the work of the church in education, in moral reform, in evangelism at home and overseas.

It is, however, in the great revivals of the eighteenth and nineteenth centuries – evangelical and tractarian – that the diversity of the English tradition has been most conspicuously renewed. Evangelicalism has its roots in earlier traditions of protestant dissent – Lollardy, Lutheranism, Calvinism. The revival of the evangelical tradition within the Church of England can be traced from the middle years of the eighteenth century. It owed something to its contact with the Methodist movement, and especially to the preaching ministry and the Calvinist influence of George Whitefield. It met with suspicion and hostility, but it secured its place within the Church of England, developing as a parallel movement alongside Methodism, but looking for its authority to scripture and to the formularies of the established church.

The moderate Calvinism of the evangelical tradition laid its chief emphasis upon the authority of scripture, the doctrine of total depravity, justification by faith in the atoning death of Christ, the necessity of personal conversion and the assurance of forgiveness. It was in large measure through the work of Charles Simeon[67] that evangelicalism was brought within the mainstream of the church's life. It contributed significantly through the work of William Wilberforce, Lord Shaftesbury and members of the Clapham Sect to important areas of social legislation. Its influence extended to British colonies throughout the world through the newly founded missionary societies.

It is in the catholic revival associated with the writings of the Tractarians and the wider influence of the Oxford Movement that connections are most obviously established once again with the traditions of the early seventeenth century divines. Cardinal Newman[68] gave his retrospective judgement that 'the essence of Tractarianism was belief in a special providential mission of the Church of England. The Church of England was called to represent a theology that was Catholic but not Roman, a theology marked by what he called "calmness and caution", though not encouraging "lukewarmness and liberalism" '.[69]

The circumstances in which the movement evolved owed much to the abandonment of the confessional state in the repeal of the Test and Corporation Acts in 1828 and in the granting of Catholic Emancipation in 1829; to the spirit of reform that dominated critical intellectual thought in the 1820s and the early 1830s; and to the suppression by parliament of ten Irish bishoprics in 1833.

The Tractarians recovered for the English tradition its sense of the church as a divine institution, of the continuity of catholic faith and order, of the significance of episcopacy. They brought an awareness of the divine transcendence and of the essential mystery of the divine revelation. They emphasised the centrality of the incarnation and of the church's sacramental theology and life. The Tractarians became associated in the public mind with ritual, with the enrichment of public worship and the introduction of liturgical forms and ceremonies that owed much to the Roman tradition. But, in common with the evangelicals, they represented also above everything else a rediscovery of the church's call to holiness, of the disciplined life, of personal piety and practical Christianity, and of new standards of pastoral ministry.

But there has also been a tradition of critical enquiry, of liberality, which has been an important ingredient within the theological life of the English church. It is undoubtedly the case that alongside the newly affirmed authority of scripture and tradition, represented by the evangelical and the tractarian movements, there must also be placed the development of critical biblical scholarship and philosophical enquiry which have attempted to take account of new thinking in science, in philosophy, in history.

Essays and Reviews, published in 1860, might properly be seen as an early contribution to a modern tradition of theological radicalism which sought nothing less than free enquiry in matters of faith. It is, however, *Lux Mundi*, published in 1889, which has been judged by some to stand more fully in the line of development that leads directly from Hooker and Andrewes.[70]

Lux Mundi was sub-titled, 'A Series of Studies in the Religion of the Incarnation'. The Preface to the first edition spoke of the writers' concern 'to attempt to put the Catholic faith into its right relation to modern intellectual and moral problems'.[71] This statement of intent was enlarged upon in later editions and told of the need 'to bring the Christian Creed into its right relation to the modern growth of knowledge, scientific, historical, critical, and to the problems of politics and ethics'.[72] The writers set their faces against any suggestion of compromise as 'tampering with principle' but argued instead for 'readjustment, or fresh correlation, of the things of faith and the things of knowledge'.[73] There is nothing here of the rigidity or the romanticism of the tractarians, but a commitment to engagement and dialogue which has been part of the church's apologetic work from the beginning and which mattered so much to the post-reformation English divines.

In making its appeal to the scriptures and to the early fathers, the English tradition had acknowledge the centrality of a Trinitarian faith and an incarnational Christology. The authority of scripture and of credal definitions remained in the foreground of theological enquiry in the early years of the twentieth century. The liberal catholicism of *Lux Mundi* continued to inform the debate as new generations of scholars[74] raised questions that were disturbing to some, but reassuring to others that faith and reason are willing to engage critically with each other.

There can be traced from the middle years of the nineteenth century a painful and continuing period of theological reconstruction. The church has been required to adjust to a wider understanding of creation, to the significance of historical and literary studies, to a new awareness of the dynamics of human personality and human society. The intellectual climate has not always been sympathetic to the insights of Christian orthodoxy. Theology cannot do its work in isolation. The traditions of all churches are bound to be set in a context that is international and multi-disciplinary and ecumenical. The English traditions of comprehension and liberality have attempted to take account of wider influences: liberal protestantism, modernism, biblical orthodoxy, social reality, existentialism, liberal scepticism, liberation theology, and – in more recent times – a resurgence of theological conservatism alongside a continuing tradition of theological radicalism.

The diversity of traditions within the English church has been found in theological enquiry, in public worship, in personal piety, in patterns of public ministry. These traditions or tendencies, which have been known by a variety of names at different times, have their origins in the reformation settlement. The circumstances of successive generations have meant that they have been informed, or modified, or ignored, or enlarged, or renewed. It is, however, through the dialogue of scripture, tradition and reason – within a framework of comprehension and liberality – that their continued existence is ensured.

NOTES
 1 The Elizabethan Book of Common Prayer (1559).
 2 The Ordinal(1559).
 3 The Thirty-Nine Articles of Religion (1571).
 4 The Second Book of Homilies (1571).
 5 The 'Canon on Preaching' (1571).
 6 John Jewel, Bishop of Salisbury, 1522–1571.
 7 Matthew Parker, Archbishop of Canterbury, 1504–1575.

8 Richard Hooker, c.1554–1600.
9 John Whitgift, Archbishop of Canterbury, c.1530–1604.
10 Lancelot Andrewes, Bishop of Winchester, 1555–1626.
11 Cited by J.E. Neale, *Elizabeth I and Her Parliaments*, Jonathan Cape 1953 and 1957, Vol. II, p. 198.
12 John E. Booty, *John Jewel as Apologist of the Church of England*, SPCK 1963, p. ix.
13 John Jewel, *An Apology of the Church of England*, Ed. by J.E. Booty, Cornell University Press 1963.
14 Henry McAdoo, *Richard Hooker*. Essay in *The English Religious Tradition and the Genius of Anglicanism*, Edited by Geoffrey Rowell, Ikon 1992, p. 108.
15 Cited by Henry McAdoo, *Richard Hooker*, Essay in *The English Religious Tradition and the Genius of Anglicanism*, Ed. by Geoffrey Rowell, Ikon 1992, p. 108.
16 John Jewell, *Defence of the Apologie of the Church of England* (1567).
17 John E. Booty, *op.cit.*, p. 6.
18 Richard Hooker, *Of the Laws of Ecclesiastical Polity*, 8 vols., Vols 1–4 (1594), Vol. 5 (1597), Vol. 6 (1648), Vol. 7 (1662) and Vol. 8 (1648).
19 Cited by Henry McAdoo, *Richard Hooker*. Essay in *The English Religious Tradition and the Genius of Anglicanism*, Ed. by Geoffrey Rowell, Ikon 1992, p. 109.
20 W. Speed Hill, *The Evolution of Hooker's Laws of Ecclesiastical Polity*. Essay published in *Studies in Richard Hooker*, Ed. by W. Speed Hill, Case Western Reserve University Press 1972, p. 118.
21 Ibid., p. 151.
22 John S. Marshall, *Hooker and the Anglican Tradition*, A. & C. Black 1963, p. 66.
23 Richard Hooker, *Laws of Ecclesiastical Polity*, V. viii. 1–2.
24 Ibid., V. xx. 4.
25 Ibid., III. viii. 18.
26 Ibid., I. xvi. 8.
27 Ibid., III. ix. 2.
28 Richard Hooker, *Sermon III*. 2. Cited by John S. Marshall, *op.cit.*, p. 86.
29 Ibid., V. liv. 10.
30 Ibid., V. li. 3.
31 See William Covell, *Just and Temperate Defence of the Five Books of Ecclesiastical Polity*, London 1603, p. 70.
32 Ibid., III. i. 14.
33 Ibid., III. ii. 1.
34 Ibid.
35 John S. Marshall, *op.cit.*, p. 167.
36 Richard Hooker, *op. cit.*, VIII. i. 7.
37 Ibid.
38 Ibid., VIII. iv. 5.

39 Ibid., VIII. iv. 6.
40 Ibid., VIII. iv. 9.
41 Ibid., VIII. vi. 11.
42 Ibid.
43 John S. Marshall, *op.cit.*, p. 172.
44 Preface to Cranmer's *Bible of 1540*. Cited by W. Speed Hill (Editor), *Studies in Richard Hooker*, Case Western Reserve University Press 1972, p. 90.
45 Ibid.
46 Ibid., p. 93.
47 P.E. More, *The Spirit of Anglicanism*, Essay published in *Anglicanism: The Thought and Practice of the Church of England: Illustrated from the Religious Literature of the Seventeenth Century*, Ed. by P.E. More and F.L. Cross, SPCK 1962, p. xxiv.
48 Ibid., p. xxiii.
49 Ibid., p. xxii.
50 John Donne, Dean of St Paul's, c.1571–1631.
51 George Herbert, Poet and Divine, 1593–1633.
52 Nicholas Ferrar, founder of Little Gidding, 1592–1637.
53 Jeremy Taylor, Bishop of Down and Connor, and Dromore, 1613–1667.
54 H.R. McAdoo, *The Spirit of Anglicanism*, A. & C. Black 1965, p. 1.
55 Lancelot Andrewes, *Responsio*, p. 70. Cited by H.R. McAdoo, *The Spirit of Anglicanism*, A. & C. Black 1965, p. 334.
56 H.R. McAdoo, op.cit., p. 335.
57 Nicholas Llosky, *Lancelot Andrewes The Preacher (1555–1626)*, Oxford 1991, p. 345.
58 Ibid.
59 P.E. More, *op.cit.*, p. xx.
60 Ibid., p. xxi.
61 William Laud, Archbishop of Canterbury, 1573–1645.
62 The Cambridge Platonists: a group of influential philosophical divines at Cambridge between 1633 and 1688. Their number included Benjamin Whichcote, N. Culverwel, John Smith, Ralph Cudworth, Henry More.
63 Latitudinarians: a term applied to a group of Anglican divines in the seventeenth century within the church of England who attached relatively little importance to dogmatic questions. Their number included John Tillotson, Edward Stillingfleet, Simon Patrick.
64 The Deists: Deism denotes the system of natural religion which was first developed in the England in the late seventeenth and the eighteenth centuries. The Deists included Lord Herbert of Cherbury, John Toland, Samuel Clarke, Anthony Collins, Matthew Tindal.
65 Joseph Butler, Bishop of Durham, 1692–1752.
66 John Walsh, Colin Haydon and Stephen Taylor (Editors), *The Church of England c.1689–c.1833: From Toleration to Tractarianism*. CUP 1993.

67 Charles Simeon, Vicar of Holy Trinity, Cambridge, 1759–1836.
68 John Henry Newman, 1801–1890.
69 Cited by Aidan Nicholls, *The Panther and the Hind*, T. & T. Clark 1993, p. 121.
70 P.E. More, *op.cit.*, p. xxxi. H.R. McAdoo, *op.cit.*, pp. 335–6.
71 Charles Gore (Editor) *Lux Mundi*, John Murray 1889, p. vii.
72 Ibid., Tenth Edition, p. vii.
73 Ibid., p. viii.
74 *Foundations: A Statement of Church Belief in Terms of Modern Thought* (1912). *Essays Catholic and Critical* (1926).

Chapter 7

The English Experience

Establishment provides the legal framework within which the English Church offers public ministry to the whole nation. Canon Law declares that the Church of England, which is established according to the laws of the realm, belongs to the true and apostolic Church of Christ.[1] This statement affirms the wider community of faith to which the Church of England belongs, but recognises the distinctive historical process whereby it has evolved. Establishment does not determine the fundamentals of faith and order – the scriptures, the sacraments, the credal statements, the orders of ministry – but it has inevitably influenced the Church of England's self-awareness and the wider perceptions, public and private, which have facilitated or inhibited the exercise of ministry.

The English tradition has affirmed the conviction of the English reformation that within a Christian commonwealth a supreme governorship of church and state properly resides in the crown. It is implicit in this understanding, however, that the authority of the crown would be circumscribed by law and by the responsibilities of parliament and the convocations. The complex pattern of constitutional dependence and independence established by the reformation settlement has had its counterparts throughout Christendom in the ancient, the medieval and the modern worlds.

But there are many questions to be asked. What has been the English experience of establishment? How did it come about that the reformation settlement was embraced, abandoned, restored, qualified, retained? Has it served the interests of church and state? What principles does it embody? What has it bequeathed that church and state might still be glad to recognise and carry forward?

It has to be acknowledged at the outset that the great ideal of the Christian commonwealth was never realised. The strength of puritanism and the presence of catholic recusancy meant that the idea of a church which was truly comprehensive of all people could not be achieved. Hooker's model of an ecclesiastical polity was not irrelevant and it continued to inform the English tradition over four centuries; but the existence of significant and determined confessional minorities served only to strengthen the rigour with which the penal legislation designed to enforce the Elizabethan settlement was pursued.

The reformed church polity with its comprehensive claims to allegiance could not fail to be perceived by some as an institution, if not an empire, which was overbearing, intolerant, exclusive. Two generations were to pass after the death of Elizabeth before the deep controversies with puritanism could be resolved. Two centuries and more were to pass before the civil disabilities imposed upon protestant nonconformists and catholics could be removed. The place of the reformed church, the *ecclesia Anglicana*, in English life appeared to be secure; but it was a consequence of all these things that puritans and catholics alike were compelled to function as sects within the realm.

The accession of James I in 1603 seemed to offer every promise that the royal supremacy would be exercised in exactly the way that Hooker had envisaged. The intermingling of the spiritual and the temporal was developed further by the notion of the divine right of kings in the early Stuart period, although the actual relation between church and state was less oppressive from the church's point of view than might have been expected because of a corresponding commitment to a high doctrine of episcopacy. James I's famous dictum, 'No Bishop – No king', expressed the ideal of how the continuing catholicity of the church might properly be reconciled with the temporal authority of a national church.

The English tradition evolved in the seventeenth century against the background of great upheavals in the life of the state. The church's controversies with protestantism in its various forms – puritanism, presbyterianism, independency – were caught up in the wider traumas of civil war, the execution of Charles I, the commonwealth of Oliver and Richard Cromwell, the restoration, the revolution of 1688. The church-state of the Tudor reformation settlement and of Hooker's *Ecclesiastical Polity* was embraced by the early Stuart kings, rejected at the time of the commonwealth, restored at the accession of Charles II, brought into question with the abdication of James II and the resignation of the non-jurors,[2] and secured – albeit in a slightly modified form – by a new constitutional settlement in which the Toleration Act of 1689 guaranteed freedom of worship to protestant dissenters within certain prescribed conditions.

The Church of England was wholehearted in its support of the crown in the years following upon the restoration of the monarchy in 1660, and its position in the life of the nation was re-established and strengthened. But the abdication of James II in 1688, the accession of William and Mary, the resignation and the ejection of the non-jurors raised important questions concerning the divine right of kings, non-resistance and passive obedience.

These were the matters that dominated the lower houses of convocation after 1688 during a period of considerable disquiet. One of the consequences of the revolution of 1688 had been that authority in ecclesiastical matters passed increasingly to parliament. This was something that touched upon the historic understanding of the relation between church and state under the personal governorship of a godly prince. The suppression of the convocations by royal writ in 1717 in the face of continuing controversy represented, therefore, a potentially serious loss of any residual independence the church might have enjoyed. The assumption was thereby strengthened that parliament was the assembly of both church and state, competent to legislate in all matters, spiritual and temporal.

The theory of the unity of the church-state was qualified by the Toleration Act, and there began to appear from that time signs of differing opinions amongst English divines concerning the supremacy.[3] The publication of William Warburton's book, *The Alliance of Church and State*, in 1736 represented the first significant breach in the thinking behind the reformation tradition. Warburton saw church and state as independent organisms which might enter into a compact for their mutual advantage, although their interests and purposes would be different. It was only on the basis of such a compact that the church would surrender its powers of appointment, legislation and jurisdiction, and receive in return public recognition, endowment and privileges in law.

But recognition, endowment and privileges in law could not alter the fact that the established church was not alone in ministering to the spiritual needs of the nation. The small catholic community in England had survived and continued to set its face firmly against the reformation settlement. Protestantism, which had produced relatively strong minorities in most parts of Northern Europe, had experienced a series of re-alignments in England over a period of two centuries. The growth of religious affiliations outside the allegiance of the established church was assisted by the success of itinerant preaching ministries in the course of the eighteenth century, by the growth of population in cities and towns from the middle years of that century, by the appearance and rapid expansion of the Sunday school movement, and by the emergence of Methodism as a significant and separate religious communion.

By the beginning of the nineteenth century large numbers of English people were members of dissenting bodies. The Toleration Act of 1689 had granted a limited degree of recognition to orthodox protestant dissenters. It was, therefore, in one sense an admission that other confessional groups must at the very least – and on certain strict conditions – be permitted within the state. The movement for the removal of civil disabilities on the grounds of religion went back to the 1780s and focussed upon attempts to secure the repeal of the

Test and Corporation Acts. The question of catholic emancipation was in many ways a consequence of the Act of Union which brought Ireland fully within the jurisdiction of the English parliament in 1800–1801. It meant that some recognition and accommodation must eventually be made for a population of some five and a half million Roman Catholics in Ireland.[4]

But the reformation pattern continued as the Church of England functioned throughout the eighteenth and the early nineteenth centuries as 'the embodiment of the state in its religious aspect'.[5] Behind the practical outworking of the religious establishment, there lay a continuing sense that church and state belonged to each other and that the church was called *inter alia* to embody and express the identity, the consciousness, the religious aspirations of the nation. It was only with the repeal of the Test and Corporation Acts in 1828 and the passing of Catholic Emancipation in 1829 that the position of absolute primacy that had previously been granted to the English Church as an expression of the unity of the church-state was finally removed.

It was the judgement of one churchman that the repeal of the Test and Corporation Acts 'pronounced religion to be, so far as the state is concerned, a thing indifferent'.[6] The evidence of the following century does not support such a dismissive judgement, but it is plain that the dominant characteristic of church-state relationships in the nineteenth century is the partial but progressive disengagement of church and state. The whole process was carried out over fifty years or more in a thoroughly piecemeal and pragmatic way, and the leaders of the church were no less pragmatic as they adjusted to new circumstances. The establishment principle was qualified but it was not abandoned.

When everything has been said about the mutual responsibility and interdependence of church and state, the century as a whole was distinguished by consistent attempts on the part of successive governments to secure the religious neutrality of the state: the removal of all restrictions on grounds of religion for election to parliament and to public

office; the abolition of the wide-ranging powers of church
courts; the abolition of compulsory church rates; the
opening up of the ancient universities; the introduction of
civil marriages; the provision of public burial grounds and
municipal cemeteries; the establishment of parish councils
that were to be separate, at least in law, from the parish
church and its officers.

In some instances, the driving force was the removal of
civil disabilities that were bitterly resented. In some instances, the driving force was a recognition by government of
the religious diversity, even the religious neutrality, of the
nation. It meant that in many areas of national life the old
ideal was finally and necessarily abandoned that in England,
a Christian commonwealth, church and state are one.

And yet the experience of the established church showed
that the law could still be oppressive: the judgement in the
Gorham Case concerning baptismal regeneration in 1850;
the four reports published by the Royal Commission on
Ritual in 1867–1870; the Public Worship Regulation Act of
1874; and the prosecution of clergymen for the use of certain
forms of ceremonial. These were all matters that were deeply
resented by those for whom such actions and judgements
represented a violation of the independence and the integrity
of the church. It would be the work of later generations
to take the initiative in securing for the Church of England
in the course of the twentieth century the appropriate degree
of independence through the Enabling Act,[7] the establishment of Synodical Government,[8] the Worship and Doctrine
Measure,[9] and the establishment of the Crown Appointments Commission.[10]

Meanwhile the relationship between church and state at
the end of the nineteenth century appeared to every disinter-
ested observer to be intimate and far-reaching. The church
retained its endowments. Its bishops sat in the House of
Lords. Its parochial clergy were deeply involved in the life of
their local communities. Church schools were integrated
within a national system of education. And more than that:
'The country continued to regard itself as possessing a

Christian government. Only small groups of intellectuals looked to a rigorous secular state. Nonconformists who said they did really retained a greater belief in the establishment of religion than they knew. For Nonconformists were among the first to demand that there be a connection between the law and Christian morality ... Nonconformists, like churchmen, expected Christianity to provide the ultimate sanction of the morality of government: the principle of Establishment in its purest form'.[11]

But public perceptions of the church as the estate of the realm which is required to embody and to articulate the religious aspirations of the nation have to be set alongside a long-standing tradition of indifference at a personal level to the claims of the church on the part of large numbers of people. It is one of the paradoxes of the English experience of establishment that there is to be found over the generations a tradition of stubborn and persistent secularism. The tradition does not take the form of violent antipathy, of militant anti-clericalism. Here also there is to be found the principle of moderation, of measure. It is as though people have been willing to operate on two levels: acknowledging the place of the church, using the occasional offices, ensuring that their children are taught the rudiments of the Christian faith; and yet remaining at the same time unresponsive to calls to active and sustained participation in the life of the church.

A study of the church in one of the great industrial English cities led to the conclusion that 'from the emergence of the industrial towns in the eighteenth century, the working class, the labouring poor, the common people, as a class, substantially, as adults, have been outside the churches. The industrial working class pattern has evolved lacking a tradition of the practice of religion'.[12] But this broad statement cannot be allowed to stand without qualification. The popular notion that church-going habits were lost in the turmoil of the industrial revolution has no substantial basis. It is possible to point to exceptional cases, but studies of the rural church suggest that 'the alienation of the urban working classes in the period of the industrial revolution has its origins in the slow alienation of the rural working classes throughout the previous century'.[13]

The voluntary census of attendance at public worship on a particular Sunday in 1851 provides hard statistical evidence regarding attendance in the middle years of the nineteenth century. The conclusion is inescapable that in a score of the largest towns in England fewer than one person in ten attended any place of worship on the census Sunday. Small industrial settlements in different parts of the country provided exceptions to the general rule, but in spite of the tremendous advances made by the Victorian Church in the final decades of the nineteenth century, nothing can contradict Bishop Winnington Ingram's[14] comment, 'It is not that the church of God has lost the great towns; it has never had them'.[15]

Reference has already been made to the enduring fact of a secular British polity.[16] It is not possible to offer an explanation of this tradition of indifference, of secularism, of alienation which has its roots deep in the life of the nation. Some will go back to the wholesale destruction of medieval catholicism, with its extraordinary combination of mysticism and superstition, in the violent fluctuations of reformation and counter-reformation. Some will direct attention to the hard rigours of public religious uniformity that became the touchstone of the new religious settlement. Some will cite the long standing traditions of non-residence, of pastoral neglect, of gross clerical abuses. Those who look at the rural church will discover situations in which the tithe dominated and embittered relationships between clergy and people. Those who look at the urban church will see the tragic lack of provision made in towns and cities caught up in the upheavals of rapid industrial development and urbanisation, and the problems posed by pew rents and free benches.

It may not be sufficient to look for an explanation merely within the confines of the ecclesiastical scene. The hard facts of economic life over successive generations provide, perhaps, the unhappy framework within which historians must pursue any analysis of alienation. Certainly there is to be found running through all the discussion of this problem over the last one hundred and fifty years a recognition of 'the remarkable influence of class on religious observance' in England.[17] One commentator speaks of a 'terribly deep-rooted notion that the church was for the rich and comfortable',[18] while another remarks that 'amongst the working classes there is a feeling that they compromise themselves in some way by going to a church'.[19] As early as 1840, the incumbent of one of the 'Million Churches' in Sheffield, writing an open letter to Sir Robert Peel,[20] complains of a tradition of unconscious secularism: 'the prevailing reason, I am assured, is the *force of inveterate habit* ... they tread in the steps of their fathers, and are neither impressed with the obligation, nor feel the desire of obtaining religious instruction'.[21]

The English experience is multi-facetted. The church which is called to be in some sense the religious embodiment of the nation is also the church from which people, while voicing assent, will actually withhold active participation. And yet the church has continued to explore the meaning of a church-state relationship which has proved to be more pervasive and more enduring than any comparable establishment in the western world.

Several themes present themselves from the beginning of the nineteenth century concerning the relation of church and state and the special responsibilities of the established church within the state. There is a sense that the English church is required to embody and to articulate the principle of nationality; that the establishment of religion is one of the essential prerequisites of a sound social order; that the comprehensiveness which informed the ideal of the Christian commonwealth from the time of the reformation should be secured within a broad-based church polity. These are the themes which interweave with one another and which, interpreted in a wide variety of practical ways, indicate something of the tradition and the experience of the English church.

It was the judgement of Samuel Taylor Coleridge[22] that a national church is an estate of the realm, 'established and endowed and treated as an essential part of the constitution because its office was to serve the interests of the nation'.[23] It was the younger Gladstone's conviction that a national church is required to be 'the centre of the national life'.[24] But the relationship between church and state is one of mutual responsibility and interdependence: the state is the guardian of the church; the church is the guardian of morality. For Coleridge, Thomas Arnold[25] and the younger Gladstone,[26] Christian morality – secured within the life of the nation by the establishment of religion – is the basis of law, of political order, of society's well-being. It was the task of the national church to bring the principles of Christianity into all the relationships of life.

The English reformation settlement bears testimony to the biblical conviction that religious faith and practice, political order and social stability, are bound up together. But the circumstances of the times served also to emphasise the need to secure social cohesion and social harmony. There was a spirit of reform in intellectual circles in the 1820s and the early 1830s; but there had also been a sense of profound shock following upon the French Revolution and the Napoleonic Wars, which had deepened the isolation of the English people, strengthened the conservatism of the nation, and brought back into the forefront of discussion the ancient connection – public and private – between religion and morality.

Hooker's great theme of comprehension or comprehensiveness was taken up again and pursued with great vigour by Thomas Arnold in his book, *Principles of Church Reform*, published in 1833. He wrote from the premise that the establishment of religion is a great blessing to a nation, but he acknowledged that in England this blessing had been largely lost because so large a part of the nation no longer adhered to the national church. He sought to give a liberal and broad-based interpretation to the established church and, committed wholeheartedly to the notion of comprehensiveness, argued that the boundaries of the Church of England must be enlarged to include the majority of orthodox dissenters. He expounded what has been caricatured as the broad church position, pleading for a church that was tolerant of diversity in faith and practice, 'thoroughly national, thoroughly united, thoroughly Christian'.[27]

Arnold's proposals were not welcomed in the Church of England and they were fiercely opposed by non-conformists; but in calling for a church that was enlarged and comprehensive he was giving new life to the conviction of Richard Baxter,[28] the seventeenth century Puritan divine, that it is the function of the Church of England to tolerate the tolerable.[29] It is of some interest to note that, nearly a century later, Bishop Hensley Henson,[30] who had become persuaded by the late 1920s that disestablishment was inevitable and desirable, hoped 'that the Church of England after disestablishment should be still firmly based on the principles of the reformation and therefore the better qualified to become the corporate expression of the nation's Christianity. 'Not disestablishment but more establishment', I used to say, meaning that I would have the established church administered in a large and liberal spirit with the definite object of widening its fellowship to include the orthodox nonconformist and thus making it more truly in fact what it was in theory, the corporate expression of the nation's Christianity'.[31]

The liberality of spirit which is implicit in Arnold's thesis found its fullest expression in the middle years of the nineteenth century in the work of Arnold's favourite pupil and biographer, Dean Stanley[32]. It was for him a matter of conviction that establishment provided the checks and balances which enabled the church to contain within itself a diversity of interpretation. The connection of church and state as it had developed in England represented, therefore, the nearest approach which could be made to 'the original and essential idea of the Christian church'.[33]

It was also Henson's judgement that establishment had shaped the 'uniquely tolerant and comprehensive' character of the Church of England, 'allowing a larger margin for private opinion than the more exacting systems with which it is contrasted. The line between essential and non-essential is otherwise drawn in the Church of England than in the churches of Rome, Wittenberg and Geneva'.[34] It is impossible to assess the extent to which this comprehensiveness is born of a continuing interaction between church and people in which national characteristics play an important part, and in which the pragmatism, the lack of dogma, the absence of written constitutions and clearly defined statements of political and ecclesiastical theory all contribute something. But a church that takes seriously God's covenant relationship with His people will understand something of the comprehensiveness of election and the all-inclusiveness of grace.

The themes persist: the interdependence of church and state; the necessity of establishment; the nature of the church's responsibility within society. The church that was not established was in F.D. Maurice's[35] judgement incomplete. 'We say that this condition was necessarily imperfect, for it left all the relations of men, as held together by the bonds of neighbourhood, as distinguished by race and religion, unaccounted for; for it did not bring their relations under church influence.'[36]

Maurice believed that the nation is an ordinance of God, and the state a servant of God. The function of the church, of the national church, within the life of the state is fundamental to the integrity of society. 'A National Church should mean a church which exists to purify and elevate the mind of a nation; to give to those who make and administer and obey its laws a sense of the grandeur of law and of the source whence it proceeds, to tell the rulers of the nation that all false ways are ruinous ways, that truth is the only stability of our time or of any time ... This should be the meaning of a national church: a nation wants a church for these purposes mainly; a church is abusing its trust if it aims at any other or lower purpose.'[37]

A church that is informed by a biblical theology will find it easy to understand that the story of a people and the story of a people's relationship with its God cannot easily be separated. This is the scriptural warrant for Thomas Arnold's conviction that, 'State and Church are then only in a perfect condition, when they are not allied, but identical; in other words, when the State is a Christian society, and the Church a sovereign society.'[38] It is a mark of the enduring nature of the church-state relationship throughout the nineteenth and the early twentieth centuries that Archbishop Benson[39] could insist that 'the Christian state is the Christian church in another character',[40] and that Archbishop William Temple[41] could urge that 'both state and church are instruments of God for establishing His kingdom'.[42]

But what is the significance of nationality within the purposes of God? Why do English divines continue to affirm that for the sake of church and state there is something in the fact of establishment which remains serviceable? Is there a theological understanding of history which illuminates and informs these classical statements of the position of the English church?

The English ecclesiastical settlement which has come down the centuries in its distinctive form, adapted and modified in all kinds of ways, has said something about what it means to be a nation. It was Archbishop Lang,[43] speaking in the debate on the disestablishment of the Welsh Church in the House of Lords in 1913, who expounded an understanding of the state which went far beyond all utilitarian and contractual theories. It recognised the 'organic unity and spirit' of the nation, the 'tradition and associations running far back into the past', the 'subconscious continuity which endures and profoundly affects the character of each generation of citizens'.[44] The question that was, therefore, posed by Lang was 'whether just there, in that inward region of the national life where anything that can be called its unity and character is expressed, there is or is not to be this witness to some ultimate sanction to which the nation looks, some ultimate ideal which it professes. It is in our judgement a very serious thing for a state to take out of that corporate heart of its life any acknowledgement at all of its concern with religion'.[45]

But the advantages of such an acknowledgement were not for the state alone but for state and church. Archbishop Davidson,[46] speaking also on the disestablishment of the

Welsh Church, argued the case for establishment on the ground that 'it compels the state in its corporate capacity to recognise the power and influence of religion ... (it) compels the church to be in touch with thoughts and interests which are wider and deeper (than its own)'.[47]

And this great ideal – the interdependence of church and state within the framework of law – has its roots in an incarnational view of history. Bishop Hensley Henson, writing out of a deep understanding of Christian history, insisted that, 'Nationality ... is the product of a long evolution into which many factors have entered. It arrives late on the stage of history, and its rich efflorescence in national character, language, art and literature is at once the garnered harvest of all the past and the seed of all the future. We must see it thus if we would see it justly ... When nationality is thus seen in its true character as an element in the developing life of the race on this planet we can see that it stands connected with the religion of the world's redeemer. For that religion includes a philosophy of history. Christians must regard the entire life of mankind as inspired by the divine spirit and directed by a divine purpose'.[48]

No one was more mindful of the dangers, and Henson was not slow to warn that, 'National Christianity may not be so national as to cease to be Christian'.[49] Certainly he was alert to the possibility of a real divergence of interests. And yet he pleaded powerfully that 'nationality has been a potent instrument of spiritual interpretation ... The distinctive contributions of Jewish, Greek, Latin, Celtic, Teutonic and Slavonic nationality to the slow unfolding of Christ's religion are recognisable and precious'.[50]

But the broad themes of nationality, of social harmony, and of comprehensiveness are nothing more than fine sentiments unless they are translated into attitudes of mind which inform the pattern and the content of the church's public ministry.

The principle of nationality must speak of the importance of locality, of the identity and the significance of each community of people, which provides the context and the focus of the church's ministry as it is experienced day by day.

The principle of social harmony must speak of the social dimension to the work of ministry, transcending the church's proper concern with individuals, enabling it to witness to the values of the kingdom, which are to be sought and expressed in the ordering of all human affairs, in private and in public.

The principle of comprehensiveness must speak of the all-inclusiveness of Christ's religion, of the church's openness to people in all their situations, of the wide range of associations with the church that people have and are capable of sustaining, of the many ways by which people might find their way home to God.

It is only in so far as these principles – of nationality, of social harmony, of comprehensiveness – are translated into the realities of public ministry that the English tradition and the English experience can be fully seen. But it is the theological principles that are implicit in all these things that are so important. The principle of locality, like the principle of nationality, speaks of an approach to ministry that is fundamentally incarnational. The principle of social harmony speaks of the prophetic dimension that can never be removed from the wholeness of the church's ministry. The principle of the all-inclusiveness of Christ's religion, like the principle of comprehensiveness, speaks of the generosity of grace, of the self-giving, which have their origin in the God who gives Himself to His creation with purpose and with infinite patience.

The Church of England has no monopoly where these things are concerned and, in common with all churches, has shown itself time and again to be a compromised institution. All churches within the mainstream of the Christian tradition will interpret these theological principles in the light of their own story and, like the Church of England, will respond with varying degrees of faithfulness and unfaithfulness. But what cannot be gainsaid is the fact that these principles, these approaches to ministry, come inescapably within the remit of the Church of England – because of the continuing story of the English Church, because of the reformation settlement, because of the responsibilities that are implicit even in the modified form of establishment that remains.

It is in the parochial system, supplemented by a wide range of sector ministries that the Church of England embraces in a comprehensive fashion the principle of locality. The parish has been from Tudor times a unit of civil administration as well as of spiritual oversight; and, although the civil functions have long since been removed, the church's commitment to the maintenance of the parochial ministry remains the first charge upon its resources. The growth of cities and large towns at the time of the industrial revolution, the movement of population, the necessity to unite parishes within a single benefice in rural areas, the secularisation of life and the privatisation of religion have all compromised the significance of the parish as the basic unit of the church's ministry; and yet it continues to testify – the parish, the parish church and the parish priest – to the church's desire to offer ministry to the whole nation.

The territorial basis of the parochial system reflects the origins of the church's ministry in an agricultural society. It has been supplemented over recent generations by large numbers of sector ministries – in education, in industry and commerce, in the armed services, in hospitals, in local government, in community relations, in prisons – but the mainstay of the church's ministry remains the parochial ministry, and the pattern of parochial life still reflects something of the achievements of the Victorian church.

It was in large measure the reforms of the 1830s which enabled the Church of England to grow beyond some of the persistent abuses of church life – pluralities, sinecures, non-residence, gross inequalities of income – and respond to the needs of a rapidly changing society. Overtaken by a rapidly escalating population and by the parallel processes of urbanisation and industrialisation, the churches – and not least of all the Church of England – provided a pattern of local ministry that was enlarged and extended in all kinds of ways.

The development of parochial ministry was distinguished by four characteristics: first, the provision of a massive

network of church buildings – parish churches, parsonage
houses, church schools, mission halls, Sunday School insti-
tutes; secondly, the provision of large numbers of clergy;
thirdly, the enrichment of public worship, and especially
through the introduction of the organ and the robed choir;
and, fourthly, the multiplication of church guilds and clubs
and societies, many of which had a biblical, educational or
evangelistic basis. The pattern of English parochial church
life, which has been known throughout much of the twentieth century, has been in large measure the legacy of the
Victorian church. Indeed, it is the achievements of the
Victorian church that have provided the criteria by which the
church in the twentieth century has sought all too often to
evaluate its work.

The Victorian age marked an important transition in
several areas of parochial life, and not least of all in regard to
the English parson and the conscientiousness with which he
pursued his pastoral duties. The eighteenth century was not
without notable instances of learning and piety and pastoral
care, but there was a prevailing sense that 'the way of the
Church of England was one of benign acceptance ... a great
national institution, a preserver of peace, good order and
culture'.[51] Dean Church,[52] writing at the end of the nineteenth century, speaks of the English parson prior to the
evangelical revival and the tractarian movement as a man
who counted for a good deal in the society around him –
'often the patriarch of his parish, its ruler, its doctor, its
lawyer, its magistrate, as well as its teacher' – but who, in
spite of much that was good and useful, was marked more
than anything else by 'quiet wordliness'.[53]

The English parish and the English parson represented and
reflected a practical out-working of the church-state relation
at a local level: the extent of lay patronage in the church; the
relationship in rural parishes between the squire and the
parson; the large numbers of clergy who took their place as
of right on the magistrate's bench; the use of parochial
administration for the purposes of poor relief and public
services. These things did not proceed from any coherent

theology or theory of establishment. They were the accepted residue of a political and social order in which church and state were intimately bound up with each other. Establishment was accepted by many as a practical and useful expression of Christian profession on the part of the state and a public means of securing and encouraging a Christian morality.

There was from the 1830s a growth in responsibility on the part of government for areas of concern that had previously come within the competence and responsibility of the church. But the emphasis upon social harmony continued to be implicit in the endeavours of generations of clergy and their congregations. Alongside the self-consciousness, even the self-righteousness, of the Victorian church with its missionary zeal and its moral fervour, there must also be set the basic work of welfare in countless parishes – through the regular pastoral work of the clergy; through the oversight of church schools; through an active involvement in local charities; through relief work in a wide variety of ways. No more striking testimony can be found than the fact that in the course of the nineteenth century large numbers of clergy appeared before Parliamentary Select Committees and Royal Commissions of Enquiry into social conditions, and could speak out of personal knowledge, and could be accepted as expert witnesses.

The comprehensiveness or all-inclusiveness of the Church of England has been experienced in two respects: first, with regard to the diversity of interpretation permitted within the church; and, secondly, with regard to the outer constituency of allegiance the church has traditionally retained.

The story of the Church of England since the reformation demonstrates its ability to contain within itself a wide diversity of interpretation. There is a framework provided by the Book of Common Prayer, the Ordinal, and the Articles of Religion; by the threefold dynamic of scripture, tradition and reason; by the legislative authority of the crown in parliament. It is within this framework that there has evolved a tradition of catholicity and comprehension. The spirit of

renaissance and reformation has remained as the continuity
of apostolic faith has engaged with a liberality of mind which
has been sensitive to new learning. What is to be found at the
heart of the English tradition and the English experience is an
affirmation of the dynamic character of scripture, tradition
and reason; a refusal to accept the infallibilities of statement
and the inflexibilities of mind which have all too often
distorted the church's presentation of the gospel. It is easy to
caricature such a church as one lacking in principle or theological rigour. It is less easy to dismiss the willingess to
contain within one community of faith differing interpretations which speak of the paradoxes of faith, of the ambiguities of human experience.

It is also one of the characteristics of the Church of
England's comprehensiveness that it has long since retained
the nominal allegiance of large numbers of people. Gladstone
spoke as early as 1838 of the responsibility of the established
church 'to preserve in a greater or a less attachment to religious ordinances and professions and even feelings, a very
large class of persons who would otherwise be without God
in the world'.[54] It would be folly to suggest that such a
constituency of opinion and support will necessarily
continue to exist; but there has been over the generations a
vague Christianity in English life, buttressed and informed
for some in earlier times by the public schools and for far
more by the Sunday Schools and by acts of worship and
religious instruction in state schools.

It was, however, the pastoral strategy pursued in the
parishes in the middle years of the nineteenth century, together with comparable strategies in churches of other traditions, that undergirded the inarticulate Christian religion of
a nation that was in fair measure non-churchgoing. The
development of parochial ministry must be seen to be at least
in part an endorsement of the principle of the comprehensiveness of the church and the all-inclusiveness of religion.

The nineteenth century saw a massive increase in the
number of parish churches, especially in the towns, as the
Church of England struggled valiantly to keep pace with the

expanding population of the country. And it was not just parish churches. It has been reckoned that Victorian England was nurtured in the Sunday Schools and the church day schools. There was a proliferation of church schools, Sunday Schools, clubs, guilds, fellowships and societies of all sorts attached to or run by the parish church. Local community life in late Victorian England would have been incomparably poorer but for the vigorous, wide-ranging ministries offered in many parishes. The introduction of a parish magazine, the appearance of religious tracts and other publications, and regular parochial meetings on weekdays for bible study, prayer, discussion and worship were all common features of parochial life. There was in many places a lively social life centred on the parish church. Institutions such as the Mothers' Union, the Girls' Friendly Society, young men's clubs, parochial libraries and reading rooms can all be traced back to this period.

There is a glimpse of what this tradition of comprehensiveness meant in practice in Alan Wilkinson's study of *The Church of England and the First World War*. One of the Anglican chaplains reflected upon his experiences at the front. His observations might serve as a tribute to a pattern of ministry that was not self-consciously and explicitly religious, but was directed to people's needs and to the opportunities that might be presented. It was his experience that if the chaplain 'stands exclusively for spiritual things his contact will be limited. If he tries to get to know the battalion as a whole he throws himself into a number of minor activities, running canteens and cinemas, and providing comforts. The Roman Catholic chaplains had decided to work on a frankly sectarian basis, dealt simply with their flocks, shunned canteens and tried to minister almost exclusively on a spiritual level. Most Anglican chaplains had chosen the wider type of ministry. Not only have I run canteens, but at advanced dressing stations I have been content for hours to busy myself with blankets and hot soup for their needs happy if just once or twice in the night I could put in a word of more articulate religion. Over against those inside and outside the church who see Christianity as something outside and beyond ordinary life we preach the all-inclusiveness of Christianity'.[55]

It may yet be that this is the most important single theological perspective in any understanding of church-state relationships in the English experience. What one Anglican chaplain was able to say out of his experience of the realities of ministry at the front in the Great War undoubtedly had its roots in an approach to ministry that was one of the products of the establishment of the Church of England, which at its best has been comprehensive in the drawing of its boundaries and all-inclusive in the exercise of its ministry.

But in what did the comprehensiveness of the Church of England finally reside? Was its basis theological or pastoral? Has the continuity of establishment been a significant factor? There is, of course, the pragmatic judgement of Dr W. E. Orchard, the High Church Congregationalist Minister, in the early years of this century, that the Church of England had 'discovered exactly how much religion the Englishman can stand'.[56] But there is also the theological and the constitutional judgement of one of the establishment's most notable exponents in recent years. Enoch Powell, speaking in the debate in the House of Commons on the Worship and Doctrine Measure in 1974, attributed the comprehensiveness of the Church of England to the fact 'that its formulae and its liturgy, being established by the law of parliament, are peculiarly rigid and difficult to change. It was because the liturgy and the articles of religion, being part of the law of England, were so difficult to alter, were near as possible permanencies, that in age after age successive waves of thought and religious feeling were nevertheless able to find a place within the Church of England and within its unity'.[57]

It is a consequence of establishment – expressed in and supported by doctrinal formulae, liturgical norms, constitutional settlements, and pastoral strategies – that the Church of England, and especially through the work of its cathedrals and parish churches, has continued to be a community church. It has provided over the generations a framework within with the religious aspirations of non-churchgoing people can find expression from time to time. It follows that a variety of traditions – the comprehensiveness of the Church of England; the network of relationships into which bishops, priests and deacons enter on taking up their charge; the opportunities for ministry and the expectations of people – ensure that there remains within the church an awareness of folk religion, and some appreciation of the need to interpret the range of religious experience, the inarticulate religion of those who may not conform exactly to the requirements and disciplines of membership.

The distinctive theological traditions that are found within the Church of England – catholic, evangelical and liberal – have not always found it easy to come to terms with folk religion. Alan Wilkinson's reflections on the failure of the Church of England to respond adequately to the theological and the moral questions posed by the Great War included an acknowledgement that the church had failed also to understand the expressions of folk religion because 'its evangelicalism was too puritan, biblicist and pietistic; its liberalism too detached and academic; its catholicism too selfconscious, dogmatic and nostalgic'.[58] Those who have responsibility for public ministry are bound to be mindful of the emptiness of a vague Christianity that attaches no vital importance to sin, to grace, to redemption, or to the church as a divine society. But folk religion, which is in the nature of things both uncritical and uncommitted, has something to say about human behaviour and human need. It challenges the clericalism and the ecclesiasticism of the church. It calls into question the assumption that the church has an absolute monopoly where God is concerned.

The Church of England's search in the course of the twentieth century for a greater degree of autonomy in ordering its affairs has inevitably continued the process of disengagement in church-state relations. It was the Enabling Act of 1919 which brought the Church Assembly into being, conferred certain legislative powers upon that body which had previously been exercised by parliament, and provided the electoral roll in the parishes as the basic electoral unit in a representative form of synodical government. It was for Bishop Hensley Henson the passing of this Act which effectively brought to a close the long story of church-state relations as they had developed in England over the centuries. His acerbic judgement on the proponents to the measure was that, 'They have exchanged the status which was in principle Christian for one which is in principle sectarian, and they have banished from the realm of practical possibilities the idea of a national church'.[59]

It may well be true that the ideal of a national church as it had previously been expressed was being abandoned, but it was far from clear that establishment and all that it represented in English life was being finally surrendered by either church or state. The church's search for a greater degree of autonomy has coincided with deep changes in the life of society, with the increasingly pervasive influence of secular thought, and with the privatisation of religion. It remains to be seen in these changed and changing circumstances if the historic pattern of comprehensiveness and all-inclusiveness can be maintained.

It has been the case throughout the course of this century that all churches have seen a significant decline in church attendance and in all the numerical yardsticks of formal association. And yet there is a continuing tradition of tentative connections, of fundamental beliefs and values, which count for something in the reckoning of large numbers of people. It is too soon to say how much will be lost if the strong base of Christian faith and practice is so far eroded that religion, and especially the Christian religion, can no longer inform and shape the minds, the spirit, the character of the English people.

NOTES
1 *The Canons of the Church of England.* Canon A1.
2 The Non-Jurors: Bishops and clergy of the church who refused to take the Oath of Allegiance to William and Mary on the grounds that by so doing they would violate their previous oath to James II and his successors. They numbered 8 bishops and some 400 priests.

3 William Wake, *The Authority of Christian Princes Over Their Ecclesiastical Synods Asserted* (1697). Francis Atterbury, *The Rights, Powers and Privileges of an English Convocation* (1701). Benjamin Hoadley, *A Preservative Against the Principles and Practice of Non-Jurors both in Church and State* (1716). George Hickes, *Constitution of the Catholic Church and the Nature and Consequences of Schism* (1716).

4 Owen Chadwick, *The Victorian Church*, A. & C. Black, 2 vols (1966 and 1970). Vol. I, p. 8.

5 Derek Jennings, *The Established Church: Has It A Future?* Essay in Allen Warren (Editor), *A Church for the Nation: Essays on the Future of Anglicanism*, Gracewing Fowler Wright Books 1992, p. 65.

6 W.R.W. Stephens, *Life and Letters of Walter Farquhar Hook*, Richard Bentley & Son, London 1878. Vol. I, p. 221.

7 The Church of England Assembly (Powers) Act (1919), popularly known as the Enabling Act.

8 Synodical Government Measure (1969).

9 Worship and Doctrine Measure (1974).

10 The Crown Appointments Commission was established in 1977 following upon the recommendations of the *Report of the Archbishops' Commission on Church and State* in 1970 and a series of conversations with the Archbishop of Canterbury, Sir Norman Anderson Q.C. on behalf of the General Synod, and successive Prime Ministers and their advisers.

11 E.R. Norman, *Church and Society in England 1770–1970*. Clarendon Press 1976, p. 219.

12 E.J. Wickham, *Church and People in an Industrial City*, Lutterworth Press 1962, p. 14.

13 A.J. Russell (Editor), *Group and Team Ministries in the Countryside*, SPCK 1975, p. 88.

14 A.F. Winnington-Ingram, Bishop of London, 1858–1945.

15 A.F. Winnington-Ingram, *Work in Great Cities*, 1896, p. 22.

16 See page 80.

17 E.R. Wickham, *op.cit.*, p. 176.

18 Walsham Howe, *Church Congress Report (1888)*, p. 662.

19 J.F. Kitto, *Church Congress Report (1881)*, p. 215.

20 Sir Robert Peel, British statesman, 1788–1850.

21 Cited by E.J. Wickham, *op.cit.*, p. 87.

22 Samuel Taylor Coleridge, poet and thinker, 1772–1834.

23 Alec R. Vidler, *The Church in an Age of Revolution*, Penguin Books 1961, p. 82.

24 William Ewart Gladstone, British statesman, 1809–1898.

25 W.E. Gladstone, *Church Principles Considered in Their Results*, 1840, p. 373.

26 Thomas Arnold, Headmaster of Rugby, 1795–1842.

27 Thomas Arnold, *Principles of Church Reform*, London 1833, p. 28.

28 Richard Baxter, Puritan divine, 1616–1691.

29 Cited by H.H. Henson, *Retrospect of an Unimportant Life*, Vol. I (1863–1920) OUP 1942, pp. 305–6.
30 Herbert Hensley Henson, Bishop of Durham, 1863–1947.
31 H.H. Henson, *op.cit.*, Vol. I, p. 209.
32 Arthur Penrhyn Stanley, Dean of Westminster, 1815–1881.
33 Cited by David Nicholls, *Church and State in Britain since 1820*, Routledge and Kegan Paul 1967, p. 208.
34 H.H. Henson *op.cit.*, Vol. II (1920–1939), OUP 1943, p.238.
35 Frederick Denison Maurice, Anglican divine, 1805–1872.
36 F.D. Maurice, *The Kingdom of Christ*, SCM Press 1958, Vol. II, p. 249.
37 F.D. Maurice.
38 Cited by David Nicholls, *op.cit.*, p. 38.
39 Edward White Benson, Archbishop of Canterbury, 1829–1896.
40 Edward White Benson, *The Church in Wales: Shall We Forsake Her?*, London 1895, p. 4.
41 William Temple, Archbishop of Canterbury, 1881–1944.
42 William Temple, *Church and Nation*, Macmillan & Co. 1915, p. 53.
43 Cosmo Gordon Lang, Archbishop of Canterbury, 1864–1945.
44 Hansard, Fifth series, iii 1195 (12 Feb 1913).
45 Ibid.
46 Randall Thomas Davidson, Archbishop of Canterbury, 1848–1930.
47 Hansard, Fifth Series, xxix 369 (10 March 1920).
48 H.H. Henson, *Bishoprick Papers*, OUP 1946, p. 36.
49 Ibid., p. 39.
50 Ibid., p. 39.
51 J.H.L. Rowlands, *Church, State and Society: The Attitudes of John Keble, Richard Hurrell Froude and John Henry Newman, 1827–1845*, Churchman Publishing 1989, p. 8.
52 Richard William Church, Dean of St. Paul's, 1815–1890.
53 R.W. Church, *The Oxford Movement*, Macmillan & Co. 1897, pp. 3–4.
54 W.E. Gladstone, *The State in its Relations with the Church*, John Murray 1838.
55 Alan Wilkinson, *The Church of England and the First World War*, SPCK 1978, p. 135.
56 Cited by G.F.S. Gray, *The Anglican Communion*, SPCK 1958, p. 165.
57 Cited by Peter Cornwell, *Church and Nation*, Basil Blackwell 1983, p. 23.
58 Alan Wilkinson, *op.cit.*, p. 196.
59 H.H. Henson, *Retrospect of an Unimportant Life*, Vol. I (1863–1920), OUP 1942, p. 306.

PART III

PATTERNS OF ENGAGEMENT

Chapter 8
Patterns of Engagement

The establishment of the Church of England represents one form of religious settlement. It is a public acknowledgement of the story of the English Church and of its place within English society. It affirms the continuity of the church in catholic faith and order. It says something about the identity and the integrity of the nation, and of the circumstances in which the church was re-shaped and re-formed in the sixteenth century. It recognises the distinctive task of the Church of England to offer ministry to all people.

The story of the Christian church demonstrates the great variety of ways in which church-state relations have been managed down the centuries. There is a distinction to be made between the response of the Christian disciple to living in the world and the response of the Christian church to the society in which it is set. The evidence of the New Testament and of the writings of the sub-apostolic age suggest that the earliest guidelines were intended to instruct and encourage Christian disciples in the profession of their faith. But the experience of the church as it moved from the early phases of experience and movement to the more developed forms of sect and institution and empire required some negotiation of the ways in which the spiritual and the temporal would relate to one another. Questions concerning the source and the nature and the boundaries of authority were bound to arise.

The prophetic tradition of a righteous remnant, mindful of its deep ambivalence to the things of the world, was not sufficient to guide the church as it took its place within the later

Roman Empire as an established institution, which provided the bond of unity. Church and state had reached the point where their ultimate purposes, although distinct, were not necessarily irreconcilable.

It was the achievement of the church that it had become in large measure co-extensive with the state. The theory of the Two Powers or the Two Swords suggested some delineation of responsibility, but it spoke also of the inter-relationship of the sacred and the secular. It acknowledged the complementarity of the responsibilities to be carried by church and state in a society which is a *corpus Christianum*.

The way in which the interdependence of church and state has actually been managed has owed something to the opportunities provided by circumstance and personality. Interpretations have been offered *ex post facto* but the practical outworking of the relationship has been determined at least in part by the exigencies of the situation. There is nothing inevitable about the historical process, but there is a dynamic at work in the life of church and state which narrows the range of options within which they both move forward.

It has been suggested that there are five ways in which the church has been seen throughout history: experience, movement, sect, institution and empire. These ways of being the church do not necessarily constitute a chronological progression. They are to be found in sequence and in parallel. They represent the directions in which the church might move at any time. But there does appear to be in both the ancient and the medieval worlds a kind of inevitability about the church's progression from sect to institution and from institution to empire, even though its movement from one to the other will be seen by some to violate fundamental theological principles about the nature of the church and its relation to the world.

The church cannot fail to be influenced by the secular environment. It is a necessary part of the church's story that it has adapted itself to human society, responding to changing circumstances, influencing and being profoundly influenced by the world. Its theology, its ethics and its institutions have all been shaped at different times by contemporary, non-ecclesial influences.

The rediscovery of the ancient ideal of a universal society that finds its bond of unity in the profession of a common religion prepared the way for the church's transition from institution to empire. Constantine, Justinian and Charlemagne represented one way in which the interests of church and state could be secured and developed within the unity of the church-state over which they presided as Christian emperors. The model was unashamedly imperial. The question that was pursued relentlessly over a thousand years related to the conflicting claims of the ecclesiastical and the temporal powers with regard to the source of authority and the primacy of jurisdiction.

In the East, the model provided by Justinian as *imperator* and *pontifex maximus* led to the tradition of caesaro-papism associated with the Byzantine Emperors. Earlier pagan notions concerning kingly authority had been taken up by Eusebius of Caesarea[1] and applied to the office of the Christian Emperor. The failure of the barbarians to disrupt the Eastern Empire meant that the theory of imperial sovereignty or imperial papacy was significant in the life of the Eastern Church during the centuries preceding the final breach between the Catholic West and the Orthodox East, between Rome and Constantinople, in 1054. This imperial oversight and jurisdiction extended in the first instance to the appointment and deposition of bishops, and to the summoning of and presiding over councils of the church whose concern was the definition of doctrine, although the Seventh Ecumenical Council in 787 declared that the emperor had no jurisdiction within the church's teaching office in defining matters of faith or morals.

The tradition of caesaro-papism bequeathed to Orthodoxy the intermingling of the sacred and the secular, the strong nationalism of the Eastern Churches, and the concept of the sacred monarch. In Russia – to take the most obvious example – there arose after the fall of Constantinople to the Ottomans in 1453 the idea of Russia as Holy Russia and of

Moscow as the Third Rome. The Tsar was invested with something of the mystique of the Byzantine Emperor; and, although church-state realtions developed along different lines, it was possible for Peter the Great,[2] mindful of what was happening in the reformed churches of Central and Northern Europe to interpret his role in relation to the church in an unashamedly ruthless fashion, subordinating the church to his imperial control.

In the West, the notion of the Two Powers or the Two Swords was retained, but the balance of power swung between the temporal and the ecclesiastical authorities in the period that followed upon the collapse of Charlemagne's Empire. The wealth and the power of the church, the controversy surrounding lay investiture, the developing tradition of canon law, and the determination of the papacy led to a new Roman imperium between the eleventh and the fourteenth centuries in which the absolute demands of the papal monarchy imposed a comprehensive jurisdiction throughout Western Europe. But the oppressive imperialism of the Roman see was required to take account of the sovereignty of the nation states and of their princes in countries that remained largely unaffected by the protestant reformation. A series of concordats with France and Spain and Austria between the sixteenth and the eighteenth centuries conferred powers upon the crowned heads of these nations with regard to episcopal appointments, taxation and jurisdiction that were not totally dissimilar to those taken by the sovereign in countries with a reformed church polity.

The fluctuations in the practicalities of church-state relations in catholic countries are best demonstrated by reference to the French Church. The Concordat of Bologna of 1516 conceded to the crown the right to nominate to all benefices in France and thereby surrendered all papal claims to taxation. The four Gallican Articles imposed upon the French clergy by Louis XIV in 1682 remained in force for no more than a decade, but they asserted the authority of the crown and the liberties of the French Church, and renounced the jurisdiction of the papacy in relation to all temporal matters.

The Civil Constitution of the Clergy, published in 1790 in the wake of the French Revolution, was designed to subordinate the church to the state, reducing the control of the papacy over the clergy, and giving to the civil electorate the chief voice in the appointment of bishops and parochial clergy.

The Concordat of 1801 between Napoleon and the papacy, although it was subject to differing interpretations, restored the power of the Roman Catholic Church in France, abandoning the election of clergy by the laity, and conceding once again to the French government the rights previously enjoyed by French kings under the Concordat of Bologna with regard to the nomination of bishops. But a growing tide of secularism and anti-clericalism towards the end of the nineteenth century led to the severance of church-state relations in 1905. The state's recognition of the church was brought to an end, together with all financial assistance. All ecclesiastical buildings were declared to be state property. The right of assembly for public worship was guaranteed to catholics and protestants alike as private citizens; but no distinction was made between clergy and others in regard to liability for military service, and pious bequests, except to individuals, were made illegal.

It is through the instrument of the condordat that the papacy has continued to regulate church-state relations in catholic countries down to the present time. The concordat is essentially an agreement between the papacy and the government of the nation concerned regarding matters of importance to both parties. It is a church-state treaty that has the force of law. It makes provision for the rights of the church, ecclesiastical jurisdiction, the appointment of bishops and pastors, marriage laws. Approximately one hundred and fifty agreements of this kind have been negotiated since the Concordat of Worms in 1122 which brought to an end the controversy concerning lay investiture.

The securing of a concordat assumes a high degree of goodwill on both sides, and one contemporary instance that might well be cited relates to Poland. The first concordat between the Holy See and the Republic of Poland was signed in 1925 and provided the constitutional foundation for ecclesiastial order in Poland. But the concordat was abrogated by the communist government in September 1945 and, until the signing of a new concordat in July 1993, church-state relations were never regularised. The Catholic Church in Poland represents a little over ninety-five per cent of the population. The new concordat acknowledges that the church and the state are 'each in its individual order, independent and autonomous'.[3] The state recognises freedom of worship, together with specific rights with regard to property, education, marriage according to the law of the church, and the propagation of the faith. The state guarantees for the Catholic church 'the free and public exercise of its mission ... in conformity with canon law'.[4]

In the churches of the reformation, a new form of imperialism could be found as the principle of nationality was embraced and endorsed by the temporal prince who presided over the reformed polity of a church-state. The English experience tells how the continued existence of dissenting minorities, catholic and protestant, ensured that in the long term the religious diversity of the nation would be recognised and the civil disabilities that had been imposed in order to secure the supremacy of the crown and the uniformity of the people would be removed. The progressive disengagement of church and state has still allowed a residual form of establishment to continue, which embodies not merely the fundamental principles of the reformation but also the experience of the ancient, the medieval and the modern worlds that the sacred and the secular can never be totally disentangled.

The Church of Sweden is a reformed church which stands more obviously in the Lutheran tradition. Its adoption of the Augsburg Confession in 1593 represented its formal commitment to Lutheran teaching, although the Swedish Church – like the English Church – retained catholic church order. The Swedish state tolerates all religions but it continues to secure the position of the Established Church. The Swedish constitution requires that the sovereign must be a member of the

Swedish Church, together with the one member of government who is responsible for church affairs. The work of the
church has been very greatly assisted by the parochial – or
church – tax which is levied through the regular system of
taxation.

Proposals are now under discussion within the Swedish
Church which might well lead over the coming years to a
public recognition of the neutrality of the state and to what
would be tantamount to the disestablishment of the Swedish
Church. It is being urged that the Church of Sweden should
be given the status of a legal person in its own right, affiliated
to neither national nor local government. The position of the
Church of Sweden would be redefined by public law and
would be expressed in the Constitution Act and in a Church
of Sweden Act which would provide certain constitutional
safeguards. It is envisaged that other churches would be able
to secure a legal status as registered denominations. The
existing parochial tax would be superseded by an ecclesiastical charge, but it is envisaged that those who are not
members of the Church of Sweden would no longer be
required to pay any tax or charge to it.

The Church of Scotland, which in its origin owed more
than other churches of Northern Europe to Calvinist influence, was caught up in the political and ecclesiastical turmoil
of the sixteenth and the seventeenth centuries, and finally
abandoned episcopacy and adopted a presbyterian pattern of
church order. By contrast with the religious settlements in
England and Sweden, the Church of Scotland represents,
therefore, an Established Church which is different in important respects. It is national in its relation to the crown and to
the people of Scotland. It is presbyterian in its form of
government. It is endowed in the sense that it retains the
historic endowments of the Scottish Church, but it is also
free in so far as Acts of Parliament in the 1920s secured its
spiritual independence.

The Scottish Church provides a model which is looked
upon by many as a good illustration of how the historic relationship with the state can be maintained without compro-

mising in any way the spiritual freedom and jurisdiction of
the church. It is right to acknowledge that throughout the
world the vast majority of churches within the reformed
tradition appear to be free in the sense that they are able to
order their affairs – nationally or locally – without direct
reference to the state.

But freedom requires definition. The reality is that all
churches are required to regularise their relationships with
the state. It may well be the case that the churches have often
enjoyed the wider liberties that have been guaranteed by the
state to all its citizens. But the church requires in all situations the freedom to worship, to teach the faith, to hold
property, and to administer its endowments and trust funds.
These are things that the church is bound to seek as soon as
it moves from experience and movement to sect. But the
more complex relationships which are implicit in the
church's transition from sect to institution will invariably
require more extensive arrangements.

The continuing form of establishment in England touches
upon the life of the Church of England in many ways, but all
churches in England come within the constraint of the law
and of the sovereignty of the crown in parliament. The
*Report of the Archbishops' Commission on Church and
State* in 1970 acknowledged that, 'All Churches have a basis
in law. Their constitutions and rules are enforceable under
the law relating to voluntary associations. Their property
and endowments are held under trusts which are sometimes
defined by reference to the doctrines and forms of worship of
the Church concerned'.[5] Indeed, the Report goes on to cite
specific instances of changes in legislation which had been
required by some churches other than the Church of England
'to secure or modify their forms of worship or standards of
doctrine; e.g. the Church of Scotland Act 1921 and the
Methodists Church Union Act 1929. The ... Sharing of
Church Buildings Act 1969 was almost as badly needed for
the purpose of modifying the trust deeds of the Free
Churches as for modifying the laws governing consecrated
property of the Church of England'.[6]

The constitutional arrangements that recognise the form of relationship between the church or the churches and the state say something about the state's understanding of society and of the place of religion within it. But there is also the question of the church's understanding of itself and of the function of religion within the wider life of the community.

The sect might well see itself as a voluntary association, but no church which has moved beyond the exclusive terms of reference by which the sect defines itself will be able to abandon the idea of the church as a public institution whose ministry relates to the whole life of society. The church as an institution has historically been an integral part of the social order and an element of stability and continuity within it. This has been the significance of establishment, which has embodied in a constitutional and legal form principles which are fundamental to the understanding of state and church.

But beyond the familiar pattern of establishment and the network of relationships which it embodies, there are some instructive patterns of engagement in different parts of the world as church and state impinge upon one another. Three instances must suffice.

The experience of the various religious traditions, Christian and Jewish, in the United States of America in shaping the nation's self-consciousness is a remarkable phenomenon in a situation in which the state has set its face from the beginning against any form of establishment.

The experience of the Orthodox Church in Russia during the period of Soviet oppression illustrates the way in which the story and the tradition of the church, inescapably bound up with the story and the tradition of the people, determined at least in part the pattern of the church's response in grievous circumstances.

The experience of the Church of the Province of Kenya, the Anglican Church in Kenya, demonstrates a tradition of engagement and confrontation, critical and prophetic, which has come out of the church's understanding of the gospel and of the things that constitute the integrity of a nation's life.

These three studies take us beyond the constitutional

arrangements that have traditionally been known in Western and in Eastern Europe. They provide commentaries upon the continuing engagement of church and state. They tell of traditions of free association, of continuity, of prophecy. They relate to the perennial questions of nationality, of authority, of the intermingling of the sacred and the secular.

NOTES
1 Eusebius, Bishop of Caesarea, c.260–c.340.
2 Peter the Great, Tsar and Emperor of Russia, 1672–1725.
3 Concordat between the Holy See and the Republic of Poland, 28th July 1993, Article 1.
4 Ibid. Article 2.
5 *Report of the Archbishops' Commission on Church and State (1970)*, pp. 1–2.
6 Ibid.

Chapter 9

The Law of Liberty

The right to life, liberty and the pursuit of happiness are the basic tenets of the American Constitution. The right to liberty included from the time of the Union equality before the law for all confessions of faith. It was the proud assertion of the Supreme Court in 1947 that, 'We have staked the very existence of our country on the faith that complete separation between the state and religion is best for the state and best for religion'.[1] The separation of church and state is fundamental to any appreciation of the story of church and state in the United States of America.

The Statute of Liberty approved by the State of Virginia in 1785 asserted that 'our civil rights have no dependence on our religious opinions in matters of religion'.[2] It was this principle which was incorporated as the First Amendment into the Constitution of the Union in 1791, requiring that 'Congress shall make no law respecting an establishment of religion, or prohibiting the free exercise thereof'.[3]

This principle was incorporated within a short time into the constitutional legislation of all member states. The churches were, therefore, free to manage their affairs – the definition of doctrine, the ordering of worship, the establishment of hierarchies, the government of their internal life, the administration of property and finance. The separation was not an act of indifference on the part of the state, but an act of benevolent and purposeful neutrality. It was related to the authority and the freedom of conscience.

The story of America is the story of the immigrants. The first settlers of the seventeenth and the eighteenth centuries were succeeded by three great waves of immigrants from Europe over a period of more than one hundred years going through to the end of the First World War. During this time more than thirty-five million men and women came to America from Central and Eastern Europe, from Italy, from Ireland, from Great Britain, from the Balkans and from Scandinavia. They constituted one of the great migrations of human history, creating in America one of the most diverse nations in the world.

The early colonists had been predominantly protestant but the new immigrants brought with them a variety of religious allegiance. For the first generation, it was religion that provided the necessary element of continuity between the old world and the new. It was in the immigrant churches that the immigrant groups found their identity and their belonging. For the second generation, religion was also an important part of their heritage as immigrants, but it was less significant in terms of their identity as they became increasingly assimilated within the wider community. For the third generation, the process of integration had continued and had required conformity in nationality, in language and in culture, but religion remained the thread of continuity and became important in so far as it distinguished and differentiated one group from another.

The immigrants brought with them strong local identities: they did not come from nations, but from provinces and districts, from towns and villages. America was to be 'the melting pot of many races';[4] and the need of the immigrants to find an identity in the new world meant that some sense of national awareness was imposed upon the diverse immigrant groups. The ethnic group mattered and continued to matter over the generations in political and economic life, in family relationships, and in the churches; but the new life in the new world could not allow these local identities to become too rigid and too permanent.

Religious affiliation played a vital role in giving to individuals and to families their sense of belonging; but the importance of the ethnic group and of the immigrant church gave

way in the second and the third generations to the importance of the major religious groupings – Protestant, Catholic
and Jewish. It is in these three great communities of faith that
the process of assimilation and integration is carried
forward. 'For being a Protestant, a Catholic or a Jew is
understood as the specific way, and increasingly perhaps the
only way, of being an American and locating oneself in
American society.'[5]

The early protestant settlers had included from the 1620s
onwards large numbers of Puritans who had come to the new
world to escape exclusion or persecution. Their hope had
been to establish their freedom in churches where they could
develop their religious life in ways that had not been possible
in Europe. They were concerned to establish a pattern of
church life based upon the radical principles of the reformation in its most rigorous form and to make the church co-
extensive with the community. But the rigidity of their
teaching and of their practice, together with the emphasis
upon the gathered church, led inevitably to the expulsion of
dissenters and the fragmentation of their church polity.

It is impossible to exaggerate the importance of the frontier either in the story of the American nation or in the life of
the American churches. The frontier represented in the first
place the advancing geographical frontier of European
settlers, but it became the potent and compelling frontier of
pioneer evangelism. Missionary activity had not been a
priority for most of the early settlers, but the spirit of the
frontier and the tradition of evangelism came together to
shape profoundly the developing life of the churches. The
Great Awakening from the mid-1720s onwards was the first
of the great revival movements in American protestantism. It
began in the settled communities of the east but it was essentially a phenomenon that belonged to the frontier, and it
determined the pattern of the revival movement and of the
religion of the frontier for a hundred and fifty years. The
significance of the frontier lay in its 'breaking the bonds of
custom, offering new experiences, calling out new institutions and activities'.[6] It was the revival movement, bound up

with the advancing frontier, that transformed American protestantism, modifying its theology, its worship, its organisation and its spirit.

One of the fascinations of this process is the way it illuminates the phases of experience, movement, sect and institution in the life of the American churches. In the settled communities of the east, the churches had already begun to take on something of the character of institutions. The revival movement ensured that experience was renewed within the life of the church in successive generations. The frontier was essentially about movement, and the established churches of the colonies either became caught up in movement or gave way to those who did. But as the frontier moved on and new communities became established, leaving the pioneer stage behind, the experience and the movement and the sect of the frontier gave way to the institution of the rural church. It is Richard Niebuhr's judgement that, 'In a very general sense it is true that under the influence of the frontier the churches of Europe after migrating to America have tended to become sects, and that with the passing of the frontier and with the establishment of ordered society the sects of Europe and America have tended to become churches'.[7]

One of the consequences of all these things was dissension within the churches and the proliferation of sects. There were important realignments as the churches responded or failed to respond to the frontier and to all that it represented. The process of economic development and rapid social change within the nation at large, together with the inevitable movement of the population either to the frontier or to the towns and cities, encouraged the emergence of new religious bodies. Ethnic, cultural, and sectional interests loomed large in these new formations, and the situation was exacerbated further by the fact that the churches as voluntary associations found it necessary to proselytize, competing with each other for support.

The great divide in American protestantism relates to the issue of race and colour. The formation of separate churches for Negroes had begun soon after the revolution and the process was accelerated by the civil war and the emancipation of the slaves. The Negro churches followed the broad institutional lines of their parent white churches, but they developed their own characteristics, retaining something of the spirit of evangelical revival from the early days. The judgement of one commentator is that, 'The church has meant more to the Negro than any other institution, since only in his church has he had an opportunity for self-expression'.[8]

Catholicism in America – by contrast with protestantism – is essentially a consequence of the large influx of immigrants from catholic countries in Europe in the nineteenth century. The immigrants settled in the large urban centres – New York, Boston, Philadelphia – and tended to form close-knit ghettoes in early years. The tradition of catholicism, reinforced by the distinctions of language and culture, together with a predominantly protestant environment, ensured that these immigrant churches would function and could only function as religious sects. Account was taken of ethnic groupings in the creation of parishes, in the appointment of priests, in the religious and educational work of the church, and in the formation of lay societies. The diversity of the immigrant groups led to friction, ethnic and cultural, with some minor schisms and defections.

From the 1830s onwards, the Irish immigrants became a significant element in the Catholic church and performed a necessary task in enabling other catholic ethnic groups to achieve some measure of integration. The Irish Catholic spoke English; he adapted more easily than many to urban life; he became active in local politics. He retained much of his ingrained hostility to protestantism, but the Irish Catholic became passionately and patriotically American.[9] There is clear evidence of anti-catholic sentiment – of rejection, discrimination and violence – which seems often to have had its roots in anti-Irish feeling; but the process of assimilation continued and it was increasingly the pattern that 'Irish, Catholic and American became almost identical in the Irish American mind'.[10]

The Catholic population of the country grew rapidly –
from 1.6 million in 1850 to 12 million in 1900 – and the
missionary status of the American Catholic Church was
ended in 1908 when it was removed from the jurisdiction of
the Sacred Congregation of Propaganda. It is only in the
twentieth century that a significant catholic middle class has
emerged, although catholics are now long since established
in the professions, in the public service, in industry and
commerce. The election of John F. Kennedy as President of
the United States in 1960 completed the integration of
catholics into national political life.

The Catholic church in America has continued to be
largely Irish in tradition and leadership; but the story of
catholicism in America tells how a conglomeration of
catholic ethnic groups from all parts of Europe became over
the generations one of the three great communities of faith,
representing over twenty per cent of the population and over
thirty per cent of church affiliation. No religious community
represents more visibly the pluralism of American society. It
has been 'one of the three great "melting pots" or population
"pools" into which America is divided',[11] but it has become
an institution rooted in the life of the nation.

It was not merely as an immigrant group but as a religious
community that the Jews came to America. The first significant influx of Jews came from Central Europe from
1820–1870. The second and far larger influx came from
Eastern Europe from 1870 until the early 1920s. It meant
that by the early years of the twentieth century there were
two distinct Jewish communities – the German and the East
European – in America; but it was the latter, who had come
very largely from Yiddish-speaking communities in Eastern
Europe, who were most concerned to establish a clearly
defined Yiddish-speaking Jewish ethnic group.

American Jewry has been distinguished by the extent to
which it has retained a corporate identity. The early Jewish
immigrants had disappeared throughout the country, settling
in a few large cities, establishing their ghettoes, and pursuing
their work. The German Jews lost within two or three

generations the ethnic and cultural distinctiveness of the first immigrants; but the third generation of East European Jews made a conscious attempt to reassert the distinctively Jewish characteristics. This did not necessary represent a rejection of the new world. The duality that had been present from the beginning of being both an ethnic group and a religious group persisted. It was in the affirmation of their Jewishness that some American Jews could now locate themselves within the wider national community.[12]

It was as the Jewish communities – German and East European – made their way in the new world and flourished that the process of assimilation and integration went forward both in relation to the wider community and to each other. By the middle years of the twentieth century, the Jewish community had become an integral part of American society, and 'the American Jew was now in the position where he could establish his Jewishness not apart from, nor in spite of, his Americanness, but precisely through and by virtue of it'.[13]

The process of transforming a large number of disparate immigrant groups into a nation state with a strong sense of identity and belonging owes much to a combination of influences and circumstances that constitute and shape the American story. It is in large measure the same complex of influences and circumstances that has transformed the same disparate immigrant groups with all the differences of tradition and emphasis that belonged to their primary religious affiliations into the three great communities of faith in which American people – Protestant, Catholic and Jewish – have found their identity.

The American dream, the American ideal, the American way of life: these have been determined by ideals and values and aspirations which are rooted in the religious faith and experience of the immigrant people. The three great communities of faith: these have evolved as the distinguishing and defining constituencies of American religious life as a result of influences – political, economic and social – which have become part of the reality of life in the new world.

The constitutional commitment to equality before the law

for all professions of faith underscores the democratic dimension which has been the vital ingredient in the political, economic and social development of the country. But it was democracy and the availability of free land that allowed political and economic development to go forward. The commitment to equality was matched by an emphasis upon opportunity and achievement. Economic and social historians have long since drawn attention to the importance of protestant or puritan or Calvinist principles in providing the ethical foundations of the capitalist system. It was in the interval between the early puritan tradition and the thinking of the enlightenment at the time of the revolution that the key principles of equality and achievement emerged to shape the institutions and the value systems of America.

The adoption of the English language was a significant factor in enabling immigrant groups and immigrant churches to adapt and to survive. But there had also been from the time of the puritan settlers a respect for learning which was expressed both in the endowment of schools and universities and in a tradition of self-improvement. It is here that the characteristics of individualism, optimism, humanitarianism, dynamism and pragmatism can all be found. But these were also the characteristics that were needed by the churches, and especially the protestant churches, who as voluntary associations found it necessary to secure a voluntary membership in an environment of free competition.

The voluntary principle shaped the pattern of the church's work in evangelism, but also in education, in moral and social reform, and in charitable work. The voluntary churches gave rise to voluntary groups which, in common with the tradition of English parochial life, were concerned to secure a Christian social order. In the absence of any formal establishment of religion and of the legitimacy it gave to Christian morality, it was through the public ministry of the churches – and especially within protestantism – that the association was made in the public mind between religion and morality.

It is the interplay of all these factors – constitutional and political, economic and social, evangelistic and moral – that has influenced the American churches and fashioned the American nation. The immigrant churches had their roots in the religious traditions of Europe. The protestant, catholic and Jewish communities have evolved to become the religions of the American democracy. There has been ample scope for competition and conflict; and tension – or at the very least self-consciousness – between the religious communities has never been entirely absent. But 'under the influence of the American environment, the historic Jewish and Christian faiths have tended to become secularised in the sense of becoming integral as parts within a larger whole defined by the American Way of Life'.[14]

The American way of life understands pluralism in society at large and in the churches. The three communities of faith co-exist as equally legitimate expressions of the religious life of the nation. The multiplicity of churches did not follow upon the breakdown of one established church – catholic or protestant – within the unity of a Christian commonwealth. The immigrants brought with them an immense variety of association and affiliation – ethnic, cultural, religious – and although, at least for the protestants, the experience of the frontier and of revivalism led to a proliferation of sects, the immense variety of religious expressions had been a vital part of the story from the beginning. 'Pluralism of religions and churches is something quite axiomatic to the American.'[15]

Religion is an important part of the ethos of American life. Some have suggested that, in the absence of the forms of establishment known in Europe, what can be traced in America is the emergence of the denomination.[16] The American experience provides ample evidence of the familiar phases of experience, movement and sect; what is also found is a multiplicity of churches as institutions, self-confident, outward-looking, secure in the regard of the local community. It is in the fact of belonging to one of the communities of faith that the institutional model of the church can be seen most clearly as its members in any locality take their place within the wider association of churches in their respective traditions.

It is the importance attached to belonging that is judged by some to lie at the heart of the extraordinary vitality of American religion. Widespread interest in religion is not a new phenomenon in America, but statistical data suggests that religious activity – church building, church attendance, church membership – has reached an exceptionally high level in the second half of the twentieth century. Will Herberg, writing a generation ago, suggested on the basis of surveys of opinion that 'virtually the entire body of the American people in every part of the country regard themselves as belonging to some religious community'.[17]

There are many interpretations that might be offered, but the intriguing question relates to the paradox of a nation which is at one and the same time self-consciously secular and avowedly religious. It is as though there is some kind of separation within the prevailing American culture which enables 'pervasive secularism and mounting religiosity' to live side by side.[18] It may well be that religion has become a symbol of association and church membership the appropriate form of belonging; but there is something in the paradox which expresses the truth of the story of church and state in America.

American society and American religion have been so intimately bound up with each other from the beginning that it is scarcely possible to understand one without reference to the other. The constitutional commitment to equality, democracy and opportunity has given the churches an environment in which they could adapt and survive. But religion has been judged even from the earliest years to be the indispensable basis of society and in particular of American society and of its democratic institutions. Religion has provided the ideals, the values, the aspirations, the symbols, the rituals that have given American people the framework of normality and meaning within which they have found their unity. Society and religion have drawn from one another. The American ideal, expressed so often as the

American way of life, encompasses a relationship that is secular and religious. 'The optimism, morality and idealism of Jewish and Christian faith in America are plain evidence of the American outlook on American religion.'[19]

The American experience is a remarkable instance of religion as the bond of unity. There is a church-state dimension which is pervasive and profound, but it does not provide a case-study of how a free church might flourish in a free state to the mutual advantage of both. It has nothing to do with the church as an institution relating to the state as an identifiable community with a history, a complex of institutions, a culture. The pattern of engagement that is to be found here is one in which the state only evolves as a result of the immigration of many different ethnic groups whose prior religious and cultural affiliations provided the bonds that held them and, in due course, the nation in being.

There are questions concerning the relation of church and state – religion and society – which remain unanswered. One interpretation of the paradox in the American experience of religion suggests that, 'The secularism that pervades the American consciousness ... is thinking and living in terms of a framework of reality and value remote from the religious beliefs simultaneously professed'.[20] It may be that the American people are merely holding up a mirror to the face of every secular democracy in the western world.

But the questions remain because the assimilation of a multiplicity of immigrant groups in the past is no guarantee that those who are the poor and the dispossessed today will achieve a comparable degree of integration. The immigrant churches ultimately became American churches, but the Negro churches continue to be detached in exactly the same way as the Negro stands on the boundary of so many areas of American life. It remains to be seen if other minority groups, even those with a religious affiliation, are able to find the same degree of assimilation and integration as their predecessors over the last one hundred and fifty years.

Could the integration of American society have taken place without the strength and the resilience of the primary religious allegiances that were brought with them by the immigrants? Is the interplay between religion and society as open and creative today as it has been in the past? Can religion still perform in America the function it has fulfilled over the generations? Is religious faith – and not merely religious affiliation – the all-important dimension which cannot be jettisoned without disrupting the processes which in other circumstances have led to integration?

America has been constitutionally committed to the separation of church and state since the creation of the Union, but some would suggest that the separation is specious and illusory.[21] The law of liberty has served the immigrant peoples and the immigrant churches. It has enabled the great communities of faith to establish themselves and in the process to establish the nation. But there is a residual concern that religion lends itself too easily to manipulation.

The American story – in common with the experience of church-state relations in many parts of the world – provides numerous instances of patriotic appeals at times of emergency, and not least of all by those who speak for the nation. There is an abiding temptation even today in American life to appeal to the moral majority when sensitive social and ethical issues arise. It is difficult to sustain the charge that, 'The state uses the church but the church cannot use the state'.[22] The story of church and state is one of such comprehensive interdependence that broad generalisations cannot be sustained. But there is an intermingling – of democracy and religion; of equality, opportunity and achievement; of individualism and morality; of secularism and religious affiliation – in which the American experience of church and state can be traced. The strength and the weakness of the law of liberty is to be found in President Dwight D Eisenhower's comment about the paramount importance of religion: 'Our government makes no sense unless it is founded in a deeply felt religious faith – *and I don't care what it is*'.[23]

NOTES

1 Judgement of the Supreme Court of the United States of America. Cited by Johnson and Yates, *Separation of Church and State in the United States of America.*
2 Cited by Sidney Z. Ehler, *Twenty Centuries of Church and State,* Newman Press 1957, p. 88.
3 Cyril Garbett, *Church and State in England,* Hodder & Stoughton 1950, p. 25.
4 H. Richard Niebuhr, *The Social Sources of Denominationalism,* Meridian Books: The World Publishing Company 1971, p. 107.
5 Will Herberg, *Protestant, Catholic, Jew,* Anchor Books, Doubleday & Co. 1966, p. 39.
6 Cited by H. Richard Niebuhr, *The Social Sources of Denominationalism,* Meridian Books: The World Publishing Company 1971, p. 137.
7 H. Richard Niebuhr, *The Social Sources of Denominationalism,* Meridian Books: The World Publishing Company 1971, p. 145.
8 William S. Sweet, *The Protestant Churches,* p. 49.
9 Will Herberg, *op.cit.,* p. 146.
10 Ibid., p. 147.
11 Ibid., p. 157.
12 Ibid., p. 189.
13 Ibid., p. 198.
14 Ibid., p. 82.
15 Ibid., p. 85.
16 Ibid., p. 86.
17 Ibid., p. 46.
18 Ibid., p. 2.
19 Ibid., pp. 83–4.
20 Ibid., p. 2.
21 Frank Gavin, *op.cit.,* p. 125.
22 Ibid., p. 126.
23 Will Herberg, *op.cit.,* p. 84.

Chapter 10
Identity and Continuity

The historic claim of the Orthodox Church to be the church of the Russian people expresses – for church and people – the ideas of identity, unity and continuity. It was the Prince and the Metropolitan who, together with the support of the monasteries, had freed Russia from the oppression of the Mongols in the fourteenth century, securing the independence of Russia and preparing the way for her emergence as a political and economic entity. The church believed itself to be co-existent with the Russian people, the arbiter of its Christian destiny.

It was in Russia that the Byzantine tradition of a church-state presided over by a Christian Emperor could be seen most clearly after the fall of Constantinople. The Patriarch of Constantinople had written to Tsar Basil I concerning the importance of the Tsar within the church in the mid-fifteenth century. 'The Holy Tsar occupies a high place in the church … From the beginning the Tsar secured and confirmed piety in the entire world. The Tsars convoked ecumenic councils. They reaffirmed in their laws the observance of that which has been said in divine and holy laws concerning the dogma and the good management of Christian life … It is impossible for Christians to have a church and not have a Tsar.'[1] It is this Byzantine tradition of caesaro-papism that has influenced the tradition of the Orthodox Church in Russia.

The ancient compact between the church and the tsar was wilfully abandoned by Peter the Great, who was determined to ensure that the power of the church would not be used to frustrate his attempts to modernise Russia. He abandoned the principle of symphony or harmony between church and state, abolishing the patriarchate and bringing the administration of the church under state control. The establishment of the Holy Synod and the management of that body through the civil office of the Chief Procurator secured the submission of the church to the authority of the Tsar.

Over the two centuries that followed prior to the Bolshevik revolution there was no aspect of church life which was outside state control. Peter had imposed upon the church an imperial control which was derived from the Byzantine tradition and which had been significantly influenced by the experience of royal absolutism in Western Europe. But the ideal of Holy Russia was maintained. The church possessed great wealth in spite of the confiscation of monastic lands by Catherine the Great.[2] The relationship of church and people continued to be significant and found public expression in the liturgy, in the monasteries, in the places of pilgrimage, in the Orthodox tradition of spirituality. But the church had become a compromised institution, subordinate and submissive.

It was in the years of Soviet oppression that the church in Russia – all churches in Russia – suffered grievous oppression and persecution. Religious freedom had been proclaimed during the brief transitionary period between the abdication of the Tsar in February 1917 and Lenin's[3] accession to power in October 1917; and the democratic government of Kerensky established a ministry of religion and transferred to the minister the duties previously performed by the Chief Procurator. The Holy Synod acknowledged that the Orthodox Church could not preserve the old pre-revolutionary order and was allowed to summon a Great Council of the Russian Church. The work of the Council was overtaken by events but it attempted to initiate a thoroughgoing reform of all aspects of the church's life.

Lenin's approach to power was unashamedly totalitarian as he translated the theory of Marx into the politics of comprehensive and radical reform. He was an uncompromising and dogmatic atheist who saw religion as both a symptom and a cause of disorder within man and within society. Religion had been an instrument of oppression, and it was inevitable in view of the long association between the Orthodox Church and Tsarism that the leaders of the revolution would seek the destruction of religion as they carried forward their reconstruction of society.

The Decree of January 1918 separated church and state and initiated the period of repression which with brief respites was to last for two generations. All ecclesiastical property was transferred to the state. The church lost its status in law so that it could no longer defend itself or be represented in the courts as a corporate body. Education was removed from the influence of the church, the teaching of religion was prohibited in all educational institutions, and religious instruction was confined to individual citizens in private.

The revolution removed from the church the support of the tsar and of the landed gentry. The nationalisation of land and buildings alienated the wealth of the monasteries. The Decree of January 1918 guaranteed the freedom to profess or not to profess a religious faith, but this decree was violated in the years that followed by subsequent decrees and by a policy of systematic persecution. Clergy were deprived of their civil rights. The law on the registration of parishes was strictly applied. Many churches were closed and adapted to secular use. Church valuables were confiscated and many icons and sacred relics were abused or destroyed. The educational, charitable and relief work of the church, and especially of the monasteries, was prohibited. Emigré church sources estimated that between 1917 and 1923 twenty-eight bishops and more than twelve hundred clergy were arrested and executed.

The first evidence of the church's continuity with its past was to be found in the sustaining of the spiritual life of the Russian people by the existence of an underground church. 'It was at this time that many priests went underground in order to continue their mission. They hid in the woods like their forefathers had done in the days of the Mongol invasion. Disguised as peasants and workers they lost them-

selves in the crowd of ever moving, ever anxious populations
driven from town to town by civil war, famine and epidemics
... They brought the sacraments to the people whose
churches were closed and whose pastors were gone: confession, communion, marriage, baptism – all these were secretly
performed. There were also laymen who wandered throughout Russia, reading Scripture and giving responses to the
priests.'[4]

This can only be an impressionistic account and clearly it
does not tell the whole story; but there is also evidence
during the years of oppression that bishops and priests were
ordained in secret, that some religious communities went
underground or registered as agricultural communes, that
worship was offered in the houses of the faithful, that the
icon took on a new significance for some in the privacy of the
home.

But there had also been a tradition of subordination in
the church's past, and the early years after the Bolshevik
revolution provided the first evidence of submission and
collusion on the part of the leaders of the church. Patriarch
Tikhon had been elected in 1917, but he was arrested in
1923 and adopted thereafter a policy of full cooperation
with the soviet authorities. 'I disavow definitely and clearly
any connection with the counter-revolution abroad and
with the monarchist and White Guardists in this country'.[5]
He remained in prison until his death in 1925 when a statement was published over his name calling on the church 'to
permit no activity directed against the government, to nour-
ish no hopes for the return of the monarchy, and to be
convinced that the soviet government actually is the power of
the workers and peasants and that for this reason it is
unshaken'.[6]

Sergei survived after Tikhon's death as the *locum tenens*
until he was acknowledge by the soviet authorities as the
administrator of the church of Moscow in 1927.[7] But the
pattern of submission initiated by Tikhon was maintained.
Sergei's concern, like that of his predecessor and his successors, was to ensure the survival of the church. His Pastoral

Letter of 1927 constituted an appeal for loyalty to the soviet authorities. 'We want to remain orthodox believers and also want to recognise the Soviet Union as our earthly fatherland ... Every blow against the Soviet Union, through war, boycott, natural catastrophe, or assassination on the streets ... we shall consider a blow against ourselves.'[8]

The public statements of the Soviet government laid great emphasis upon proletarian principles and proletarian revolutionary action. The philosophy and the strategy of the Soviet authority in regard to the churches and to religious faith found clear expression in the Programme of the Communist International in 1932. 'The proletarian power must destroy all government support of the church, which is an agent of the governing classes, must destroy all participation by the church in the government organised work of upbringing and education, and must mercilessly suppress the counter-revolutionary activity of church organisations. At the same time, the proletarian power, allowing freedom of confession and destroying the privileged position of the former state religion, conducts by all possible means anti-religious propaganda, and reconstructs all upbringing and educational work on the basis of the scientific, materialistic world.'[9]

Stalin,[10] who had succeeded Lenin in the mid 1920s, presided over a period of great oppression which lasted until the early years of the Second World War. Stalin's first Five Year Plan, which was announced in 1928, required that every aspect of the nation's life should be brought under rigorous scrutiny. The Law on Religious Associations, which was published in the same year, was intended to strengthen the state's control over the churches and to facilitate the elimination of religion. All religious societies were required to register and wide powers were granted to regional agencies and committees for religious matters. All activities – with the exception of worship – were prohibited, and a propaganda programme was relentlessly pursued whose sole purpose was the systematic vilification of religion.

The churches were not alone in bearing the brunt of persecution. There were purges at all levels of society in the late

1930s as opponents – actual or potential – were removed. Large numbers of people in the churches, in schools, in collective farms and in industry became the victims of local trials or of administrative action. One of the consequences of this whole period since the revolution was the savage emasculation of the Orthodox Church. Estimates are necessarily unreliable, but it is reckoned that the number of parish churches had been reduced from about fifty thousand in 1917 to less than ten thousand in 1938; and the reduction in the numbers of clergy and of religious might well have been even more drastic.

The church's continuity with its past has been found in two areas – the emergence of an underground church and the pattern of submission and collusion. But there is a third strand in the response of the Orthodox Church which cannot be discounted. It is the activity and the witness of the church in exile. The Russian Orthodox Theological Institute, founded by Metropolitan Eulogius in 1925, was a potent influence in the tradition of the emigré church which took upon itself 'the task ... of keeping alive and developing the lively currents of Russian Orthodox theology and religious philosophy ... Men abroad felt it to be their duty to nation and to church to carry on, to think, speak, write and publish'.[11]

It was the circumstances of the Second World War which signalled a revival in the church's fortunes and ushered in a period of relative peace. The German invasion of Russia in 1941 gave the Orthodox Church an opportunity to demonstrate in the most practical way its wholehearted commitment to Russia. The war effort received the unqualified support of the church which took an active part in the propaganda war against the Nazis, raised money to equip armoured divisions for the Red Army, blessed military units, and gave every encouragement to those who fought for the fatherland.

Stalin recognised what had been done by the church during the war and what it might yet do in the period of post-war reconstruction and in the cold war confrontation after

1945. The oppressive legislation of earlier years remained in place and the government never abandoned control. The church remained under surveillance and government approval was necessary for senior appointments and for all significant developments; but the church had recovered a good deal of ground by the end of the war. One estimate suggests that the number of bishops, parish priests and churches was restored to nearly one half of what they had been before the Bolshevik revolution.[12] It was a consequence of the concessions made by Stalin that the patriarchate was restored; the theological academy at Zagorsk, together with other seminaries, was allowed once again to function properly; some of the older churches were restored; and some Christian publications were permitted.

The expansion of the Soviet Empire in Eastern Europe after the war emphasised the potential importance of the Russian Orthodox Church as an intergrating force in satellite countries where there was a large Orthodox community. But it became apparent that the church might also be useful as an instrument of Soviet propaganda in the western world. It was an act of cynicism on both sides – church and state – that there were selected church leaders who were prepared to visit western countries, becoming involved in the peace movement, testifying to the positive features of the Soviet system, and speaking of their religious freedom. Alongside the established pattern of submission there must now be set what seemed to many to be the cynical and self-seeking acquiescence of the church in the distortions of Soviet foreign policy and propaganda.

The détente in church-state relations lasted until the late 1950s, enabling the church to return to some kind of regular life. The statistics for 1959 suggest that there were thirty-five to fifty million practising Orthodox Christians in Soviet Russia, thirty-three thousand priests, five hundred religious, seventy-three dioceses and three seminaries. The city of Moscow is believed to have had fifty churches available for worship which were crowded to capacity at the great festivals. But the late 1950s saw the beginning of a new period of vigorous oppression which reversed the substantial gains the church had made in recovering its former position of activity and influence.

Krushchev's persecution of religion contrasted with moves in a more liberal direction in other areas of society. The Council for the Affairs of the Russian Orthodox Church, which had been established by Stalin in consultation with church leaders in 1943 as a liaising body, became the instrument used by government in the first instance to undermine the work of the church and to enforce penal legislation. Christians were purged from the party and its organisations. Children under the age of eighteen years were forbidden to attend worship or take part in religious ceremonies or receive formal religious instruction. There was a great increase in propaganda against religion, and an attempt was made by the state to provide secular substitutes for the festivals and the rites of passage.

In 1961, Krushchev required Patriarch Alexei and a synod of bishops at Zagorsk to amend the statutes of the church so that parish priests were deprived of the leadership of their churches and congregations and could no longer serve on parish councils. The meeting had been convened at short notice and without any prior consultation. The new decree was subsequently published by the Holy Synod and the severity of this new attack upon the church was greatly assisted because parish councils could now be penetrated by party members who would use their membership to carry forward the policy of repression. It is reckoned that one half of the parish churches of the Orthodox Church were closed during a three year period and many were undoubtedly destroyed. There are no figures concerning the numbers of priests who were removed or imprisoned or executed; but many bishops and priests were dismissed and their replacements tended to be men who were entirely subordinate to government influence and policy. There was a wholesale closure of the monasteries.

There is no doubt that the bishops had been required to act speedily and in the light of government directions, but the charges of collusion and collaboration that were made against the leaders of the Orthodox Church in respect of this decree and of the persecution of the church at this time are very substantial.

It has been alleged that many bishops dissociated themselves entirely from any attempt to secure for Christian people their full rights as citizens under the law. It has been suggested that some bishops were actively involved in the closure of churches and the amalgamation of parishes, even when congregations were well able to maintain their churches and their priests. In the spring of 1964, the Metropolitans Nikodim and Pimen made statements when travelling abroad denying that the church was suffering persecution and alleging that churches were being closed only because people were abandoning their faith. It is believed by many that the government succeeded so completely because of the compliance of the leaders of the church in carrying out the requirements of government officials and agents.

There are those who have found some explanation of the behaviour of the leaders of the church in the tradition of Orthodoxy which, with its sense of history and of the continuity of the church, is able to look beyond the expediency of short-term protests in order to ensure that the church might actually survive.

The most compelling evidence comes from Josif, the Metropolitan of Alma-Ata in Siberia, who had spent twenty years in labour camps. He reflected upon the situation of the church and what seemed to be the passivity and the collusion of its bishops. 'I often ask myself, Are we doing right to remain silent, not exposing what is happening in the Church? ... Sometimes I get sick of it and want to throw it all up and retire. When that happens my conscience objects. It says you cannot abandon the faithful. You cannot abandon the Church. If I speak up and say all, even if I criticise publicly, I should be out and nothing would be changed. So – while I have strength – I do what I can and work quietly for the Church.'[13]

This personal and poignant rationale, which undoubtedly

expresses something of the truth of the situation as it was seen by many, was soon to give way to more strident interpretations which also attempted to explore the tradition of Orthodoxy and find some explanation of this repeating pattern of submission.

An Open Letter which was sent to Patriarch Alexei by two Moscow priests in the mid-1960s recalled the persecution suffered by the church in recent years, and lamented the failure of the patriarchate to protect the church against the ruthless oppression of the government. 'Today the bitter truth is obvious to everyone who loves Christ and His Church. It is clear that the Russian Church is seriously and dangerously ill, and that her sickness has come about entirely because the ecclesiastical authorities have shirked from fulfilling their duties ... The Orthodox Church has always recognised the absolute right of the state to leadership in the civil life of society, and for this reason has always instilled in her members the obligation to submit themselves, according to their conscience, to the state ... However, during the period 1957 to 1964 the Council for the Affairs of the Russian Orthodox Church radically changed its function, becoming instead of a department of arbitration, an organ of unofficial and illegal control over the Moscow patriarchate ... We feel that it is our duty to say that such a situation in the Church could occur only with the connivance of the supreme ecclesiastical authorities, who have deviated from their sacred duty before Christ and the Church and have clearly violated the apostolic command by compromising with the world.'[14]

Bishops and priests who protested found invariably that they were dismissed. The protest contained in this Open Letter was taken up seven years later by Alexander Solzhenitsyn in a Lenten Letter to Patriarch Pimen, asserting that no attempt had been made to refute the allegations concerning the enslavement of the Russian Church, and attempting also to offer some interpretation of the failure of the leaders of the church. 'A study of Russian history over the last few centuries convinces me that it would have followed an incomparably more humane and harmonious course if the church had not renounced its independence and the people had listened to its voice ... We have lost the radiant ethical atmosphere of Christianity in which for a millenium our morals were grounded; we have forfeited our way of life, our outlook on the world, our folk-law, even the very name by which the Russian peasant was known. We are losing the last features and marks of a Christian people ... The Russian Church ... never has anything at all to say about things which were wrong here at home ... The church is ruled dictatorially by atheists.'[15]

The principle of separation between church and state enshrined in Lenin's decree of January 1918 had been persistently violated over the years by Lenin, Stalin and Krushchev. The situation stabilised from the mid-1960s onwards and, although there continued to be administrative interference in the affairs of the church, the size of the country and the inefficiency of the Soviet system meant that it was impossible for effective control to be maintained over every aspect of Soviet life.

The new constitution of the Soviet Union in 1977 maintained the separation of church and state and freedom for religion and for propaganda against religion. But the restrictions imposed on the church were extensive: churches were to be registered; the names of church members were to be supplied to the state; the religious education of children was prohibited outside the home; no religious activity was permitted outside church buildings; the charitable and social work of the church remained forbidden. Religious liberty in this extenuated form amounted to the right of public worship in churches leased to the congregations without charge by the state.

New circumstances in the 1980s appear to have brought to an end the persecution of two generations. The important markers along the way were Gorbachov's coming to power in 1985, the spirit of *perestroika*, the Millenium celebrations in 1988, and the collapse of the Soviet Empire in 1988–1989. But it is also helpful to trace step by step the abandonment of restrictions and the positive encouragement to the Orthodox

Church to take its place again in the life of the Russian people.

The church was invited to move tentatively but purposefully beyond the constraints of the law. A policy of co-operation and toleration was judged to be a matter of urgency, and the Orthodox Church was seen as a potential ally in the regeneration of society. The spirit of *perestroika* found practical expression in the greater availability of bibles, in the granting of amnesties to prisoners of conscience, in the lifting of censorship, in the repeal of secret laws prohibiting religious sects, and in the restoration of confiscated property to parishes, theological seminaries and monasteries.

It is not easy to evaluate the role of the church throughout Eastern Europe in bringing about the collapse of the Soviet Empire. It may well be the case that the foundations – political, economic and ideological – of the Soviet autocracy were too shallow to sustain the overbearing edifice that had been established since the Second World War. It is not immediately obvious that the churches can claim too high a measure of responsibility for the break-up of this totalitarian regime; but there is evidence – in Poland, in Romania, in Eastern Germany – of the involvement of Christian clergy and lay people in movements that were eventually significant in the liberation of their countries. The churches – orthodox and catholic – had been the bearers of a tradition which was deeply rooted in the story and the identity of the disparate peoples of the Soviet bloc. It may be the achievement of the churches that they have been able to represent an alternative ideology, facilitating 'others who were not particularly religious but cared passionately about freedom and human rights'.[16]

The gradual liberation of the church in Russia in the late 1980s appeared to owe practically everything to a new spirit of toleration and accommodation. The Millenium celebrations in 1988, focussing inevitably on the story of Russia and of the Orthodox Church, ensured that the church assumed an increasingly high public profile. The Orthodox Church had never lost its hold over the Russian people, even though two generations had been subjected to virulent propaganda against the faith. Estimates suggest that thirty million baptisms had taken place between 1971 and 1988;[17] and the published figures for 1989 indicate a notable degree of resilience when comparisons are made with the previous year: 70 (67) dioceses; 70 (70) bishops in office; 8100 (6674) clergy; 9374 (6893) churches; 32 (21) monasteries; and 19 (5) theological academies and seminaries.[18]

But the strengths and weaknesses of the Russian Orthodox Church had been demonstrated as the bitter saga of church-state relations was played out over a period of seventy years. Questions were bound to be asked about the application of the spirit of *perestroika* to the church. 'Who will bring restoration not only to the destroyed churches but also to the trampled and crippled souls of both ordinary believers and the Russian Orthodox Church hierarchy?'[19]

The story of the Orthodox Church in Russia during the period of Soviet oppression suggests a pattern of engagement in church-state relations which cannot be compared with anything else that has been considered. Inferences cannot be drawn from this experience which can then be applied un-critically in other situations. The story of the church through-out the world tells of the many different ways in which the church engages with the state. Account must always be taken of the different models, each one of which might be entirely appropriate – or, at the very least, unavoidable – in a parti-cular setting. Judgements must not be made on the basis of assumptions which are unrelated to the historical circum-stances in which the church is placed at any time.

It is the paradoxes of experience that are most telling in any critical appreciation of the Orthodox Church in Russia. The Church had been co-existent with the story of the nation over a thousand years. It had been deeply rooted in the piety of the people. And yet it had also been intimately associated with the traditions of Tsarist Russia. It had shared as an insti-tution in the corruptions of wealth and power. But the church bore witness to the Byzantine tradition of harmony or symphony between church and state. It understood that orthodoxy and patriotism are inter-connected; and yet it had also been placed in a relationship of subordination and submission to the state, at least since the time of Peter the Great. The church was characterised by a tradition of innate conservatism, of quiescence, of pragmatism; but it demonstrated its resilience as an institution and the vitality of its spiritual life. The church had participated in the structures and the realities of power. And yet it pointed beyond these things in its liturgy, in its tradition of prayer and meditation, in its awareness of the mysteries of faith and of the supernatural life, in the symbolism of its art, and in its sense of being within and beyond time.

It was the denial of the freedoms and the functions that traditionally belonged to the church as an institution that condemned the Orthodox Church to the status of a persecuted sect during the period of Soviet oppression. But the Church refused to function as a sect. Such a response would have been fundamentally at variance with its history and its tradition.

The church's determination to survive and to fulfil its historic role was demonstrated repeatedly. It moved swiftly to adjust to changing circumstances in 1917 in acknowledging, at least in public, that the old order could not be restored. Successive patriarchs issued statements in support of the Soviet authorities. It participated wholeheartedly in the war effort at the time of the Second World War. It showed its resilience and its vitality during the periods of remission from persecution. It responded confidently as the spirit and the policies of *perestroika* and *glassnost* removed the restrictions and encouraged the churches to share in the work of reconstruction.

There is evidence of complicity and collusion on the part of the hierarchy, and it is not easy to understand the extent to which some of the leaders of the Orthodox Church were prepared to go in being agents of government policy at home and instruments of Soviet propaganda abroad. Such was the degree of compliance at certain times that what was presented appeared to some observers to be tantamount to a state church within an atheist state. It was, perhaps, inevitable in the later years that questions would be asked about the areas of weakness within the tradition of Orthodoxy which were exposed at a time of great testing.

The tradition of any church, although it might find formal definition in certain accepted ways, has a life of its own, and those who are concerned to discover its inner meaning must move beyond public statements and public actions. It is not easy – looking back over the years of Soviet oppression – to evaluate the importance of those who worked in the underground church, moving quietly from place to place, keeping the rumour of God alive. It is not clear how much significance might be attached to the church in exile, holding up before other communities of Christian faith a tradition of thought and spirituality which had its own integrity. It is impossible to measure how much is owed to the fidelity and heroism of the victims of persecution, of those who were dispossessed or imprisoned or executed.

The continuing insecurities of Russian life, political and economic, suggest that the period of great upheaval for the Russian people and the Russian Church has not necessarily passed. It is too early discern how the church will move forward in changed and changing circumstances. Two generations have been largely alienated from the church, and the Russian people will not be unaffected over the years ahead by the influences that have brought about a decline in religious observance in the western world during this century. Time will be needed to repair the damage, to set the course, and to see if the church is able to find again a strong foothold in the piety of the people. The tradition of engagement between church and state is one that has counted for a great deal in Orthodoxy. It remains to be seen if the period of persecution has set the Russian Church free from earlier traditions of submission and subordination, enabling it to stand more confidently alongside the secular powers as an institution which is rooted in the life of the Russian people.

The church in Western Europe has wrestled over the centuries with questions concerning the boundaries of authority between church and state. What is presented in the experience of the Orthodox Church in Soviet Russia concerns the boundaries of loyalty. There is an inevitability about the historical process that requires the church to move beyond experience, movement and sect to institution. There is a proper responsibility to be carried by the leaders of the church for the life of the church as an institution and for its survival. Questions concerning the boundaries of loyalty are raised for the church in its relation to the state by the fragility of all institutions, by the compromises that are part and parcel of serious engagement, and by the corruptions of power. In what circumstances and by what criteria should the church impose limits upon its loyalty to the state? How many concessions can be justified to secure survival? How does the church ensure that its response in any situation is informed and shaped by its tradition of faith and piety?

The answers to these questions might appear to be self-evident, but the questions are posed in this way because they draw attention to one other matter which is the concern of church and state. The experience of the Russian Church raises questions also concerning freedom and the recognition of human rights. There is a facile assumption in many places that these things go hand in hand with a secular democracy and that they are ultimately independent of religion and of any theological interpretation of life that the church might offer. The churches of Eastern Europe over recent decades have something to say about 'religious conscience as an ultimate safeguard of human freedom'.[20]

There have been successive phases in the life of the church: experience, movement, sect, institution and empire. It has to be acknowledged that when the church has become an empire it has proved itself well able to be a totalitarian power, unashamedly authoritarian and oppressive in the constraints it imposes upon human freedom. But when the church functions in society as an institution, taking seriously the world in which it is set, it brings to its work an authority which is supernatural and supra-national. It has a story, a hierarchy, a code of law, a discipline. It embodies the principle of nationality or locality; but it represents also the principle of continuity, bearing the tradition of faith, making connections for people between the past, the present and the future. It is the one institution which can never be entirely taken over by an alien philosophy. It is for this reason that the church will, therefore, appear at certain times to be a challenge – actual or potential – to the state, and especially to totalitarian powers.

The story and the institutional life of the Orthodox Church in Russia speak of this principle of continuity. Its response during the period of Soviet oppression exhibited the weaknesses of submission and compliance and collusion that have been the subject of vehement attack within Russia. It may be, however, that the final judgement upon this chapter in its history must take some account of all that it represented in terms of the continuity of church and nation, recognising the threat that it posed and the challenge that it offered to those who would deny the story and the freedom of the Russian people.

NOTES

1 Helene Iswolsky, *Christ in Russia*, The Bruce Publishing company 1962, pp. 79–80.
2 Catherine the Great, Empress of Russia, 1729–1796.
3 Vladimir Ilich Ulyanovsh Lenin, 1870–1924.
4 Helene Iswolsky, *op.cit.*, p. 132.
5 Cited by Trevor Beeson, *Discretion and Valour*, Fountain Books, 1974, p. 56.
6 Ibid.
7 Subsequently elected as Patriarch of Moscow by a synod of bishops in 1943.
8 Cited by Trevor Beeson, *op.cit.*, pp. 56–7.
9 Paul B. Anderson, *People, Church and State in Modern Russia*, SCM Press 1944, p. 51.
10 Joseph Stalin, 1879–1953.
11 Paul B. Anderson, *op.cit.*, p. 142.
12 Trevor Beeson, *op.cit.*, p. 63.
13 Cited by Jane Ellis, *The Russian Orthodox Church: A Contemporary History*, 1986, pp. 23–4.
14 Cited by Trevor Beeson, *op.cit.*, pp. 70–71.
15 Ibid., pp. 72–73.

16 Owen Chadwick, *The Christian Church in the Cold War*, The Penguin Press, 1992, p. 207.
17 Cited by Michael Bourdeaux, *Gorbachev, Glasnost and the Gospel*, Hodder & Stoughton, 1990, p. 61.
18 Ibid., p. 56.
19 Ibid., p. 100.
20 Owen Chadwick, *The Christian Church in the Cold War*, The Penguin Press, 1992, p. 207.

Chapter 11

Critical Encounter

It is exactly the same issues – loyalty to the state and the relation of religious conscience to human rights – that are raised by the experience of the church in Kenya during the last decade or so. The issues are addressed in Kenya in entirely different ways by church leaders who represent young churches in a young country. Kenya has no experience of any constitutional relationship between church and state, although the churches are deeply rooted in the life of local communities and have pioneered the provision of education and primary health care.

The problems that are inseparable from leading a newly independent African nation towards full political, economic and social development lead all too easily to authoritarian government whose overriding concerns are order and stability. The response of the churches in Kenya – and especially the Anglican church – has been to engage critically with the state, taking full advantage of its independence within the state, in order to speak passionately and prophetically against all attempts to subvert the democratic process and to infringe fundamental human rights.

Kenya achieved independence from British colonial rule in 1963. The first fifteen years of independence were dominated by Jomo Kenyatta, who appeared to combine freedom and democracy with political development and economic growth. Parliament and the civil service and the dominant political party – KANU : Kenya African National Union – provided the structure of power at a national level, while the inherent problems of containing the diverse ethnic and

174

cultural groupings of Kenyan life were addressed through a series of alliances at district level. Kenyatta established a centralised state in which great authority was vested in the civil service which, while it had no direct political role, influenced every area of national life and development.

The accession of Daniel arap Moi to the presidency in 1978 initiated a new phase in the government of Kenya. The blatant corruption of Kenyatta's years had not eroded the confidence and the popular support that surrounded this early period of relative stability and growth. But the continuing task of nation-building would become precarious in the face of rising inflation, national debt, a rapidly increasing population, substantial unemployment, and the havoc caused by the AIDS epidemic. Moi's release of political detainees at the beginning of his administration, together with his initial drive against corruption, raised the hope that he would preside over a more liberal regime. But Moi was intolerant of opposition from the beginning and the following years were to see the establishment of a one-party state and an increasingly repressive political autocracy.

Kenya had been for all practical purposes a one-party state in Kenyatta's time, but the freedom of parliamentary debate that had been permitted by Kenyatta was eroded by Moi's use of the party and of party discipline. The fundamental change concerned the use of KANU as the primary instrument in managing the work of government at all levels. The relation between the institutions of Kenyatta's centralised and patriarchal administration – parliament, the civil service and KANU – was drastically changed. The centre of political gravity shifted and the party began to control as fully as possible all organs of the state. The National Assembly passed an amendment to the constitution in June 1982 that Kenya would become *de jure* a one-party state, but it was in the district that the work of government by the party was managed and secured. It was Moi's achievement to turn KANU into a broad-based party with a national organisation and a strong internal discipline.

Continuity between the two administrations was

expressed by Moi in his repeated references to *Nyayo* or footsteps. The intention at the outset had been to suggest that he would walk in Kenyatta's footsteps, although *Nyayo* came to represent the footsteps of Moi in which Kenyans were required to walk. *Nyayo* might be properly considered in the first instance as little more than a political slogan, but it was invested by Moi with philosophical overtones and *Nyayoism* expressed the prevailing political philosophy of the decade between the establishment of the one-party state in June 1982 and its abandonment in December 1991.

It is this period that has become known as the *Nyayo* era. Moi's exposition of *Nyayoism* suggests that it drew upon an African tradition of public affairs, upon Christian faith, and upon a fair degree of pragmatism where the realisation of political goals was concerned.[1] It required loyalty to Kenya, to the head of state, and to the government. It placed great emphasis upon strong leadership in carrying forward the work of development. It did not envisage a centralised administration, but it was profoundly hierarchical and worked within the structures of national life through Provincial Councillors, District Councillors, District Officers, Chiefs and Sub-Chiefs. Moi defined *Nyayoism* as the spirit of Peace and Love and Unity; but it was primarily a plea for nation-building. The party was the vehicle; Nyayo was the moving spirit; *Nyayoism* was the philosophy. Moi introduced an ideological note into what was essentially a rallying cry. It became the public symbol of a decade in which Moi exercised an increasingly autocratic leadership.

The political and public consequences of *Nyayoism* were to be seen most clearly in the work of KANU in the 1980s. The party had not been a significant instrument of government under Kenyatta. It had served as the arena in which conflicting interests could compete at district level. Moi acknowledged the primary importance of the district in political management and used KANU to secure and control the work of government.

Great authority was given to the districts and to the local branches of the party – through membership recruitment drives; through the registration of members at polling stations; through the conferring of life membership by the branches; through regular elections within the party; through the screening of candidates for national office; through the enforcement of party discipline.

The powers conferred upon KANU at a local level – together with the development of queue-voting in the mid-1980s – meant that the scope for manipulating the electoral system was very considerable. It followed that the open and free discussion of public policy was virtually impossible. But it also meant in practice as events unfolded that distinctions between the executive, the judiciary, the legislature and KANU were blurred. Indeed, it was Moi's proud boast in November 1986 that KANU was 'the supreme institution in the land, higher than all other organs of state, including the legislature and the judiciary'.[2]

All these matters were brought together in the issue of queue-voting. Elections within KANU for party posts in June 1985 had been managed in the district by party members forming lines of queues behind their chosen candidates. This system of open elections represented an alternative to election by secret ballot, compromised community leaders who needed to retain their professional impartiality, and laid itself open to widespread abuse. This method of queuing was introduced for preliminary elections in order to eliminate weak candidates prior to the general election of 1988.

Queue-voting was a technical matter but it became a symbol of the confrontation between church and state and, in so far as this issue was concerned, church leaders were joined by the Law Society of Kenya in calling for a thorough debate. The constitutional significance of the development lay in the fact that the effective decision was taken not by parliament but by the party. It was the new KANU constitution in May 1987 which made provision for election by queuing. The procedure was judged to be an internal party matter which only required the approval of the party's own councils.

It was in the events of 1987 and 1988 that the constitutional situation deteriorated and that confrontation between church and state became a matter of public concern. The working of the electoral system at a local level was vitiated by allegations of manipulation and fraud, and by the intimidation of voters. The activities of the KANU disciplinary committee at a national level raised constitutional questions concerning the sovereignty of parliament.

There had been great emphasis from the beginning of Moi's presidency on personal loyalty. Dissent was interpreted as disloyalty. What was seen in the mid-1980s was a heavy-handed response on the part of government to any suggestion of opposition. Critics were discredited and intimidated. Publications were censored. There were frequent allegations of subversive activity and MwaKenya, a dissident group that was becoming a rallying point for opponents to the regime, was proscribed. Detention without trial became a feature of government. Constitutional amendments in August 1987 removed the security of tenure that judges had previously enjoyed.

There was continuing public controversy between the government and leading churchmen, and especially Bishop Alexander Muge of Eldoret and Bishop David Gitari of Mount Kenya East, including public vilification and physical assault. A council of KANU delegates called on the churches to refrain from abusing what was termed the 'privilege' of freedom of worship; and, prior to Moi's intervention to end the public dispute, KANU officials threatened to remove the freedom of worship that had been guaranteed by the constitution.

The churches of Kenya probably represented seventy-five per cent of the people, of whom it was estimated in 1980 that sixty per cent were practising Christians.[3] But the significance of the churches was not only to be found in their numerical strength. The churches – many of the churches – were deeply involved in very practical ways in the lives of people through the provision of education, of primary health care, of land reclamation, and of agricultural development. The churches constituted, therefore, 'an awkward obstacle for politicians to negotiate: too large to ignore; too deeply rooted to remove'.[4]

The challenge that was offered to the *Nyayo* state was confined in large measure to a handful of church leaders within two Christian traditions. The Roman Catholics, who comprised twenty-seven per cent of the population, confined themselves almost entirely to occasional pronouncements on political matters in pastoral letters from Episcopal Conferences. Some of the mainstream Protestant Churches were equally reluctant to engage in public dialogue with the government. The continuing influence of the East African Revival Movement, which had done much to shape the Protestant and the Pentecostal Churches in Kenya, remained steadfastly indifferent to all political and social concerns. The African Churches were largely loyal to the government. The responsibility of providing a loyal opposition fell almost entirely upon the Anglicans (CPK – the Church of the Province of Kenya) and the Presbyterians (PCEA – the Presbyterian Church of East Africa), together with the National Council of Christians in Kenya which brought together most of the Protestant Churches.

The overriding concern of the churches – and this most certainly included the Anglicans and the Presbyterians – was evangelistic and pastoral and developmental. The prophetic work of critical engagement came within the broad parameters of these primary responsibilities. But the Anglicans and the Presbyterians were well placed to question what was happening in the nation: 'the CPK and PCEA leaderships were fully African and self-confident. Their pastoral and developmental activities brought them into close contact with the state without making them dependent on the state. They were familiar with the exercise of power in large organisations. They both had structures which encouraged the local organisation to assert its autonomy in the face of central authority'.[5]

There was no concern in any public criticism of the Nyayo state to denigrate the legitimate authority of government. There was emphasis upon the need to recognise and applaud the achievements of government and to accept its legitimate demands for taxation and loyalty.[6] What was questioned was any claim to absolute authority on the part of the state and any claim to immunity from criticism on the part of government.[7] It was only in so far as the actions of the state impinged upon questions of justice and righteousness that the church was bound to protest.[8]

The public confrontation with the practical consequences of *Nyayoism* required church leaders to distinguish the spheres of authority that properly belong to church and state, to explore the nature of loyalty, and to examine the appropriate relationship between a leader and his people. But there was nothing theoretical about these matters. The prophetic word of judgement was set firmly within a pattern of ministry which placed great emphasis upon the exposition of the scriptures, the pastoral work of the church, and a deep involvement in the life of local communities. 'The incarnational model invites us to proclaim the Gospel not from a distance but rather by penetrating communities and cultures, cities and villages, so that we can see for ourselves the harassment and helplessness of God's people and then stand in solidarity with them.'[9]

There is an innate religious awareness which permeates all areas of African life. The authority for the church's confrontation with the state lay in the imperative of the Gospel, but it was buttressed by an indigenous tradition which regarded 'the regulation of social relationships, the administration of justice, the acquisition and use of land and flocks, and the making of war and peace as sacral activities'.[10]

But the abiding theme is justice and it is related to all that is understood about judgement. The church's duty to the state includes the prophetic ministry of judgement.[11] There is much emphasis upon the goodness of creation, upon the dignity of human life, upon the meaning of incarnation, and upon the demands of the kingdom of God. The call is to conversion and conversion implies public responsibility; but public responsibility is to be defined by the kingdom of God and not by the state.[12]

It is, however, within the twentieth century understanding of a realised eschatology that judgement is experienced as impending judgement. The most outspoken churchmen owed much to their own evangelical tradition and to the insights of liberation theology. But there is a common thread in their emphasis upon the righteousness of God, the importance of the present time, the significance of every action, the requirements of natural justice, and the fact of judgement in the destiny of nations.

Nothing should be allowed to minimise the magnitude of the task confronting the government during the *Nyayo* period. It was inevitable that every attempt should be made to secure order and stability. There was nothing in this situation – the churches and the *Nyayo* state – that remotely resembled the thoroughgoing persecution of the church by an atheistic state in Russia during the period of Soviet oppression. It was, rather, a question of fundamentally different perceptions, values, criteria for judgement as politicians and churchmen disagreed over the things that make for political development, social harmony and the integrity of the nation.

Moi's understanding of the Christian faith owed much at the beginning to the revivalist tradition of the African Inland Church. He refers frequently in his study of *Kenya African Nationalism* to the importance of Christianity, although he never speaks of the church as an institution. It is not possible for him to conceive of the church as an entity that stands over against the state. Implicit in Moi's understanding of nation-building and of *Nyayoism* is a concept of leadership in which all leaders within the community are required to share. There is a sense in which the churches challenge the Nyayo state merely by their existence as 'separate institutions outside the framework of the *Nyayo* leadership core'.[13] It was, perhaps, inevitable that public criticism should be interpreted as public and personal disloyalty.

The church challenged what it saw as injustices in the life of the state. Specific concerns would arise from time to time: irregularities concerning the allocation of building plots for church development; the destruction of shanties in Nairobi;

the concerns of the coffee farmers at the dissolution of the Kenya Planters' Co-operative Union. General concerns persisted and provided the mainstay of public criticism: the increasingly authoritarian character of government and of KANU; the continuing corruption of Kenyan life; the intimidation of government critics; the suppression of freedom of speech; detention without trial; the abuses that were inseparable from queue-voting; and the wilful manipulation of elections and election results.

Any examination of this period of critical engagement is bound to take account of the Presbyterian pastor – Timothy Njoya, and of the Anglican bishops – Henry Okullu, Alexander Muge and David Gitari. These men were primarily preachers and pastors, rather than theologians or political theorists. They were willing to take full advantage of the church's position in Kenyan society as 'one of the few organisations with licence to dissent'.[14] It was only in the process of addressing the specific and the general concerns in the course of their public ministries that they provided reflections upon the relation of church and state, the meaning of power, the priority of justice.

The approach of these prominent and persistent critics varied a good deal. Njoya was strident in his condemnation of the presidential personality cult as idolatry. He deplored the emasculation of the institutions of government and the manipulation of mob feeling and mob violence at mass meetings. But his main emphasis in his writing was upon the dignity of human life as the key to an understanding of the world.[15] All institutions, including church and state, are provisional and serve only to enhance the dignity of human life.

Okullu attached far greater significance to church and state and spoke of their distinctive but God-given responsibilities.[16] 'The state is created to keep law and order in society ... The church is instituted by God to bring the mind of God to bear upon total human life and to contribute to the building of value systems upon which a sound human society may be built.'[17] He acknowledged the complexities of nation-building and the difficulty of containing forces that work against justice. It was his commitment to justice, rooted in the righteousness of God, that led him to condemn the one-party state, the violation of human rights and any infringement of freedom of speech.

Muge was a vehement and persistent critic. He spoke fearlessly out of his knowledge of local issues – the allocation of land for development; the detention of members of his staff; the existence of famine. He condemned the government for its violation of human rights. He was critical of the confidantes with whom the president surrounded himself. He spoke passionately against the threat to withdraw the freedom of worship. His death in tragic and suspicious circumstances in August 1990 cut short a conspicuous ministry.

Gitari has written extensively on the interconnection between Christian faith and community life.[18] There is no theory or theology of the state in his writings, but he affirms the role of the state. 'Because God is not a God of chaos but of order, it is within His will that there should be governing authorities to protect the citizens from wrongdoers and to punish the latter.'[19] Gitari lays great emphasis upon the independence of the church within the state. The characteristics that should mark the church's relation with the state are distinctive separation, creative participation and justice. It was Gitari who insisted that Justice should stand alongside Peace and Love and Unity in any exposition of *Nyayoism*.

Gitari's public criticism of the government became focussed in the four sermons preached in June 1987 and subsequently published under the title, *Let the Bishop Speak*. His sermons addressed the routine inadequacies of life as they were experienced by ordinary people. He spoke of those who could not pay school fees; of those who were denied goods by hoarders; of those who were treated inconsiderately on matatus; of those who lacked space in hospital. But his sermons also addressed wider questions relating to the political integrity of the nation's life: the suppression of the Kenya Planters' Co-operative Union; the denial of registration as voters of those who were not members of KANU; the wilful distortion of the truth to discredit critics; secret meetings; ill-considered and speedy changes to the constitution.

It would be inaccurate to suggest that the church, although it had been influential during these years, was the major factor in bringing the one-party state to an end. International events and international pressure were far more significant. It is not easy to know how much importance should be attached to events in Eastern Europe in 1989, which undoubtedly had consequences – ideological and psychological – for Africa, and especially for Kenya, where a one-party state had become the norm. There was undoubtedly growing unrest in Kenya; but it was almost certainly financial pressure from the United States and from the World Bank which finally tipped the balance and encouraged the National Assembly to repeal Section 2A of the constitution in December 1991, thus making it possible for a multi-party state to emerge again. This date effectively marked the end of the *Nyayo* period, although the divided nature of opposition politics at the time of the general election in 1992 ensured the continuing dominance of KANU.

The church had been influential throughout Kenya, and especially among politicians, during this decade. The public protests voiced by church leaders had not formed part of some coherent strategy of opposition, and their impact was weakened both by inconsistency and by government distortion. Perhaps all that can be claimed is that the confrontation of churchmen contributed to the downfall of *Nyayoism*. But the witness against injustice had been heard and there is substance in the claim that the church stood almost alone in providing a loyal opposition. In April 1992, the Justice and Peace Commission of the Church of the Province of Kenya issued a pastoral letter reflecting upon the experience. 'Fear was the order of the day and before very long that fear became a new culture in the national life – the *culture of fear*. Other institutions which were critical of the government were also intimidated and some succumbed to silence. In the final analysis it appeared as if only the Church and the Law Society had the courage to speak on behalf of the people'.[20]

The response of several church leaders in confronting this culture of fear represents another pattern of engagement in the continuing story of church-state relations. There are circumstances in which the constitutional relationship which is enjoyed by an established church might inhibit the leaders of the church from responding critically at a time of great political sensitivity to questions of national and local concern. But there is no guarantee that the absence of such a relationship will necessarily set the church free to engage in such a way.

It has been convenient to speak of the church, although the truth of the matter is that it was individuals – bishops and pastors – who were outspoken in their condemnation of injustice in the *Nyayo* period. There are questions to be asked about a prophetic ministry and the extent to which it can ever be a function of the church as an institution rather than the response of individuals who are rooted within it. These are not matters that can be thought through in advance; but it is, perhaps, one of the signs of maturity that a church is able to establish a culture of tolerance within its own internal life which enables some people to exercise this wider ministry of critical encounter.

The work of the Church of the Province of Kenya is well documented, and it is not the least intriguing aspect of the whole episode that this young and relatively small church should have taken such a prominent part in confronting the Nyayo state.

The established pattern of experience, movement and sect is one with which the CPK was familiar. Its strong evangelical tradition ensured the continuing importance of personal conversion as the experience of faith and repentance in which the life of the church is visibly renewed. Its spiritual vitality and its numerical growth ensured that it still had something of the character of a movement. Statistical returns in Bishop Gitari's diocese of Mount Kenya East for the mid-1980s indicated annual increases in the number of worshippers of almost fifteen per cent and of conversions measured by adult baptism of over thirteen per cent.

It would have been easy for the church in these circumstances to confine itself to the position of a sect in Kenyan
society. It represented only seven per cent of the population.
It had no constitutional relationship with the state. But it had
been able to grow beyond the constraints of being a sect in its
theology, in its ecclesiology, and in its approach to ministry.
The work of Okullu, Muge and Gitari enabled the church
within the context of Kenyan life to address the principles of
nationality, social harmony and comprehensiveness in new
and prophetic ways. It was their achievement to take
forward the evolution of the church as an institution in this
young province of the Anglican Communion.

The experience of the Church in Kenya has been instructive in one additional respect. Gitari has taken as the basis of
his thinking on church and state the work of the colloquium
organised by the World Council of Churches and the
Ecumenical Institute at Bossey in 1976, which proposed the
four approaches that might be adopted by the church in its
relation to the state and to secular power.

First, there is the response of *active adaptation* in so far as
the church identifies itself with the goals and the intentions
of the state. Secondly, there is the response of *passive adaptation* in so far as the church withdraws into the sphere of the
purely religious, and abstains from any statements on the
decisions and activities of the state. Thirdly, there is the
response of *critical and constructive collaboration* with the
state by evaluating, on the basis of its understanding of the
gospel, the political decisions and the proposed programme
of the state. Fourthly, there is the response of *resistance or
opposition* to the state if circumstances arise which require
the church to act in such a way because the state has lost
sight of its vocation to be the servant of God and of the
people.

Gitari explores these four approaches in the experience of
Africa[21]. He brings his own interpretation of events to bear
upon the situation in different countries over a period of fifty
years. He discusses the responses that have been adopted at
different times by churches of various traditions in Angola,

in Mozambique, in Ethiopia, in South Africa, in Zambia, in Kenya, in the Sudan, and in Uganda.

Gitari's firm judgement is that the first two approaches – active or passive adaptation – constitute either 'imposed captivity or accepted captivity'.[22] He is clear that in most instances the church is called to adopt the third approach – critical and constructive collaboration – and he is well able to cite instances of the way in which he and other church leaders in Kenya pursued this path during the *Nyayo* period. The fourth approach – resistance or opposition – can never be discounted if the church is to fulfil its task of being the conscience of the nation.[23]

It may well be that Gitari's emphasis upon the independence of the church within the state owes much to the tradition of conservative evangelicalism in which he was nurtured. This tradition had been broadened and deepened by his openness to the insights of liberation theology and his wholehearted commitment to a holistic approach to ministry. The theological emphasis that undergirds his approach to church and state is the conviction that the church is called to be both 'an agent of liberation and a community of hope'.[24]

Every situation is different. The experience of the Church in Kenya – like that of the communities of faith in America and of the Orthodox Church in Russia – cannot be easily transposed to other places. The various patterns of engagement that have been identified do not provide broad principles which can be taken out of context and used as the basis of some universal theory of church and state. These three case studies serve a limited purpose, but they illustrate the different ways in which church and state engage with each other.

The experience of the three great communities of faith in the United States of America tells of an engagement between church and state which is extraordinarily pervasive and profound. The commitment to equality, democracy, opportunity and achievement provided the context in which a great diversity of immigrant groups could exist and adapt and find a wider association and belonging But it was a two-way process. The American dream, the American ideal, the American way of life were shaped in fair measure by the aspirations and the values of these communities of faith. The law of liberty speaks, then, of a relationship which owes nothing to any kind of constitutional establishment but which binds church and state together in a way that has been without parallel in the modern world. The American experience tells of how in one nation and over a period of two or three centuries religion can be a bond of unity.

The experience of the Orthodox Church in Russia during the period of Soviet oppression presents a totally different experience of engagement between church and state. A church that had been co-existent with the nation over a thousand years, intimately associated with the tsars and with the people, found itself exposed to systematic persecution. The strengths and the weaknesses that are contained within all traditions are exposed in times of testing; and it remains to be seen if responses which appear to tell of subordination, collusion and acquiescence have actually enabled the church to survive and to resume its historic task. The vitality and the resilience of Orthodoxy with its deep sense of being within and beyond time introduce an entirely new dimension into all thinking about church and state. Identity and continuity speak, then, of a story in church-state relations which possesses greater complexity, subtlety and depth of meaning than might be immediately apparent.

The experience of the Church in Kenya during the *Nyayo* period takes up in a different way the questions of loyalty and human rights which have been presented by the Russian story. It is not primarily the story of the church or the churches but of a handful of prominent churchmen who exercised a prophetic ministry. Their starting point was the conviction that everything they believed about the righteousness of God and the dignity of human life required them to confront an authoritarian state. They did not intervene as political theorists but as preachers and pastors whose young churches in a young country were deeply involved in the life of their local communities. Critical encounter speaks, then, of a prophetic tradition in which the church is able and willing to take advantage of its independence within the state to be the conscience and the voice of the people.

Establishment represents one form of religious settlement. Every church is bound to regularise its relationship with the state in one way or another. Church and state will engage with each other to their mutual advantage or disadvantage. There might appear to be little in common between the experience of the church in America, in Russia and in Kenya. If there is a connecting thread it is to be found in the relationship between church and people. Bishop Gitari speaks out of his knowledge of the church in Kenya but his words might well have been addressed to the situation in the other nations. 'The Christian community must be rooted in the society in which it has grown up, and its members must be a part of that society, sharing its traditional points of view, influenced by its history, involved in its strength and its weakness.'[25] In each case – America, Russia and Kenya – there has been evidence of the church being rooted in the society to which it belongs, being influenced by its history, and being involved – at times unwittingly – in its strength and its weakness.

NOTES
1 Daniel arap Moi, *Kenya African Nationalism*, Macmillan 1986.
2 Weekly Review, 1st May 1987, p. 6. Cited by Patrick Benson, *Church Confrontations with the State during Kenya's Nyayo Era, 1982–1991: Causes and Effects*. A thesis submitted to the Open University for the degree of Master of Philosophy, March 1993, p. 37.
3 Patrick Benson, *op.cit.*, p. 88.
4 Ibid.
5 Ibid., p. 2.
6 David M. Gitari, *Let the Bishop Speak*, Uzima Press 1988.
7 Ibid.
8 Ibid.
9 Ibid.
10 Patrick Benson, *op.cit.*, p. 88
11 David M. Gitari and G. P. Benson (Editors), *The Living God*, Uzima Press 1986, p. 135.

12 David M. Gitari, *Church and Politics in Kenya*, Article published in *Transformation*, July-September 1991.
13 Patrick Benson, *op.cit.*, p. 85.
14 Ibid., p. 57.
15 T. Njoya, *Human Dignity and National Identity*, Nairobi Jemisik Cultural Books 1987.
16 J.H. Okullu, *Church and Politics in East Africa*, Nairobi: Uzima Press 1974. J.H. Okullu, *Church and State in Nation Building and Development*, Nairobi: Uzima Press 1984.
17 J.H. Okullu, *Church and Politics in East Africa*, Nairobi: Uzima Press 1974, pp. 15f.
18 David M.Gitari, *Church and Nationhood in a Changing World.* Article in *Church and Nationhood*, Edited by Lionel Holmes, Papers from WEF Theological Commission at Basel, September 1976. David M. Gitari, *Mission of the Church in East Africa.* Article in *Crossroads Are for Meeting*, Edited by P. Turner and F. Sugeno, Sewanee: SPCK/USA 1986. David M. Gitari, *The Unity and Diversity of the World-Wide Church.* Article in *New Frontiers in Mission*, Edited by P. Sookhdeo, Exeter: Paternoster 1987. David M. Gitari, *The Church's Witness to the Living God in Seeking Just Political, Social and Economic Structures in Contemporary Africa.* Article in *The Living God.* Edited by David M. Gitari and G.P. Benson, Nairobi: Uzima Press 1987. David M. Gitari, *Let the Bishop Speak*, Nairobi Uzima Press 1988. David M. Gitari, *Evangelisation and Culture*, Article in *Proclaiming Christ in Christ's Way: Studies in Integral Evangelism*, Edited by V. Samuel and A. Hauser, Oxford: Regnum 1989. David M. Gitare, *Kenya: Evangelism Among Nomadic Communities.* Article in *One Gospel – Many Clothes*, Edited by C. Wright and C. Sugden, Oxford: Regnum 1990.
19 David M. Gitari and G.P. Benson (Editors), *The Living God*, Uzima Press 1986, p. 130.
20 CPK Justice and Peace Commission. *A Pastoral Letter to all CPK Congregations.* Easter 1992, p. 16.
21 David M. Gitari, *The Church's Witness to the Living God*, Appendix to *Let the Bishop Speak*, Uzima Press 1988.
22 Ibid., p. 84.
23 Ibid., p. 86.
24 Ibid., p. 85.
25 Ibid.

PART IV

A CONTINUING ESTABLISHMENT

Chapter 12
A Continuing Establishment

Observers of the English constitutional scene are bound to acknowledge the resilience of English institutions. Traditions of law, of balance, of tolerance have ensured that there is a reluctance to address constitutional questions. The circumstances in which institutions came into being may have been long since left behind; but there is a pragmatic spirit which is able to identify the elements of continuity in the English story and to make connections between the past and the future. The purposes which institutions were originally required to fulfil may well have been forgotten; but there is a practical turn of mind which is concerned to identify their inherent strengths and to ensure that adjustments are made so that they might develop in new ways. The English monarchy, the House of Lords, and the British Commonwealth of Nations are three instances of institutions that have demonstrated over the centuries – and not least of all in recent generations – a capacity to survive, to adapt, and to continue to fulfil some useful purpose.

The continuing establishment of the Church of England is no exception to this general rule concerning the resilience of English institutions. The English Church and the English nation had been intimately connected for a thousand years before the canon of 1603 spoke of the Church of England as being 'by law established'.[1] Establishment referred, therefore, in its original form to the constitutional and religious settlement that had been achieved in the reformation period, and especially under Elizabeth I. Wider questions concerning the identity and the unity of the nation had been caught up in this settlement, but the establishment of the church gave formal expression to the Christian faith of the English people and to the role of the church within English society. Circumstances have changed dramatically in church and state over four centuries, but the establishment of religion survives and continues to speak, albeit discreetly, of the religious dimension that is built into the structures, the conventions, the symbols of national life.

Circumstances have changed, and so has the nature of the Church of England's relation to the state. It is one of the achievements of church-state relations in England over the last one hundred and seventy years that much of the form, the tradition, the symbolism, the expectations of establishment have remained; while the state has recognised the religious diversity of the nation and the church has secured a fair degree of freedom in the management of its affairs and the development of its life. 'The phenomenon of a reformed established church, witnessing to a continuing tradition of total involvement with the state, and at the same time adjusting itself to a liberal and secular society, in which all subjects under the crown have equal rights, duties and privileges – this is a subtle and complex development which can all too easily be taken for granted.'[2]

The changing nature of the relationship between church and state over the centuries has said much about the way in which they have both seen themselves and seen each other. It is, however, a modern phenomenon in the history of western Europe that church and state should regard themselves as distinct entities, separate societies. They do not necessarily represent alien or conflicting principles. They share large areas of common concern. They may well buttress and support each other. But the emphasis falls increasingly upon their complementary but distinctive roles as they attempt to engage with the structures and the institutions, the relationships and the individuals, the conventions and the values that constitute human society.

Any contemporary critique of the modified form of establishment that now exists in England is bound to take account of the changes in church and state which have required substantial modifications to the original compact. The reformation settlement was a constitutional settlement and it spoke of the unity of church and state within a Christian commonwealth. This ideal has long since been qualified, compromised, abandoned. The state has long since been required to acknowledge the religious diversity, even the religious neutrality, of the nation.

Fundamental changes in the very bed and basis of society in more recent decades have challenged all the presuppositions concerning the establishment of religion. Church and state are bound to reflect upon the meaning of a nation state in an international world order; upon the meaning of an established church in a multi-racial, multi-faith, society; upon the meaning of the establishment of the Christian religion in a secular society. These are some of the factors that have compromised still further the exclusive claims that the Church of England has justly made in earlier generations simply on the basis of its position as the established church.

The ideal of an established church that is co-extensive with the state has long since been overtaken by the changing demography of religious allegiance. A multiplicity of churches and religious traditions has ensured that the Church of England does not have any monopoly of concern for the spiritual well-being of the nation. A long-standing tradition of secularism has meant that the Church of England as the established church does not count for much in the consciousness of large numbers of people. Churches – all churches – struggle to retain their footholds in the affections of people.

The reformation settlement rested on certain assumptions about church and state which have also lost their original meaning. The form of establishment provided in England embodied the ancient tradition of the godly prince. But the emergence of a parliamentary democracy meant in practice that the crown, however well intentioned, no longer possessed the power to do the one thing that was required of the godly prince – namely, to protect and defend the church.

The transition from the supremacy of the crown to the supremacy of the crown in parliament in all areas of national life has avoided the excesses of royal absolutism; but parliament is no longer competent to exercise the ancient jurisdiction envisaged by Hooker's exposition of the Tudor settlement. Parliament is bound to be sensitive to public opinion. The church can no longer require that its values, judgements, disciplines shall be imposed upon the nation as a whole. Parliament cannot be expected to act primarily and exclusively in the interests of the church.

The steady movement towards self-government within the Church of England over the last one hundred and forty years rests on something more fundamental to the church's life than either the multiplicity of churches and religious traditions or the changing dynamics of the English constitution. What has been secured is nothing less than freedom within the outward forms of establishment, and it speaks powerfully of the recognition that the church possesses and must be seen to possess 'an inherent original power of self-development'.[3]

The frustrations of an earlier age were expressed by John Keble in 1850, prompted by the judgement in the Gorham Case. He protested vehemently against the inability of the Church of England, 'To declare our own Doctrines; to confirm, vary and repeal our own Canons; to have a voice in the nomination of our own chief Pastors; to grant and with-hold our own Sacraments according to our own proper rule'.[4] The principle was one of self-determination and self-development, and this was the point seized upon by R.W. Church, reflecting upon the relation between church and state and writing at exactly the same time as Keble: 'still the claim – that what the English Church would have a right to, *were she but a sect*, she has a right to, as a power in the English State as the *Church*, recognised by the English nation – namely the right to be really represented as a Church – is so strong and so reasonable'.[5]

R.W. Church was mindful of the way in which English institutions are able to develop. The change that he sought was entirely in harmony with 'that principle of improvement

which has worked so long and widely in England; which
does not destroy, but adds on; which alters with as little
visible change and break as possible; which, leaving what it
finds, reinforces what appears to work'.[6] The important
question for the vast majority of churchmen in the middle
years of the nineteenth century onwards did not relate to
establishment or disestablishment but 'whether or no (the
church) be conceived as possessing any living power of self-
development'.[7] The issue was ultimately one of the inherent
freedom and authority at the heart of the church's life.

The evolution of representative organs of church government can be traced from this period. The Convocations of
Canterbury and York were allowed to meet again from 1852
and 1861 respectively, and Houses of Laity were attached to
these Convocations in 1885 for Canterbury and in 1892 for
York. A Representative Church Council, combining the two
Convocations and the Houses of Laity, was formed in 1904;
but the all-important step forward was taken with the establishment of the Church Assembly following upon the
Enabling Act of 1919.

It was the question of the church's inherent authority
which was acknowledged in the *Report on Church and State*
in 1916, and which prepared the way for the Enabling Act.
The Commission had been concerned to secure for the
church the appropriate degree of freedom without jettisoning
the historic relation between church and state. It acknowledged freely the limitations of the present situation in which
'Parliament has neither the leisure, fitness or inclination, to
perform efficiently the function of an ecclesiastical legislature'.[8] It was, therefore, concerned to provide the church
with 'such organs and with such a procedure in its relation to
the state as would leave it free to determine its own requirements, and, under the sanction of the state, to give effect to
its wishes, while the due authority of the state would be safe-
guarded, and the basis of its historic relationship with the
church would remain undisturbed'.[9]

The extent of the freedom and the authority envisaged for
the church was considerable: 'After careful consideration we

do not think that it would be found possible to delineate with any precision the sphere within which the Church Council is to be recognised as having power to legislate. We believe that the Church of England has inherent authority to deal with all matters of doctrine, worship, and ritual, as affecting its own members, and to determine all questions of membership'.[10] The ultimate power of a parliamentary veto would be retained but, saving this qualification, the church would be given 'full power to legislate on ecclesiastical affairs'.[11]

The Church of England Assembly (Powers) Act – the Enabling Act – of 1919 followed closely in its provisions the recommendations of the *Report on Church and State* of 1916. It conferred legislative powers upon the Church Assembly, especially with regard to the preparation and modelling of ecclesiastical measures and their presentation to parliament. It established an Ecclesiastical Committee, representative of the two Houses of Parliament, to which its measures would be submitted before proceeding to parliament. It provided that while parliament might accept or reject a measure it could not amend a measure passed by the Assembly.

The powers retained by parliament were fully demonstrated in the rejection of the church's attempts to seek a revision of the Book of Common Prayer in 1928 and 1929. The residual powers remain, but this rejection might well be seen in retrospect as the high water mark of church-state relations in the sense that never again would an issue of fundamental importance within the life of the church be disposed of in such a manner.

The process of continuing self-determination and self-development continued after the Second World War. The revision of the canons of the Church of England was commenced in 1947 and occupied the Church Assembly for the next twenty years. The Ecclesiastical Jurisdiction Measure of 1963 removed the Judicial Committee of the Privy Council as the highest court of appeal in matters of doctrine and ritual and substituted a court of appeal devised by the Church Assembly. The Alternative and Other Services

Measure of 1965 permitted the Convocations and the House of Laity to sanction new forms of worship for an experimental period.

The Synodical Government Measure of 1969 was concerned to achieve a more coherent system of self-government for the church. It reconstituted the structures of representative government in the parishes, the rural deaneries and the dioceses. The Church Assembly ceased to exist and, although the Convocations remained, the newly established General Synod of the Church of England took over the powers of the Church Assembly and some of those of the Convocations. The special responsibilities of the House of Bishops with regard to doctrine and worship and the administration of the sacraments were fully recognised; but the House of Laity was far more fully integrated in a pattern of government that brought bishops, clergy and laity together, and ensured that the delays previously caused by the dual control of the Convocations and the Church Assembly would be avoided.

The Archbishops' Commission on Church and State, appointed under the terms of a resolution passed by the Church Assembly in 1965, was required to make recommendations as to modifications in the constitutional relationship between church and state which might be desirable and practicable. Ecumenical and pastoral considerations weighed heavily with the Commission in arguing that the self government of the Church of England should be taken forward in two major areas: the worship and doctrine of the church, and the appointment of bishops.[12]

The Commission recommended, subject to certain safeguards, that 'All matters affecting the worship and doctrine of the church should become subject to the final authority of the General Synod'.[13] This recommendation was subsequently implemented through the Worship and Doctrine Measure of 1974. The Measure left a residual authority with parliament regarding the status of the Book of Common Prayer of 1662, but in all other respects the church secured full authority to order its worship and its doctrine.

The Commission had also argued for greater participation on the part of the church in the nomination of diocesan and suffragan bishops. It proposed that a Committee or Electoral Board, representing both the diocese concerned and the church at large, should be formed to present the church's view when a bishop is to be nominated for election.[14] This recommendation, at least in so far as the appointment of diocesan bishops is concerned, was embodied in the agreement that led to the establishment of the Crown Appointments Commission in 1977, which secured for the church the decisive voice in the submission of names to the prime minister, while retaining the historic convention of appointment by the crown on the advice of the prime minister.

The process of disengagement, initiated by successive governments in the nineteenth century, has been carried forward by the church over the last eighty years and has secured a substantial measure of independence for the church, even though the fundamental commitment to establishment remains. The extent of the legislative authority vested in the church was tested in the courts in 1993, following upon the decision of General Synod to submit to parliament a measure permitting the ordination of women to the priesthood. An action brought by the Church Society alleged that the Ecclesiastical Committee of Parliament had exceeded its authority in declaring the measure to be expedient. It argued that such a development in the life of the church represented a fundamental change in the doctrine of the Church of England and could therefore be dealt with only by an act of parliament.

The judgement given in the Queen's Bench Division in the High Court on 28th October 1993 rejected the application on the grounds that the Enabling Act had given to the Church of England the authority to submit to parliament a measure on *any matter*, subject only to technical constraints concerning the composition of the Ecclesiastical Committee and parliamentary procedure.[15] Parliament's intention had been that 'the church should have the right to consider, debate and decide such a question if and when they wish to do so, and to put that measure before parliament for its approval or rejection'.[16] The principle of legislative freedom and the practice of proceeding by measure found full endorsement, and the judgement of the High Court referred to the report of the Ecclesiastical Committee on this particular item of legislation in which a majority had expressed the view 'that the more important a matter is within the church the more important it is to adhere to the convention that matters concerning the church should be dealt with by measure'.[17]

It was inevitable that the realisation of the principle of self-determination and self-development should give rise to critical comment and should bring into the forefront of discussion over the years the larger questions that remained concerning a continuing establishment. Bishop Hensley Henson condemned the implicit sectarianism of the Enabling Act and feared that the Church of England would be relegated to the role of 'one more autonomous sect within a nakedly secularist State'.[18] By the early years of the twentieth century it had become impossible to continue any longer with a reformation settlement in which parliament was required to act as 'the House of Laity in a National Assembly';[19] and yet questions concerning responsibility for the religious aspirations of the whole nation continue to present themselves.

The ideal of a national church has never been abandoned. The relationship between church and state has changed and will continue to change. Synodical government, although it has suffered from the indifference and the cynicism that surround all representative and governmental institutions, has served the church well. But the question that has to be asked is whether a relatively small number of elected people, clerical and lay, who might well speak for the active membership of the church, are necessarily competent to speak for 'the inarticulate religious life of the nation'.[20]

There are other issues to be explored which raise in their turn deeper questions concerning the continuing church-state connections. Some regret the reserved position of the Book of Common Prayer and the ultimate authority that resides in parliament. Some resent any suggestion that 'General Synod deliberates and legislates not only by *permission* or *consent* of the Queen in Parliament, but also by *delegation*.[21] The question might well be asked if delegated power was all that was intended when an earlier generation spoke of the church as 'a society with a principle of inherent life'.[22]

Hooker's exposition of the Tudor settlement laid great emphasis upon its essential wisdom in ensuring that the royal supremacy would be circumscribed by parliament *and the convocations*. The achievement of freedom within the framework of establishment has been a significant accomplishment. It is inconceivable that church or state would ever seek to return to the *status quo ante*. It might be argued that the legislative freedom devolved by parliament upon the church's own representative bodies in the course of this century has enabled the Church of England to recover the position implicit in Hooker's *Ecclesiastical Polity*. Hooker argued for parliament *and* the convocations in order to secure a balanced constitution within the unity of the church-state. A generation which is bound to address large questions concerning the meaning of the nation state and the nature and function of religion in society might well be grateful for the balance and the freedom that have been restored.

But the balance and the freedom can only be explored within the fast-changing situation in which church and state find themselves in the closing years of the twentieth century. A continuing establishment raises many questions and can easily lend itself to misrepresentation and caricature. The fundamental problem does not relate to the multiplicity of churches and religious traditions, nor to the fact that Christians who are active in the profession and the observance of their faith now constitute a minority of the population. Indeed, the problem is not even confined to England where, by contrast with other churches in western Europe, the Church of England has retained to a significant degree its constitutional relationship with the state, its historical privileges, and a vital place within the network of expectations and opportunities that are part and parcel of the life of local communities.

It is, rather, a question of what appears to be a fundamental change throughout the western world where the validity of religion and the credibility of religious institutions are concerned. It is manifestly the case that since the age of the enlightenment there has emerged within what might still be called Christian Europe an increasingly large body of people who are unconnected in faith and practice with the institutional life of the church. It is as though there is a feeling after 'an entirely new mental frame of reference'[23] within which questions of value and meaning and purpose are to be explored.

The distinction has properly been made between 'the open Christian civilisation of the modern period and the compulsive or conscriptive civilisation that preceded it'.[24] The religious aspirations and assumptions of earlier generations were shaped in a culture of authority and conformity, of hierarchy and subservience. But in the open and philosophically uncommitted relationships of contemporary life there is no invariable and axiomatic deference to religion. Authority and convention count for little in matters of faith and practice; and the presuppositions of the church in matters of public and private concern are inevitably exposed to the judgements of a secular democracy which in the nature of things may well be hostile or indifferent.

It is precisely here that the arguments against any continuing form of establishment are most searching. It is still entirely appropriate to argue that church and state have complementary roles and are – at least potentially – 'divine agents for human perfection'.[25] But the prevailing culture in which church and state are required to function is now so far removed from the Christian world-view of earlier centuries that all attempts to retain the historic links are held by some to be anomalous and inappropriate.

The establishment of religion gave formal expression to the primary commitment – public and personal – to a Christian understanding of life. Establishment was subsequently judged to be indispensable to 'the upholding of a diffused Christianity throughout the land'.[26] It is acknowledged that

the church as a public institution must be brought into some
relation with the law; but the abandonment of the historic
frame of reference – the Christian world view – together with
the gradual erosion of a diffused Christianity are bound to
call in question the validity of any modified but continuing
establishment.

NOTES

1 *Constitution and Canons Ecclesiasticall* (1603).
2 Leslie S. Hunter (Editor), *The English Church: A New Look*, Penguin
Books 1966, p. 63.
3 J.N. Figgis, *Churches in the Modern State*, Longmans, Green & Co.
1913, p. 99.
4 Cited by Georgina Battiscombe, *John Keble: A Study in Limitations*.
Constable 1963, p. 301.
5 R.W. Church, *op.cit.*, p. 58.
6 Ibid.
7 J.N. Figgis, *Churches in the Modern State*, Longmans, Green & Co.
1913, p. 44.
8 *Report of the Archbishops' Committee on Church and State* (1916),
p. 39.
9 Ibid.
10 Ibid., p. 50.
11 Ibid., p. 49.
12 *Report of the Archbishops' Commission on Church and State* (1970).
13 Ibid., para. 211 (1), p. 64.
14 Ibid., para. 211 (4), p. 64.
15 High Court of Justice: Queen's Bench Division. Regina v the
Ecclesiastical Committee of Both Houses of Parliament: Ex Parte The
Church Society. Judgement (28th October 1993).
16 Ibid.
17 Ibid.
18 H.H. Henson. *Disestablishment: The Charge delivered at the Second
Quadrennial Visitation of his Diocese, together with an Introduction.*
Macmillan & Co. 1929, p. 9.
19 Ibid., p. 13.
20 John Habgood, *Church and Nation in a Secular Age*, DLT 1983,
p. 103.
21 Mark Santer, *The Freedom of the Gospel*, Essay in Donald Reeves
(Editor), *The Church and the State*, Hodder and Stoughton 1984,
p. 115.
22 J.N. Figgis, *Churches in the Modern State*, Longmans Green & Co.
1913, p. 33.

23 John Baillie, *What is Christian Civilization?*, University of Durham: Riddell Memorial Lecture, OUP 1945, p. 26.
24 Ibid., p. 34.
25 P.T. Forsyth, *Theology in Church and State*, Hodder and Stoughton 1915, p. 255.
26 Thomas Chalmers, Scottish Theologian, 1780–1847. Cited by John Baillie, *op.cit.*, p. 47.

Chapter 13
A Contemporary Critique

Establishment has a limited and technical meaning. It speaks of the special relationship, the constitutional relationship, between the Church of England and the state. But the word has taken to itself associations and connotations which all too easily distort the debate. It speaks for some of a constitutional settlement in which the church is made subservient to state control. It speaks to others of a privileged status which is inappropriate for the church, and especially in a situation in which the church – all churches – appear to count for little in the consciousness of many people.

These popular misconceptions about the true nature and meaning of establishment give place for others to far more legitimate concerns. The historic emphasis upon the unity of church and state within a Christian commonwealth can lead to collusion on the part of the church, actual or perceived, with the established order – politically, economically, socially, culturally. The pastoral opportunities provided by establishment can lead to a self-importance on the part of clergy and congregations which will inhibit the growth of all the churches into a greater unity. Establishment might give a significant public profile to religion, but all institutions – secular and ecclesiastical – are vulnerable to nostalgia and self-deception, high handedness and servility.

Antagonists will insist that establishment is nothing more than a noble facade; that the seductive pressures of establishment have consistently compromised the character of the church; that important things are lost when a church's relationship with the state is institutionalised; that independence is essential to spiritual vitality.

It is freely acknowledged that circumstances may well arise either within the developing life of all the churches or within the constitutional life of the wider community which make disestablishment desirable or expedient or inescapable. It is readily conceded that if the establishment had not survived, then a religious settlement would not be provided in anything like its existing form. But such approaches to the question of establishment suggest that the continuing connections are little more than historical anomalies, part of the story of church and nation in this land, which might yet serve some useful purpose, but which cannot be judged to be vital to the life of church or state.

And yet there are important ingredients in establishment which speak unequivocally of the church's commitment to the world, to creation, to the realities of power, to communities, to people, to the values by which people live. Here are things that go beyond the historic role of the Church of England as the church of the English people, although they acknowledge the importance of a common story, of shared memories and associations and traditions, of the living symbols of national life. Many who are not Anglicans are grateful for a continuing establishment because of the public recognition it provides of the place of religion, and especially the Christian religion, within English society. Indeed, the leaders of other faiths that are now settled in this country, over and above the members of other Christian churches, will often welcome the establishment as a means whereby the Church of England can initiate action with them or on their behalf in the public domain.

The idea that church and state are one has long since been abandoned. The religious diversity, the religious neutrality, of the nation have been fully recognised. But the ideal of a Christian commonwealth remains, even though it appears all too often to be contradicted by the hard facts of life as it is experienced in England today. Religion is still judged to be a feature – at times a necessary feature – of human society. Certain assumptions remain concerning the nature and the

208 A BROAD AND LIVING WAY

end of human life and human society. There is an implicit
Christian faith in large numbers of people. Establishment
provides a living witness to the boundaries of the secular and
to the relationship of the sacred and the secular. Establishment keeps open the possibility that the church might still
provide for those who seek it some over-arching vision or
philosophy or approach, which gives value and meaning to
all that is attempted through the conflicts, the contradictions,
the compromises of political life.

It is the predominance of a secular culture which makes
the continuing establishment of the Christian religion seem
all the more important. It is impossible to dissent from the
judgement that 'huge areas of our common life are de-
Christianised; (that) growing numbers of people (are) cut off
from real contact with Christian values; (that we are becoming) a society increasingly anchorless and bereft of shared
ideals; (that) the Christian contours of society and the
humane values they perpetuated can no longer be taken for
granted, and are daily eroded'.[1]

But the Christian churches remain the largest voluntary
associations in the country. They provide the context – theological and liturgical and ethical – within which large
numbers of people are glad to live their lives. They continue
to inform the attitudes and values by which the life of society
is maintained and renewed. 'There is still – in the tolerant,
pluralist, democratic kind of society which we now have and
want to maintain and strengthen – value and validity in the
idea of a national church, recognised as such by the state.'[2]

It is, however, in the parishes, in the church's relation to
people as individuals and in its relation to the institutions of
community life, that it is possible to discern the inherent
strength of a public ministry that is based upon the establishment principle. It is in the drawing of the line between the
inclusive and the exclusive that the church as an institution
continues to distinguish itself from the church as a sect. The
call to new life in Christ remains; but there must also be a
recognition of the anonymity which some seek in the profession of their religion, and an awareness of the different

degrees of association with the church that people want and are capable of sustaining. 'Non-religious Christians, semi-detached believers, and semi-attached agnostics, so far from being excluded, are welcome in so far as they wish to be.'[3]

It was Augustine of Hippo who expressed so clearly the all-important insight that, 'Many seem to be within who are in reality without and others seem to be without who are in reality within'.[4] The all-inclusiveness of religion has already been identified as one of the distinguishing characteristics of the English tradition; and recent generations have valued Archbishop William Temple's reminder that the church is the one institution that exists for the sake of those who do not belong. Temple was looking beyond the confines of the Church of England, but this understanding of the church and its relation to people is exactly what is meant in practice by the establishment principle.

There are large numbers of people who do not regularly attend church but who yet retain some sense that the Church of England is their church, and that its ministry is available to them at times of need. It was the awareness of this outer constituency which did so much to shape the main thrust of the Report of the Archbishops' Commission on Church and State in 1970. 'The people of England still want to feel that religion has a place in the land to which they can turn on the too rare occasions when they think they need it, and they are not likely to be pleased by legislation which might suggest that the English people as a whole were going un-Christian.'[5]

The prevailing culture of contempt that surrounds all institutions must not be allowed to call in question the conviction of those who continue to believe that establishment has served both church and nation; that civil order and religious order remain profoundly inter-connected; that the special vocation of the church to serve the world has been kept alive; that the church has been required to keep in touch with thoughts and interests wider and deeper than its own; that the nation has had held up before it the conviction that 'the ultimate ends and sanctions of politics lie in a realm which is beyond politics'.[6]

The establishment of the Church of England speaks of the relationship between church *and state*. No critique of the appropriateness of a continuing establishment can simply confine itself to questions relating to the church and its self-awareness. There must also be a full recognition of the state, of the continuing debate concerning the nation state, of the things that constitute a society and hold it in being, of the public values – the points of reference – by which people live their lives.

It is easy to enunciate a doctrine of the state which acknowledges that church and state, although complementary to each other, are forms of human society which are fundamentally separate and distinct.[7] It is, however, at the boundary of church and state, where their legitimate areas of concern overlap, that the debate concerning the continuing meaning and value of establishment is bound to take place.

'Exceedingly deep and powerful dynamics are at work in human collective loyalties, especially at the level of a people and a nation'.[8] There are the realities of land and language and story; the perceptions of identity and integrity; the experiences of custom and tradition and corporate memory.

The sixteenth century reformation endorsed the principle of nationality, and the circumstances in which the Church of England was re-formed are not entirely irrelevant in a world which is still trying to understand what it means to be a community of nations. It is through the life of the nation – its institutions, its conventions, its assumptions, its local communities – that the world impinges upon the church and provides the framework within which the church is called to pursue its apostolic task.

But it is not only the churches of the reformation that have embodied the principle of nationality or locality. 'Nationality is part of our earthiness',[9] and the faith and culture of the church have been shaped from the beginning by national characteristics and national expressions. This is not to suggest that nationality should be given absolute or ultimate value. There are limits beyond which the church cannot go in embracing the society in which it finds itself. A church that is nothing more than a national church can never adequately proclaim a catholic faith.

Questions relating to national identity are bound to be subsumed within a wider debate in which the international dimension is increasingly dominant. It may be that a proper commitment to the principle of nationality is an essential prerequisite to a proper commitment to the principle of universality. But universality, so far as the church is concerned, must relate to the community of faith as well as the community of nations.

The earliest apologists of the English reformation settlement placed great emphasis upon continuity in catholic faith and order. Scripture, tradition and reason provided the resources and the disciplines whereby the church was able to recover an ecclesiastical polity, a Christian commonwealth, which was true both to the developing life of an apostolic community of faith and to the political realities of the situation in which the church found itself. In England, the historic role of the established church is now addressed increasingly in partnership with other churches. In the wider world, the evolution of the Anglican Communion will ensure that Anglicanism is delivered from the insularity that can so easily imprison and impoverish a national church. These ecumenical and international dimensions are essential. It is vital to its developing life that Anglicanism holds within itself the perspectives of an international community of faith and of an international community of nations.

Every state has always been 'a vast hierarchy of inter-related societies'.[10] But the modern state is required to hold in balance forces which appear at times to be irreconcilable: the evolution of a new order in which power passes to a network of multi-state institutions; the call for full recognition – political, economic and cultural – on behalf of ethnic groups and indigenous cultures; the destructive outbursts of distorted and perverted forms of racism and nationalism. The interplay between the forces of integration and fragmentation is vitiated further by the loss of a coherent world-view, a shared tradition, a common culture, which is rooted in an inclusive religious faith.

It is not only the continuing debate about the nation state that calls in question the place of an established church, a national church; it is far more the changes in the *mores* of society. Throughout the world – in ancient, medieval and modern times – religion has penetrated the whole fabric of society, shaping its structures and the ideas and values and goals to which people aspire. The heritage of the nation – all nations – has been informed by its sense of identity, its traditions, its culture; and these things have been determined in large measure by the religion of the people.

But the culture of the modern world has become profoundly secular, and societies such as England which are nominally Christian are for all practical purposes secular in thought and feeling and action. It is not merely the loss of authority, of credibility, that has been suffered by religious institutions; it is far more the gradual erosion of any sense that the religious tradition, and especially the Christian tradition, has a unique and comprehensive and compelling interpretation of life. It is difficult to avoid the conclusion that 'the dominant *mores* of society are of greater importance than (the) vestigial remains of an earlier Christian culture'.[11]

Three generations have passed since an earlier student of church and state observed that 'what we have to face is a hurly-burly of competing opinions and strange moralities'.[12] There remains in England an awareness of national identity, a core of values and beliefs, 'a residual sense that there are some things which still hold us together as a nation'.[13] But these things are to be found today in a society which is both secular and pluralist; where a variety of beliefs and values and cultures exist side by side; where religious symbols have lost their power; and where religious faith is seen to be little more than a matter of private choice.

It would be inaccurate, however, to infer that the churches are nothing more than voluntary associations. Functions that have previously been exercised by the churches, and especially in education and social welfare, have been handed over in large measure to the state; but some would suggest that this process might be interpreted as 'strong evidence of the transposition of Christian values into society as a whole'.[14] What appears to some to be the marginality of the churches in society takes little account of the deep involvement on the part of Christian people in a wide range of statutory and voluntary services. The Christian values of English society – and, indeed, of the western world – constitute one of the legacies of the inter-relationship of church and state over the centuries. A church that has surrendered the totalitarian claims of empire and struggled to come to terms as a institution with the complexities and the ambiguities of the modern state might well be judged to have been one of the primary influences in the emergence of a secular society that is open to new developments and tolerant of diversity.

It may no longer be appropriate to look for the coherence, the uniformity of religious faith, of earlier ages; but the contemporary scene raises urgent questions which lie at the heart of any debate concerning the establishment of religion. Can society remain philosophically and morally neutral without degenerating into some form of paganism? Where does society now turn to find its stability, its rootedness? Can the Christian religion continue to inform the public values by which society attempts to live? Can any one church or religious faith be the custodian, the interpreter, of the things that make for cohesion in a society and a culture which are so disparate and fragmented?

It has long since been the conviction of some that, 'It may be the fate of the church throughout the world to sink again, as regards the state, into the condition of a *sect* as she began'.[15] It is unquestionably the case that the perceived impotence of the churches has led in some places in recent decades to a predominant emphasis upon a ministry to individuals, the nuturing of the congregation, and a pastoral stance which is essentially sectarian.

The historic tension between the church as a sect and the church as an institution persists. It has been suggested that, 'Europe is currently confronted by a fragmentation and privatization of Christianity';[16] and such a development, if it is sustained, can only lead to a thoroughgoing separation of church and state, to the abandonment of the idea of the church as an inclusive institution, and to the regression of the church back into the status of an exclusive sect or cult.

Some observers of the ecclesiastical scene have pointed to the emergence of a denominational pluralism in which the denomination would stand half-way between the sect and the institution. It would be essentially a voluntary association which the individual joins by personal choice, but it would attempt to engage with society as a whole, and in its theology and approach to ministry it would carry forward the earlier traditions of an inclusive church.[17]

This may or may not prove to be an accurate account of what is actually happening at the present time. What emerges, however, is a recognition that the issue is not one of establishment or disestablishment. It is, rather, a question of the theology by which the church informs its approach to society and to the work of ministry. Self-conscious attempts to purify the church should take account of Dietrich Bonhoeffer's judgement that, 'A state-free church is no more protected against secularization than is a state-church'.[18] A church does not become free – nor does it become more like the kingdom of God – merely by being disestablished. Churches, established or disestablished, are required to live in an open system in which they are vulnerable to all prevailing influences. Churches, established or disestablished, which count for anything in the national life will always be vulnerable to interference on the part of the state if public opinion or political expediency requires it.[19]

It would be premature to reach firm judgements. There are so many questions which cannot yet be answered, so many matters which provide the parameters within which all discussions regarding church and state must take place. It may well be the task of this generation to discern the meaning of the debate concerning the sovereignty of the nation state; the forces of integration and fragmentation; the prevailing culture; the impact of secularism and pluralism;

the complexities of society; the anonymity of life; the ambiguities of moral decisions; the public role of religion; the
perennial search for meaning and purpose; the continuing
awareness of core values; the perceived impotence of the
churches; the sectarianism which may be sought by the
churches or may yet be imposed upon them.

But the existence of all these things, the emergence of new
forms in church and state, the progression to new patterns of
relationship: all these are still be set with the sovereignty of
God and the prevenience of grace. 'The fact that the church
is becoming a diaspora everywhere, that she is a church
surrounded by non-Christians, and hence living in a culture,
in a state, amidst political movements, economic activity,
science and art which are conducted not simply and solely by
Christians – all this is a "must" in the history of salvation'.[20]

It is recognised in the context of a secular democracy that
no one religious tradition – let alone one church – can easily
or fully represent the aspirations of a whole nation. But there
is evidence throughout the world that the church, established
or disestablished, is still able to articulate the values, the
anxieties, the hopes of a people. Governments are glad to
look to the churches for validation, especially at times of
armed conflict, and there are circumstances in which the
churches are able to give legitimacy and critical endorsement
to the struggles of a nation at precisely the point when questions of public and personal morality are most sensitive.
There is evidence also – especially in Eastern Europe, in
South Africa, in Latin America – of the churches providing a
voice of dissent, resisting the pretensions of the state to
claims of absolute obedience, and speaking the prophetic
word of judgement. There is still, perhaps, in England at the
end of the twentieth century the fact that the Christian religion is judged by many to be a symbol of unity, of toleration,
of the values that serve to integrate.

The public affirmation which establishment provides of
the place of religion, and especially the Christian religion, in
English society has not yet been disowned by church or state.
The English experience is undoubtedly unique. The situation

may well be anomalous, but it is not immediately self-evident that the Church of England should attempt to remove this dimension from the nation's life prematurely. Disestablishment at the present time would represent an unnecessary repudiation of a large part of the nation's story. The protracted legal process of disentangling church and state would preoccupy the church for a generation. Such a development would undoubtedly strengthen the drift towards a new sectarianism, a loss of the comprehensiveness, the all-inclusiveness, which has been the abiding hallmark of the Church of England. 'It would be in favour of nothing, the relegation of religion to the realm of the private, and the emptying of our common life of some of the values and assumptions which have shaped it for a thousand years.'[21]

It remains to be seen if the establishment of the Church of England represents the broad and living way into the hearts of the people that has been claimed for it in earlier generations. The questions that have been raised in the course of these reflections do not invalidate the establishment, but they provide the context in which it must be evaluated. It is an attenuated form of establishment that has survived, and its continued existence can only be justified if it proves itself able to adapt to the dynamics of a changing society. 'It is a good thing to have a religion established by law as long as most members of the state take religious questions seriously, as long as dissent is permitted, as long as the established religion is concerned to encourage constructive conversations with other religious communities, to permit diversity of interpretation within itself and to show a concern to formulate a broad-value base for the state as a whole.'[22]

NOTES
1 Eamon Duffy, Article in the *Tablet*, 22nd January 1994.
2 Alec R. Vidler, *Religion and the National Church*, Essay in *Soundings*, Edited by Alec R. Vidler, CUP 1963, p. 262.
3 Ibid., p. 260.
4 Cited by Yves M – J. Congar, *The Mystery of the Temple*, Burnes & Oates 1962, p. 197.

5 *Report of Archbishops' Commission on Church and State* (1970), p. 65.
6 F.R. Barry, *Church and Leadership*, London 1945, p. 46.
7 Alec R. Vidler, *The Orb and the Cross*, SPCK 1946, p. 136.
8 Keith W. Clements, *What Freedom? The Persistent Challenge of Dietrich Bonhoeffer*, Bristol Baptist College 1990, p. 71.
9 Ibid.
10 P.T. Forsyth, *op.cit.*, p. 176.
11 D.L. Munby, *The Idea of a Secular Society*, OUP 1963, p. 15.
12 J.N. Figgis, *Churches in the Modern State*, Longmans, Green & Co. 1913, p. 120.
13 John Habgood, *op.cit.*, p. 30.
14 Robin Gill, *op.cit.*, p. 48.
15 R.W. Church, *op.cit.*, p. 57.
16 Robin Gill, *op.cit.*, p. 45.
17 Ibid., p. 54.
18 Cited by Keith W. Clements, *op.cit.*, p. 102.
19 See Bertram Pollock, *Church and State: A Review of the Report of the Commission on Church and State*, Eyre and Spottiswoode 1936, p. 31.
20 Karl Rahner, *Mission and Grace: Essays in Pastoral Theology*. Sheed and Ward 1963. Vol. I, p. 24. Cited by Peter Cornwell, *Church and Nation*, Basil Blackwell 1983, p. 64.
21 Eamon Duffy, *op.cit.*
22 Keith Ward. *Is a Christian State A Contradiction?* Essay published in *Religion in Public Life*, Edited by Dan Cohn-Sherbok and David McLellan, St. Martin's Press 1992, p. 16.

Chapter 14

A Broad and Living Way

It is entirely consistent with the English tradition in church and state that questions concerning the establishment of religion should be determined ultimately by considerations that are practical rather than theoretical. It is not easy to find the criteria by which such considerations may be judged; but Gladstone, writing autobiographical notes at the time of the disestablishment of the Irish Church in 1869, provided a series of observations which might be brought into service.

His commitment to the establishment principle remained, provided it could be shown that establishment is actually meaningful. 'An Establishment that does its work in much, and has the hope and likelihood of doing it in more: an Establishment that has a broad and living way open to it, into the hearts of the people: an Establishment that can commend the services of the present by the recollections and the traditions of a far-reaching past: an Establishment able to appeal to the active zeal of the greater portion of the people, and to the respect or scruples of almost the whole, whose children dwell chiefly on her actual living work and service, and whose adversaries, if she has them, are in the main content to believe that there would be a future for them and their opinions: such an Establishment should surely be maintained.'[1]

These personal reflections constituted for Gladstone a bridge in his thinking between his earlier position regarding the necessity of an ecclesiastical establishment[2] and his active prosecution in parliament of the disestablishment and disendowment of the Irish Church. But the rhetorical flourishes with which he expressed himself do not conceal the underlying conviction that an establishment – if it is to continue – must be serviceable, accessible, evocative, worthy of respect, and tolerant. It remains to be seen if the Church of England continues to meet these requirements.

One of the overriding concerns for all Christian churches in England today must be the significant decline throughout much of this century in the numerical support that they enjoy. The statistics of church life do not begin to indicate the full range of connections and associations that large numbers of people have with the churches. They serve, however, as sobering reminders of the relatively small numerical base from which the churches pursue their ministries.

The census returns for 1991 suggest a total population for the United Kingdom of 54.8 million. Some account must obviously be taken of the significant increase in the number of people from non-Christian ethnic minorities in recent decades. But an independent survey by MARC Europe[3] for 1990 suggests that the total number of baptised persons within the various Christian churches in the United Kingdom is:

Anglican	26,855.000
Roman Catholic	5,624.000
Presbyterian	1,289.000
Methodist	468,000
Baptist	201,000

It is necessary, however, to set alongside these figures the findings of the research that was also conducted by MARC Europe[4] regarding church attendances in England in the previous year. The research suggests that disparities on the grounds of age and gender are less significant than are often believed to be the case, but the figures indicate nonetheless the sombre realities of church life.

Age	Church Going (%)	Non-churchgoing (%)
Under 15	14	86
15–19	9	91
20–29	6	94
30–44	9	91
45–64	10	90
65 and over	13	87
Overall	10	90

These percentage figures suggest that 43 million people in England – over 35 million adults and 8 million children – remain outside the regular worshipping life of the churches as measured by church attendance.

It is against this background of the total population of the provinces of Canterbury and York, excluding the diocese of Europe, that the decline in all the primary numerical yardsticks of church life within the Church of England can most easily be seen.

POPULATION

1931	37,510,817
1951	41,329,643
1971	46,215,123
1991	48,297,000[5]

ELECTORAL ROLL[6]

1930	3,693,000
1950	2,959,000
1970	2,559,000
1990	1,396,000

EASTER COMMUNICANTS

	Numbers	Per 1000 of population Aged 15 years & over
1930	2,426,000	85
1950	2,004,000	69
1970	1,814,000	51
1990	1,549,000	40

SUNDAY ATTENDANCE[7]

	Numbers	Per 1000 of population Aged 15 years & over
1970	1,542,000	33
1980	1,240,000	27
1990	1,143,000	24

INFANT BAPTISM

	Per 1000 live births
1930	699
1950	672
1970	466
1990	275[8]

CONFIRMATION

	Numbers
1930	197,000
1950	142,000
1970	113,000
1990	60,000

MARRIAGE[9]

	Numbers	Percentage
1929	176,113	56.2
1952	173,282	49.6
1971	106,165	39.6
1991	102,840	33.5

The Church of England has been able to claim with some justice over many centuries that it has had a special relationship with the people of England. This relationship has traditionally found expression through the parochial ministry; through the occasional offices; through a substantial involvement in education and social care; through an intimate connection with the crown and with parliament and with the leaders of the nation's life; through ties that are legal and historical, public and personal, local and sentimental.

There has been no other country in the world where there has been the equivalent of the man in the street who without hesitation could call himself 'C of E'. It is easy to caricature this self-designation, but it has represented something within the minds of people which should not be gratuitously discarded. There has unquestionably been a long-standing tradition of indifference, of unconscious secularism; but the Church of England has provided a framework within which the religious aspirations of non-churchgoing people might also find expression from time to time.

But the point has now been reached when it has to be asked if the decline in all the numerical yardsticks of church life is not so great that the Church of England has ceased for all practical purposes to be in any meaningful sense the church of the nation. The Church of England might well continue to be established by law, but can it honestly claim to be established in the hearts of the people?

It was Hensley Henson's anxiety more than sixty-five years ago that, 'If ... the Church of England as a spiritual society had become a relatively small factor in the Nation, it could not but follow that its traditional character as a National Church had largely lost meaning, and that its legal establishment might easily involve it in humiliating and even intolerable paradoxes'.[10] Henson was speaking and writing in the aftermath of parliament's rejection of the Revised Prayer Book in 1927 and 1928. There has been no comparable humiliation for the Church of England since that time, and Henson's apprehension concerning intolerable paradoxes has proved to be unfounded; but the Church of England *as a spiritual society* has become an increasingly small factor in the nation's life and questions about the *raison d'etre* of a continuing establishment are bound to arise.

It is not sufficient in these circumstances to place one set of statistics over against another. But there is substance in the argument that the Church of England still attempts to provide a nationwide ministry. There are over sixteen thousand Anglican churches, excluding cathedrals, extra-parochial and private chapels, and peculiars.[11] There are nearly eleven thousand clergy – bishops, priests and deacons – in full-time stipendiary ministry.[12] The work of these clergy is assisted by over fifteen hundred part-time non-stipendiary clergy;[13] by nearly three hundred and fifty Church Army officers;[14] by two hundred and fifty accredited lay ministers;[15] and by more than seven and a half thousand licensed and active readers.[16] These are significant figures which suggest an unqualified determination by a national church to maintain a national ministry.

The financial burden of maintaining such a large stipendiary ministry is very great, and the responsibility is passing increasingly to congregations. It remains to be seen if parishes will respond fully, but there is at least some evidence that the ordinary annual income of parochial church councils is beginning to increase and might enable the church to meet in full the responsibility of providing a nationwide ministry.

ORDINARY ANNUAL INCOME OF PCCs[17]

	Annual Income £000s	*In real terms of 1991: £000s*
1964	22,108	208,679
1970	26,396	190,152
1976	49,000	164,265
1980	85,880	171,502
1986	196,034	244,866
1991	256,796	256,796

What is expressed in these figures – the number of churches, the number of clergy and ministers, the income of parochial church councils – is the commitment of the Church of England to a national *parochial* ministry. The numerical yardsticks of church life suggest in so many cases a pattern of continuing decline, but parochial ministry – at its best – still represents the concern of the Church of England to minister to the whole life of the nation. Parochial ministry recognises the identity and the needs of the local community and the primary importance of the worshipping congregation within that community. It attempts to hold in balance the church's traditions of worship, teaching, pastoral care and evangelism. It attempts to minister to the needs of individuals and, in partnership with others, to assist in ministering to the needs of the local community as a whole. The work of the parochial ministry has been complemented throughout much of this century by a wide range of sector ministries, which are responsible attempts to diversify the work of the church and to rediscover something of the totality of ministry.

It is self-evident that significant changes have taken place within the life of the church and the life of the nation. The Church of England has no monopoly of concern where all these things are concerned, but it retains a unique position – and, therefore, a unique responsibility – within the total life of English society.

The statistics of church life must be set in a wider context. An entirely different picture is presented by a survey of attitudes in Britain published in 1992.[18] It suggests that of the people who were interviewed:

70% believe in God;
70% are in favour of school prayers;
58% have confidence in the churches;
43% call themselves religious;
40% declare themselves members of the Church of England;
25% say that they pray every week.

It is easy to dismiss such figures, but what is undoubtedly being presented is 'a general diffused, inarticulate assent to Christianity as an ideal in the body of the nation'.[19]

There are large numbers of people who believe that they have some kind of Christian affiliation and association. They will identify with the Christian tradition if they are asked to do so in questionnaires, even though they may take little part in the regular life of the churches. It is in this sense that active churchgoers might properly be seen as 'the most visible and articulate part of a much more widespread phenomenon'.[20]

The church has been a formative influence in England over fourteen hundred years. There is a heritage of Christian faith which is embedded within the life of society. It does, therefore, follow in such a situation that hard and fast distinctions between the church and the world are not easily sustained. This vague Christianity is not always comprehended by the churches, but it is a denial of the story of church and state to disparage it as something of little consequence. 'I believe it is wrong to hold as of no account the Christianity which pervades the life of a community before it is confirmed in the personal decision of every individual citizen'.[21]

What is being put before the churches as an important ingredient in the allegedly secular culture in which they are required to operate is the inarticulate religion which is held, tenaciously or tentatively, by a surprisingly large number of people. What is frequently termed folk religion is a complex phenomenon. It embraces superstition, a basic human religiosity, and forms of experience and expression which are inherently Christian in their presuppositions. It speaks of needs that are deeply rooted in human nature and human society.

The primary statistics of church life do not take account of these wider constituencies of faith and feeling with which the churches are bound to engage. These constituencies are defined and informed both by a general diffusion of Christian values in society at large and by the manifestations of folk religion in a variety of forms. Reference has already been made to the tentative connections, the fundamental beliefs and values, which count for something in the reckoning of large numbers of people. It is unquestionably one part of the wider ministry of all the churches – unless they are prepared to settle for ministries that are sectarian and congregational – to acknowledge the importance of inarticulate religion; to interpret the range of religious experience; to meet the needs of communities, institutions and individuals for celebration, ritual and symbol.

It is exactly at this point that the question might properly be asked, Does establishment – the establishment of the Christian religion – provide 'a broad and living way ... into the hearts of the people'?[22] It would be manifestly untrue to suggest that the Church of England stands alone in attempting to wrestle with these things. But its ancient traditions of comprehension and liberality ensure that it is uniquely well qualified to take advantage of the position it continues to occupy in the life of the nation.

There are inevitably many situations in which the ministry of the Church of England as it is experienced day by day will give rise to frustration, despair, anger. The Church of England is not alone in this respect. 'We have our treasure in earthen vessels.'[23] But the tests that have been proposed for a continuing establishment might properly be applied and the question asked, Is the Church of England – the established church – still serviceable, accessible, evocative, worthy of respect, and tolerant?

It is serviceable. The ancient ideal that church and state belong to one another finds practical expression in the network of relationships and expectations which constitute the raw material of public ministry. The Church of England is resolutely determined to maintain a nationwide parochial ministry. It has steadfastly refused to abandon the inner cities and the small rural communities. It has taken a large measure of responsibility, ministerially and financially, for work in new development areas and in the sectors of community life. It has proved itself willing to enter into working relationships with institutions, agencies and individuals where there is a mutual desire to do so. It is woven into the fabric of society as a whole through the activity, the anonymous activity, of its members.

It is accessible. It may no longer be the case that there is a unity of church and state within a Christian commonwealth, but the inherited traditions of comprehension and liberality ensure that the Church of England rejects pressures from within society and the church to erect clear boundary fences. It engages with large numbers of people through the administration of the occasional offices. It attempts to work with the implicit Christian faith that is to be found in so many places. It remains marvellously open at the edges of membership. It is sensitive and courteous in exercising the disciplines of church life. It holds firmly to the principle of the all-inclusiveness of Christ's religion. It continues even today through the work of its clergy and lay people to touch the life of the nation and of every local community at so many points.

It is evocative. It may no longer be appropriate to speak of the established church as the religious embodiment of the nation, but it is still required to articulate the religious aspirations of individuals and communities. The Church of England is mindful of the religious dimension that is built into the structures, the conventions, the symbols of national life. It is sensitive to the power of its ancient buildings to speak to people; and it is scrupulous in the disciplined care with which it supervises their maintenance and development. It sustains through its cathedrals a tradition of church music which is without parallel in the world. It explores – and not least of all through its cathedrals and greater parish churches – a continuing association with all forms of artistic endeavour. The Church of England, like all national churches, forgets at its peril the extent to which it is woven into the fabric of the society it is called to serve.

It is worthy of respect. The integrity of the Church of England rests ultimately upon the conviction that the principles of catholicity and reformation are fundamental to the life of the church. It has developed a theological tradition which holds together faith and reason, scripture and tradition, nature and grace. It has evolved a theological method which is reasoned, ordered, measured, devout. It has demonstrated a willingness to engage intellectually and critically with the world. It has certainly reflected changes in public opinion in the course of this century – contraception, abortion, marriage, divorce; and in focussing attention upon questions raised, for example, by the *Report of the Archbishops' Commission on Urban Priority Areas*, it has also drawn public attention to fundamental issues relating to the priorities and the values of community life. It has a tradition of practical divinity; of quiet, unselfconscious spirituality; of humanity, of earthiness, even – in the best sense – of worldliness.

It is tolerant. It is here also that the traditions of comprehension and liberality count for so much. The Church of England is tolerant of a wide diversity of faith and practice within its own internal life. It allows a wide margin for private interpretation. It understands the paradoxes of faith, the ambiguities of discipleship, the realities of compromise. It is thoroughgoing in its commitment to ecumenical dialogue and ministry. It has shown itself to be sensitive and just in its relationship with the communities of other world faiths. It is alert and responsive to changes in public opinion. It attempts to affirm the sacredness of the secular.

A wholehearted commitment to ecumenism must not be allowed to diminish the claims that might properly be made by all the churches where their distinctive traditions and styles of ministry are concerned. The continuing establishment of the Church of England can be justified if it can be demonstrated that it remains serviceable, accessible, evocative, worthy of respect, and tolerant. There is much in all these things that might be justly claimed by other churches, but it is to a unique degree though this combination of traditions that the Church of England offers public ministry to the life of the nation.

The church is required to live in an open relationship with society. It is not able to take for granted the preconceived ideas and attitudes that have buttressed its work in previous

generations. It will be mindful of the outer constituencies of
support that it still enjoys, but it will know how easily the
general diffusion of Christian values in society can be eroded.
But establishment continues to provide the context within
which the church might hold responsibility for the nation. It
represents an element of continuity in the nation's story and
the nation's *psyche*. It offers a framework in which the principles of catholicity and reformation – 'guardianship of the
Christian heritage and radical re-appraisal of it'[24] – can be
pursued.

There is not – and there cannot be – any permanent settlement where church-state relations are concerned. Church
and state 'are not "entities" which exist in pure form; their
purposes overlap. Consequently their mutual relations are
subtle, intricate and ever-changing'.[25] The changes that are
taking place in England today are both *between* and *within*
the churches. The commitment to establishment remains on
the part of church and state; but the changes within the
churches and within society are bringing about profound
changes of emphasis.

First, it is becoming plain that distinctions *between* the
established and the non-established churches have become
increasingly less important over recent decades.

The progressive disengagement of church and state in
England has meant that the imperial claims – indeed, the
imperial status – of the Church of England has long since
been abandoned. Catholic recusants and puritans had both
been required to function as sects, even though – as some
would suggest – Roman Catholics never acquired in the post-
reformation period a sectarian mentality, retaining instead a
sense 'of still constituting in waiting the church of the
nation'.[26] The development of Methodism – and in part of
Congregationalism – shows how the churches of the poor
and the dispossessed can move over the generations beyond
their original status, accepting a new role within society,
functioning as institutions rather than sects. But sectarian
attitudes have continued to present themselves – in the
Roman Catholic Churches of the Irish immigrants; in the

mainstream Free Churches which had maintained in earlier times a measure of detachment from the national life; in the independent churches which have remained with their self-elected status as sects and continue to function as voluntary associations which choose to be in varying degrees of isolation from each other and from the wider community; and, in more recent times, in the house churches.

It is the judgement of one historian that it was only in the First World War that Free Church Nonconformity opted decisively for conformity to the establishment by giving wholehearted support to the war effort and abandoning the pacifist and internationalist tendencies of earlier years.[27] Whereas in more recent years it has been the emergence of the Roman Catholic Church as an international community of faith, which is able and willing to take its place alongside other churches in this country, which has brought about such a significant change in the relations between the churches.

Secondly, there are subtle changes *within* the self-awareness of the churches. The problem is especially acute for the Church of England as the established church, but it is to be found in all churches.

It has been suggested from the beginning that the five ways of being the church – experience, movement, sect, institution and empire – are like magnetic points. They represent the directions in which the church – all churches – might be drawn at any time. These phases or modes of being are well-established and continuing aspects of the church's life. One phase will predominate at any time, but other phases may also be present in a developed or an embryonic form. They can be found in sequence and in parallel with one another. They are always bound to be present. They vie with one another for expression.

The imperial model continues to exercise a powerful fascination. It speaks of the international dimension that must be present at the heart of the church's life. It conveys the unmistakable note of authority. But it is theologically corrupt.

The objection might be expressed in the form of a question. Does the church have the confidence, the maturity, to hold steadfastly to the all-inclusive claims that must be made for *God's* sovereignty without intruding and demanding for the church as an institution an absolutism – in faith, in morals, in structure, in law – which is fundamentally at variance with all that we know about the God who gives Himself to His creation?

If it is true that God gives to the world the freedom to make itself,[28] handing Himself over in vulnerability and in sacrificial love,[29] then the imperial model is so far removed from this pattern of the divine life and the divine activity that it must be rejected out of hand. When the church clings to this model it fails to give both to the world in general and to men and women in their various relationships in particular the degree of freedom that God gives to the creation as a whole.

There was a kind of inevitability about the historical process that led to the evolution of the Roman imperium – the papal monarchy – in the middle ages, and to the imperial pretensions of some of the churches of the reformation – including the Church of England – in the sixteenth and seventeenth centuries. The Church of England might well be grateful for the fact that this model is simply not available as an option in contemporary society.

It is inevitable, however, that the situation in which the Church of England is placed today raises questions about the way in which is it now called to be the church. Is the church an institution or a sect? One commentator applauds in broad terms the general stance adopted by the Church of England in acknowledging the different degrees of association that people want with the church, but he goes on to suggest that, 'Profound conviction at the centre and an indefinite boundary at the periphery might be thought to be a sociological monstrosity, combining the features of sect and church'.[30]

There are those who believe that in a pluralist society all churches are required to function as sects. The Christian profession of faith becomes a matter of personal choice, and the church – if it is to remain alive – cannot fail to be a community whose members participate actively in its life.[31]

Troeltsch has long since insisted that 'the church-type' – the institution – is passing through a time of decay and even of destruction. 'The days of the pure church-type within our present civilisation are numbered.'[32]

The church must always be mindful of its identity, its integrity, its authority. But it is in the drawing of the line between inclusive and exclusive, between what can be permitted and what cannot be permitted, that the church declares itself to be an institution or a sect. It is necessary to be reminded that, 'A sect was originally defined as such not merely by theological peculiarites but by its lack of relation to the state'.[33]

The institution is essentially inclusive. It is a comprehensive, all-embracing institution. The dividing line between church and community is not always clearly drawn. There is implicit in its pastoral strategy a strong sense of the incarnation, because the institution is rooted in the life of the world. The institution understands the complexities of life with all its ambiguities and contradictions. Indeed, 'To be a church ... (an institution rather than a sect) ... is to share in the ambiguities of society at large.'[34] The church as an institution embraces, or attempts to embrace, everyone and everything.

The changing dynamics of society's life may disable the church as it goes about its work. It cannot be forgotten that 'there are situations in which sectarianism represents the only genuine Christian response to society'.[35] This is not the situation in which churches in England, and especially the Church of England, find themselves today. If the Church of England continues to exercise its ministry in ways that are serviceable, accessible, evocative, worthy of respect and tolerant, then it will be saying in the most unambiguous way that it rejects sectarianism and chooses to function as an institution, a continuing part of the life of society, an element of continuity and stability within it.

Few writers have understood more clearly than T.S. Eliot the significance of the boundaries of faith and association within the life of the nation. He distinguished in his study, *The Idea of a Christian Society*, between the Christian State, the Christian Community, and the community of Christians. The Christian State refers to the traditions of public life and the framework within which laws are made and administered. The Christian Community speaks of the values that are embedded within society and which find expression in largely unconscious behaviour. The community of Christians relates to those who are consciously attempting to live according to the insights and the disciplines of the Christian faith.

Eliot was writing over fifty years ago but, in delineating the things that belong to the Christian State, the Christian Community and the community of Christians, he was describing with some accuracy the situation that prevailed in England until relatively recent times and that still survives today, albeit it in an attenuated form. Eliot's distinction related not merely to the profession of faith that might be made by individuals, but to the temper and traditions of a people, to value systems, expectations, patterns of behaviour. It is in these things that society finds its coherence.

It was his awareness of the subtleties of all these things that led Eliot to endorse the continuing responsibility of the established church. His analysis of the situation that he found in England led him to reject clear cut distinctions between Christians and non-Christians: 'if one believes, as I do, that the great majority of people are neither one thing nor the other, but are living in a no man's land, then the situation looks very different; and disestablishment, instead of being the *recognition* of a condition at which we have arrived, would be the *creation* of a condition the results of which we cannot foresee'.[36] He believed that disestablishment would represent a visible and dramatic withdrawal on the part of the church from the affairs of the nation. It would be tantamount to an abandonment of all who are not wholeheartedly within the fold of Christian faith.[37]

Eliot acknowledged the greater advantages and the greater difficulties experienced by an established church, but his judgement was clear that 'a church, once disestablished, cannot easily be re-established, and that the very act of disestablishment separates it more definitely and irrevocably from the life of the nation than if it had never been established'.[38]

Many who have reflected upon the nature of the state have gone beyond contractual theories and found the life and unity, even the personality, of the nation in the shared story of its people. Society is a complex of institutions, relationships, values. There is a plurality of interests in which established authorities form a network of containment, of management. It has been the pragmatic genius of state and church in England over long centuries to preserve the forms of constitutional life, while allowing the substance and balance to change dramatically. Those who seek disestablishment must have good reason for removing from this complex whatever place and function remain for the church and, therefore, for the Christian religion.

Questions are inevitably raised from time to time which touch upon the constitutional position of the Church of England. The oath that is sworn by the sovereign at the coronation speaks of a firm commitment to maintain and defend the reformed religion established by law in England. It is, however, the Act of Settlement of 1701[39] which is the subject of most frequent comment. The Act remains as the most notable legacy of the turmoil of the post-reformation politics of the seventeenth century. It was designed to make provision for the succession to the crown after King William III and his heir presumptive, the Princess Anne. Its effect was to exclude all other descendants of King Charles I and to transfer the succession to the descendants of the protestant princess, Sophia, the Electress of Hanover, the grand-daughter of King James I. The Act invalidated the claims of anyone who was in communion with the Roman Catholic Church or who was married to a Roman Catholic. All who might subsequently succeed to the crown were required to be in communion with the Church of England.

The exclusive claims that are made in the coronation oath and in the Act of Settlement for the Church of England as the established church are judged by some to be inappropriate or unacceptable or offensive. But there is a deep reluctance to make changes which touch upon the constitution of church and state unless they are required by the force of circumstance. 'What it is not necessary to change, it is necessary not to change.'[40] It is the English experience that in constitutional matters it is better to be re-active rather than pro-active. Institutions which are valued have survived because at times of crisis and transition men and women have been compelled to take account of the things that have served the nation well, to make the necessary modifications, and thus to ensure some measure of continuity between the past, the present and the future.

It may well prove to be the case that church and state have already entered upon a transitional phase. The existing constitutional forms remain. But circumstances could arise in which a rigorous interpretation of the Act of Settlement would be judged to be a gross act of discrimination which is totally at variance with the spirit of the age. And circumstances could also arise in which an oppressive interpretation by parliament of its residual rights with regard to ecclesiastical legislation would be universally condemned as an act of political interference which could no longer be justified or sustained.

There is a reluctance in church and state to embark upon what must inevitably be a protracted period of constitutional change. Contemporary distinctions between church and state, between the sacred and the secular, are far more pronounced than has been the case in earlier ages. There is a post-establishment culture in which the religious conventions of public life, of community life, are easily disregarded. There is, however, an acknowledgement, that the church-state relationship is of concern to church and state; and the absolute secularization of the state would be widely seen as 'an admission that civilization, or society, cannot become Christian but can only have a Christian society, in the shape of a church, beside it or within it'.[41]

The legal forms of establishment can never constitute in themselves a broad and living way into the hearts of the people. They are the residual elements of an earlier and far more thoroughgoing connection between church and state. They represent one thread in a tapestry of relationships, conventions, expectations.

And yet the establishment of the Church of England continues to embody so many of the interconnections of church-state relationships which have been such a feature of European life since the conversion of Constantine. There is a representative role to which the Church of England is increasingly sensitive as its acts in a variety of situations on behalf of all the churches. But establishment acknowledges the role of the church and the significance of the Christian faith in the story of the English people over more than fourteen hundred years. It represents the church's commitment to the nation – its history, its institutions, its communities, its relationships.

The all-important test remains: Is a continuing establishment serviceable, accessible, evocative, worthy of respect, and tolerant? These words have been used to explore the meaning of the public ministry that is offered by the Church of England. They might also be used to indicate areas of the nation's life where a self-conscious dismemberment of all that remains of establishment might prove to be unhelpful and disadvantageous to the state.

It is serviceable. There remains a significant moral element in the traditions of public and political life which derives from the Christian faith. The churches are still able to provide a framework for morality within which there is an acknowledgement of values, priorities, obligations, responsibilities.

It is accessible. There is a demand in many places for the active involvement of people in a voluntary capacity who have a representative role within the wider life of the community and who can be trusted to be informed, sensitive, compassionate and objective. It is one of the more intriguing aspects of the contemporary scene that the fact of having status without power actually enables the churches, and not least of all the Church of England, to represent something that is still judged to be important in the life of the nation or the local community.

It is evocative. There is a continuing place for all that is understood by civil or civic religion. It provides a public recognition and public hallowing of institutions and relationships. Its forms of expression are dignified and uncontroversial, but they draw freely upon the traditions, the associations, the symbolism of the church's and the nation's heritage.

It is worthy of respect. The benign pragmatism that all too often informs public debate cannot adequately respond to the sensitive and complex questions which society is bound to address. The churches have secured the necessary degree of detachment from vested interests within society. Establishment – either in law or in the minds and hearts of people – does not inevitably mean compliance or collusion. The churches are well able to ask critical questions, to be the conscience of the nation, to speak the prophetic word.

It is tolerant. Church and state are both concerned with human life lived in community. The churches have been concerned to articulate the concerns of minority groups which can so easily be marginalised. There is, moreover, a proper role for an established church – where such a church already exists – in representing the legitimate concerns of *all* communities of faith within society.

All these things indicate sensitive areas of public concern where the churches, and especially the established church, are bound to be mindful of the influence that might be exercised. They pre-suppose the open relationship with society with which the church as an institution is bound to work. They come unequivocally within the broad traditions of comprehension and liberality. Historical nostalgia, pious sentiment and wishful thinking must never be allowed to cloud the church's judgement concerning the limitations that are imposed upon this wider ministry by an increasingly secular culture. It cannot be assumed 'because the outward substance of a Christendom situation remains (that) the inward reality is there'.[42] But a broad and living way remains for churches that have the imagination, the courtesy, the patience and the sensitivity to work with institutions and individuals in areas of common concern.

It may well be that a servant model of the church requires a continuing commitment to the remaining forms of establishment while the state requires it and while the Christian conscience is able to countenance and permit it. There will undoubtedly be future modifications to the church-state connection over the years, but there are at the present time significant domestic reasons why the Church of England might find it expedient to retain the wider framework of reference that establishment provides.

There should be no illusion about the magnitude of the task confronting the Church of England at the end of the twentieth century. There is the maintenance of a nationwide parochial and stipendiary ministry; the securing of an appropriate balance between episcopal and synodical authority; the management of the ambiguities and the pain inherent in the decision to ordain women to the priesthood; the facilitating of an extended period of liturgical development; the engagement with the complex ethical issues confronting men and women in their relationship to each other, to society and to the environment; the voicing of questions that relate to public values and priorities.

These things suggest to many that the interests of church and state will best be served by keeping open all the existing relationships. The abandonment of the establishment – not merely the legal form but the expectations which it properly sustains – could so easily lend support to sectarian pressures which encourage the church to withdraw into itself, nurturing its interior and institutional life to the exclusion of that wider ministry and mission which at its best the church has always attempted.

It is patently untrue to suggest that the character of Anglicanism is now determined by the legal forms of establishment. The identity and the integrity of the Anglican tradition rest ultimately upon the conviction that the model of a reformed catholicism is fundamentally correct. There is a great deal within the Anglican tradition which enables the Church of England to embody and to interpret the church-state relationship. The broad and living way remains open, at least in part, because the inherent character of Anglicanism has equipped the Church of England to take its place within the wider community.

The primary commitment to the principles of catholicism and reformation ensures that Anglicanism embraces much that is good in both the pre-reformation and the post-reformation church. There is a tradition of sound learning, based upon the resources and the disciplines of scripture, tradition and reason, which has enabled the church to avoid the pitfalls of superstition and fanaticism. There is a tradition of practical divinity which has repeatedly found expression in a positive endorsement of the voluntary principle. There has been from the beginning an engagement with history – the story, the traditions, the laws, the language, the culture of a people. Nothing is real unless it is local. The principle of locality has found practical expression in the identifying of the *zone humaine* as the primary constituency for public ministry. The distinctive traditions of comprehension and liberality – both within the church and the wider community – have expressed a profound awareness of the all-inclusiveness of grace.

It has been emphasised by prominent churchmen from time to time that there is an inherent provisionality in the existence of the Church of England and of the Anglican Communion. This is undoubtedly true; but it must be asked if the same judgement ought not to be made in respect of all communions of faith within Christendom. All churches which remain grievously separated from one another bear witness to their incompleteness. The situation has been exacerbated over five long centuries in Western Europe because 'for better or for worse, the fact is that since the reformation each tradition in the west – Catholic or Calvinist, Lutheran or Anglican – has lived its life, ordered its affairs, arranged its understanding of the gospel, without waiting on agreement or permission from the rest'.[43] The fragmentation of Christendom requires that all traditions shall acknowledge their provisionality and incompleteness – and carry the tension and the travail in their souls.[44]

The Anglican theological method equips the church to carry the tension and the travail with integrity. This method has been associated in the popular mind with the *via media*. But 'the *via media* is not a compromise; it is a living theological system fashioned in the crucible of sixteenth century religious life; holding the tension between Romanism and Calvinism'.[45] Indeed, it has been described as being in its origin 'a narrow way of suffering and tears'.[46]

It is, however, peculiarly vulnerable to certain predicaments. The emphasis in the post-reformation period upon continuity in apostolic faith has led to the assumption that the Church of England lacks theological clarity, doctrinal definition, because it appears to do little more than carry forward the teaching of the early fathers, the tradition of the primitive church. 'It is a major and central feature of modern Anglican apologetic to deny that Anglicans have special and distinctive doctrines of their own.'[47]

There is also the absence of a systematic theological tradition. It has been both the strength and weakness of Anglicanism that there has been no counterpart to the theological systems of Aquinas, Luther or Calvin in the light of which all subsequent developments might be tested. One consequence is that 'Anglican theology has been essentially *occasional*. Theologians have spoken because they were moved by the needs of the moment – to meet this attack, to defend that line of action; they have spoken because events themselves have cried aloud for theological interpretation'.[48]

The diversity of interpretation permitted within the church suggests to some both ambiguity in matters of faith and a lack of intellectual rigour, as responsible traditions of comprehension and liberality degenerate from time to time into a 'lazy comprehensiveness'.[49]

There are finally questions that must properly be asked concerning authority within Anglicanism. The development of the Church of England and the evolution of the Anglican

Communion have both seen great emphasis placed upon a dispersal of authority with all the checks and balances which such a dispersal implies. Traditions of independence and interdependence live alongside each other.

The constitutional framework of establishment has assisted the Church of England in earlier generations in keeping open the idea of a church which exists for the sake of those who do not belong. This constitutional relationship will survive while it is desired by church and state; but the church's understanding of public ministry will be determined primarily by its understanding of the gospel. There is an urgent need for Anglicans to think through their way of being the church and to provide a coherent ecclesiology. The resolution of the dilemma – to be an institution or a sect – will be determined so far as the Church of England is concerned by the seriousness with which it is willing to rediscover its traditions of comprehension and liberality.

There are hidden strengths in the Anglican theological method which enable the church to pursue its work with integrity. The doctrinal formularies of the church speak unequivocally of a trinitarian faith, of an incarnational Christology, of redemption through the death and resurrection of Jesus. These are the all-important boundary markers, even though the way in which the church understands and speaks of these mysteries of faith continues to evolve. But there is a reluctance to inhibit the development of the tradition by dogmatic pronouncements. The Report of the Doctrine Commission of the Church of England, *Believing in the Church : The Corporate Nature of Faith*, urged that 'doctrine should be authoritatively defined as little and seldom as possible'.[50]

It is here that some awareness might be found of what provisionality and incompleteness mean for the Church of England. 'A church which still values establishment, in the sense of a conscious responsiblity for the nation, must inevitably express its beliefs more by implication than by explicit confessional formularies and be singularly disinclined to excommunicate or deprive for heresy'.[51] There is implicit in its commitment to the freedom of scholarship an expectation that the theological tradition shall remain open to the world and to the insights of so-called secular learning.

It was the achievement of the Church of England in the post-reformation period to steer a middle course between 'the rival dogmatisms of Geneva and Rome'.[52] It continues to set its face against the absolute claims that are made by some churches and some traditions of faith and experience. But this is not a complacent commitment to the *via media* It is, rather, an acknowledgement that the church is always called to be a church *in via*.

There is an understanding of the church within the Anglican tradition which is implicit in the importance that is attached to the scriptures, the dominical sacraments, the creeds, the orders of ministry, the prayer books, the articles of religion and the canons. It is an undemonstrative ecclesiology but it incorporates significant elements. It affirms the authority of the church to determine its faith, or – to be more precise – 'to define what is a sufficient statement of the Christian faith.'[53] It acknowledges the importance of the episcopate in the custodianship and the interpretation of the tradition. It builds into its corporate life the tension between episcopal and synodical authority by securing the active engagement of bishops, clergy and lay people in the ordering of its affairs. It makes provision for the dispersal of authority and – not the least of its virtues – it acknowledges that the development of the tradition requires recognition and consent.

It is in the drawing together of all these things that Anglicanism finds its identity as an authentic interpretation of the catholic tradition. There is pain in the containment of the paradoxes with which the church is required to live. But it may be that these disparate traditions of freedom within a framework of faith and order assist the church as the established church in remaining serviceable, accessible, evocative, worthy of respect and tolerant.

There is a continuing tension between authority and freedom in the wider world. Secular communities are struggling to come to terms with the changing meaning of unity and

diversity. Individuals are mindful of their personal autonomy. There is an experience of God – of religion – that is
tentative, hidden, fragmented, evasive. A church that lives
with these things *and is glad to do so* may yet find that it has
'a broad and living way open to it, into the hearts of the
people'.[54] Only the wounded healer heals! Bonhoeffer's plea
that God shall be found at the centre of life[55] is one that the
Church of England should be supremely well qualified to
understand. It requires, nonetheless, a practical outworking
in a thoughtful, passionate, worldly holiness. 'It is only by
living completely in this world that one learns to believe ... I
mean by worldliness – taking life in one's stride, with all its
duties and problems, its successes and failures, its experiences and its helplessness. It is in such a life that we throw
ourselves utterly into the arms of God'.[56]

But catholicism and reformation, comprehension and
liberality, require a wide interpretation. Something of what
this might mean was envisaged early in this century by the
Free Church theologian, P.T. Forsyth. 'The day of the sects is
over. The day of the denominations is passing. The
commanding church idea returns. We look forward to an
ecumenical Christianity composed not of national churches
but of national types of Christianity; and, within each
national type, a variety of cohesive and co-operant bodies,
which shall be ... at least as much concerned about their
unity as about their variety.'[57] This prophetic statement has
not been realised, but the Church of England chooses today
to pursue its national responsibilities in co-operation with
other churches. No discussion of a continuing establishment
can fail to take account of ecumenical hopes and possibilities.

It is necessary to acknowledge how much the Church of
England has been influenced by catholic and protestant
traditions – theological, pietistic, evangelistic – over the
centuries. But the ecumenical possibilities include an increasingly important international dimension. There is a balance
to be held because 'the church ... finds its truest life, its
catholicity, only if it is rooted both in the culture of its own

country and also transcends that culture in unity with Christians of other cultures and nations.[58]

Catholicity and ecumenicity require that all churches shall take account of 'the wholeness and the world-wideness of the church and the gospel'.[59] The authority of the Anglican tradition must be tested ultimately by the authority of the Christian tradition. Ecumenical discussions will continue to run their course. The Anglican Communion will discover if it is able to find greater theological coherence and appropriate structures for consultation and decision making. The Church of England has proved itself well able to accommodate a variety of cultural and national strands. The continuing evolution of the Church of England will require a continuing awareness of the significance of ecumenism and of the place of the Anglican Communion as an international communion of faith.

Any study of church and state, especially from the standpoint of the western world, is bound to leave open large questions concerning the ways in which the various patterns of engagement might develop. There are so many imponderables. Churches have been abandoned in earlier centuries in areas of the world where they have previously been privileged and powerful. The militancy of Islam throughout the world, and in particular the incursions of Islam in Western Europe, may yet have profound consequences for the church's self-understanding and its relation to the state. This century has been an age of great expansion for the church in the third world, and it is impossible to know what the consequences might be in the long term if the initiative in taking forward the life of the church should pass to the nations of Africa and Asia and Latin America. The church is a community of faith whose developing life lies hidden in the purposes of God.

The numerical weakness of the church in Western Europe, and not least of all in England, gives cause for concern. There is a long-standing tradition of indifference, of conscious or unselfconscious secularism. The influences at work in society at large appear to demand that the churches should identify themselves increasingly by their separation from the world. Experience, movement, sect, institution – and even empire – are still the directions in which the church might be drawn at any time as pressures from without or within determine the ways in which it moves forward.

The establishment of Church of England is one of the peculiarities of English life, but it continues to represent something that is important in the life of church and nation. It is able to embody and to articulate the religious dimension which a secular age has not yet totally discarded. It acknowledges the varying degrees of association that people want with the church and are capable of sustaining. It constitutes one of the elements of stability, of continuity, in the nation's story.

Any discussion of church and state is bound to isolate one aspect of church life, but the changing forms of church-state relationships represent serious attempts to give practical and public expression to the relation of Christianity to the whole of life. 'What Christians do, collectively and individually, in the world, and for it, depends upon their working idea of what the world is and of how it is related to God.'[60] Patterns of ministry that are rooted in the life of the local community presuppose an awareness of God in his creation. Patterns of ministry that are related to institutions and individuals, without regard to church membership and church attendance as prior conditions of ministry, presuppose a commitment to the transcendent dimension of grace in all situations and relationships. The wider frame of reference that is provided by a continuing establishment in England enables the church to interpret its primary commitment to catholicism and reformation with generosity and courtesy as it offers public ministry in a spirit of comprehension and liberality. Such a church might be accounted serviceable, accessible, evocative, worthy of respect and tolerant.

The church will always carry within itself something of the ambivalence that is bound to determine the relationship of Christ's disciples to the things of this world. Jesus bore passionate witness to the sovereignty of God's kingdom and the church is called to be a sign of the kingdom. The church will continue to wrestle with what it means to be a community of faith. The paradox of being the church in the world requires the church to take its place in all the structures and relationships and experiences of life – humbly, confidently, gladly – and yet to look for the age that is to come.

NOTES

1 W.E. Gladstone, *A Chapter of Autobiography*, London 1868, p. 7.
2 W.E. Gladstone, *The State in its Relations with the Church*, John Murray 1838.
3 Peter Brierley, *Christian England*, MARC Europe 1991.
4 Ibid.
5 Figures for 1931, 1951 and 1971 were for the total number present on the census night. The corresponding figures were not available when this table was compiled. The figure shown for 1991 is the mid-year estimate for the normally-resident population from OPCS converted to diocesan areas using the 1981 census base.
6 The lowering of the age from 18 to 17 years in 1957 and from 17 to 16 years in 1980 means that these figures are not directly comparable with each other.
7 These figures represent the normal Sunday attendance at all services for adults and children.
8 As from 1978 returns have specified infant baptism as pertaining to those under 1 year of age.
9 These figures refer to marriages solemnized in the Church of England and the Church in Wales as a percentage of all marriages in England and Wales.
10 H.H. Henson, *Disestablishment: The Charge Delivered at the Second Quadrennial Visitation of his Diocese, together with an introduction*, Macmillan & Co, 1929, p. 43.
11 *Church Statistics (1994): Some Facts and Figures about the Church of England*, Published by the Central Board of Finance.
16,303 Anglican churches, excluding cathedrals, extra-parochial and private chapels, and peculiars.
12 Ibid.
10,817 clergy-bishops, priests and deacons – in full time stipendiary ministry.
This figure reflects the number at the 31st December 1993. There were also at that date 849 ordinands in training for stipendiary ministry at theological colleges and on courses.
13 *Numbers in Ministry (1994)* Advisory Board of Ministry, GS Misc. 434.
1563 licensed non-stipendiary and local non-stipendiary clergy.

This figure reflects the numbers at the 31st December 1993. There were also at the 31st December 1993 283 ordinands in training for non-stipendiary ministry at theological colleges and on courses.

14 *Church Statistics (1994)*.
This figure reflects the number at November 1994.
15 *Numbers in Ministry (1994)*
256 accredited stipendiary and non-stipendiary lay ministers.
16 *Church Statistics (1994)*.
This figure reflects the numbers at the 31st December 1993. There were also at that date 1620 candidates in training for ministry.
17 Church Statistics (1993).
18 *A Survey of British Attitudes* (1992), Cited by Archbishop Habgood in an interview in *The Observer*, 11th April 1993.
19 Owen Chadwick, *The Link Between Church and State*, Essay published in Donald Reeves (Editor), *The Church and the State*. Hodder and Stoughton 1984, p. 41.
20 John Habgood, *op.cit.*, p. 78.
21 John Baillie, *op.cit.*, p. 35.
22 W.E. Gladstone, *A Chapter of Autobiography*, London 1868, p.7.
23 2 Corinthians iv 7
24 John Habgood, *op.cit.*, p. 75.
25 Leslie S. Hunter, *op.cit.*, p. 52.
26 Adrian Hastings, *Church and State: The English Experience*, University of Exeter Press 1991, p. 36.
27 Alan Wilkinson, *Dissent or Conform? War, Peace and the English Churches 1900–1945*, Chapter 2, SCM Press 1986.
28 Austin Farrer, *The Service of God*, Geoffrey Bles 1966, pp. 90–91.
29 W.H. Vanstone, The Stature of Waiting, DLT 1982.
30 Ronald H. Preston, *Church and Society in the Late Twentieth Century: The Economic and Political Task*, SCM Press 1983, p. 138.
31 Karl Rahner, *Mission and Grace*, Sheed & Ward, 1963, Vol. I. p. 36.
32 Ernst Troeltsch, *op.cit.*, Vol. II. p. 1008.
33 P.T. Forsyth, *op.cit.*, p. 237.
34 Robin Gill, *Prophecy and Praxis*, Marshall Morgan and Scott 1981, p. 20.
35 Ibid.
36 T.S. Eliot, *The Idea of a Christian Society*, Faber & Faber 1939, p. 49.
37 Ibid.
38 Ibid.
39 12 & 13 William III. c.2.
40 Lord Falkland, Cited by *The Times*, 12th February 1994.
41 P.T. Forsyth, *op.cit.*, p. 122.
42 Ronald H. Preston, *op.cit.*, p. 135.
43 Nicholas Lash and Eamon Duffy, Article in the *Tablet*, 15th May 1993.
44 'The credentials of Anglicanism are its incompleteness with the tension and the travail in its soul'. (Archbishop Michael Ramsay).

45 J.H. Jacques, *Confessional Theology and the Anglican Church*, Article in *Theology*, March 1944, p. 52.
46 R. Cant, Letter to *Theology*, (Re. *Confessional Theology and the Anglican Church*), May 1944, p. 112.
47 Stephen Sykes, *Anglicanism and the Anglican Doctrine of the Church*, Anglican Theological Review, Supplementary Series, Number 10, March 1988, p. 157.
48 R. Cant, *op.cit.*, p. 111.
49 Peter Cornwell, *Church and Nation*, Basil Blackwell 1983, p. 84.
50 Report of the Doctrine Commission of the Church of England, *Believing in the Church: the Corporate Nature of Faith* (1981), p. 144.
51 Ibid., p. 148.
52 R. Cant, *op.cit.*, p. 112.
53 Stephen Sykes, *op.cit.*, p. 161.
54 W.E. Gladstone, *A Chapter of Autobiography*, London 1868, p. 7.
55 Dietrich Bonhoeffer, *Letters and Papers from Prison*, SCM 1971.
56 Ibid., p. 370.
57 P.T. Forsyth, The Church and the Sacraments, 1917, Cited Alec Vidler, *The Orb and the Cross*, SPCK 1946 p. 104.
58 Victor de Waal, *The Two Kingdoms*, Essay in Donald Reeves (Editor), *The Church and the State*, Hodder and Stoughton 1984, p. 58.
59 David Jenkins, *Affirming Catholicism*, Spring 1993.
60 Richard A. Norris, *God and World in Early Christian Theology*, A & C Black 1966, p. 1.

Bibliography

Anderson, Paul B., *People, Church and State in Modern Russia*, SCM Press 1944.

Arnold, Thomas, *Principles of Church Reform*, London 1833.

Augustine of Hippo, *De Civitate Dei*. A select Library of the Nicene and Post-Nicene Fathers of the Christian Church, Edited by Philip Schaff, Wm. B. Eerdman Publishing Company. Michigan 1973.

Baillie, John, *What is Christian Civilization?*, University of Durham: Riddell Memorial Lecture, OUP 1945.

Bainton, Ronald H., *The Religion of the Sixteenth Century*, Hodder and Stoughton 1963.

Barker, Ernest, *Introduction* to Gierke Otto, *National Law and the Theory of Society: 1500–1800*, CUP 1934.

Barth, Karl, *Church and State*, Trans. by G.R. Howe, SCM Press 1939.

Barth, Karl, *The German Church Conflict*, Lutterworth Press 1965.

Beeson, Trevor, *Discretion and Valour*, Fontana Books 1974.

Benson, Patrick, *Church Confrontations with the State during Kenya's Nyayo Era. 1982–1991: Causes and Effects*. A Thesis submitted to the Open University for the degree of Master of Philosophy, March 1993.

Bindoff, S.T., *Tudor England*, Penguin Books 1951.

Bonhoeffer, Dietrich, *Sanctorum Communio*, Collins 1963.

Booty, John E., *John Jewel as Apologist of the Church of England*, SPCK 1963.

Bourdeaux, Michael, *Patriarch and Prophets*, Praeger Publishers 1970.

Bourdeaux, Michael, *Gorbachev, Glasnost and the Gospel*, Hodder and Stoughton 1990.

Brunner, Emil, *Christianity and Civilization*, Volumes I and II, Gifford Lectures 1947 and 1948, Nisbet & Co., 1948 and 1949.

Brunner, Emil, *The Misunderstanding of the Church*, Lutterworth Press 1952.

Chadwick, Henry, *The Early Church*, The Pelican History of the Church, Volume I, Penguin Books 1967.

Chadwick, Henry, *Church Leadership in History and Theology* (March 1989); *Some Theological and Historical Considerations* (April 1992). Papers prepared for the Working Party on Senior Church Appointments established by the Standing Committee of the General Synod of the Church of England.

Chadwick, Owen, *The Reformation*, The Pelican History of the Church, Volume III, Penguin Books 1964.

Chadwick, Owen, *The Victorian Church*, Volumes I and II, Adam and Charles Black 1966 and 1970.

Chadwick, Owen, *The Christian Church in the Cold War*, The Penguin Press 1992.

Church, R.W., *On the Relations Between Church and State*, An Article reprinted from the Christian Remembrancer, April 1850, Macmillan & Co. 1899.

Church, R.W., *On Some Influences of Christianity Upon National Character*, Macmillan 1873.

Collinson, Patrick, *Archbishop Grindall 1519–1583: The Struggle for a Reformed Church*, Jonathan Cape 1979.

Clements, Keith W., *What Freedom? The Persistent Challenge of Dietrick Bonhoeffer*, Bristol Baptist College 1990.

Cohn-Sherbok, Dan, and McLellan, David (Editors), *Religion in Public Life*, St Martin's Press 1992.

Coleridge, S.T., *On the Constitution of the Church and State*, William Pickering 1839.

Cornwell, Peter, *Church and Nation*, Basil Blackwell 1983.

Creighton, Mandell, *The Church and the Nation*, Longmans, Green & Co., 1900.

Dickens, A.G., *The English Reformation*, B.T. Batsford 1989.

Duffy, Eamon, *The Stripping of the Altars*, Yale University Press 1992.

Ehler, Sidney Z., *Twenty Centuries of Church and State*, Newman Press 1957.

Eliot, T.S., *The Idea of a Christian Society*, Faber & Faber 1939.

Figgis, J.N., *Erastus and Erastianism*, Journal of Theological Studies, Vol. II, October 1900.

Figgis, J.N., *Churches in the Modern State*, Longmans, Green & Co. 1913.

Figgis, J.N., *The Political Aspects of St. Augustine's City of God*, Longmans, Green & Co. 1921.

Forsyth, P.T., *Theology in Church and State*, Hodder and Stoughton 1915.

Garbett, Cyril, *Church and State in England*, Hodder and Stoughton 1950.

Gavin, Frank, *Seven Centuries of the Problem of Church and State*, Princeton University Press 1938.

Gill, Robin, *Prophecy and Praxis*, Marshall Morgan and Scott 1981.

Gitari, David M., *Let the Bishop Speak*, Appendix: *The Church's Witness to the Living God*, Uzima Press Ltd 1988.

Gitari, David M., *Church and Politics in Kenya*, Article published in *Transformation*, July–September 1991.

Gladstone, W.E., *The State in its Relations with the Church*, John Murray 1838.

Gray, G.F.S., *The Anglican Communion*, SPCK 1958.

Habgood, John, *Church and Nation in a Secular Age*, Darton, Longman and Todd 1983.

Hammond, Peter, *Dean Stanley of Westminster*, Churchman Publishing 1987.

Haigh, Christopher (Editor), *The English Reformation Revised*, CUP 1987.

Hastings, Adrian, *A History of English Christianity*, Collins 1987.

Hastings, Adrian, *Church and State: The English Experience*, University of Exeter Press 1991.

Head, R.E., *Royal Supremacy and the Trials of Bishops, 1558–1725*, SPCK 1962.

Henson, H.H., *Disestablishment: The Charge Delivered at the Second Quadrennial Visitation of the Diocese, together with an Introduction*, Macmillan & Co. 1929.

Henson, H.H., *Retrospect of an Unimportant Life*, Vol. I: 1863–1920, Vol. II: 1920–1939, Vol. III: 1939–1946, OUP 1942–1950.

Henson, H.H., *Bishoprick Papers*, Geoffrey Cumberledge: OUP 1946.

Herberg, Will, *Protestant Catholic, Jew*, Anchor Books, Doubleday & Co. 1966.

Hill, W. Speed (Editor), *Studies in Richard Hooker*, Case Western Reserve Univerity Press 1972.

Hooker, Richard, *Of The Laws of Ecclesiastical Polity*, 8 Volumes, 1594–1662.

Hunter, Leslie. (Editor), *The English Church: A New Look*, Penguin Books 1966.

Iswolsky, Helene, *Christ in Russia*, The Bruce Publishing Company 1962.

Jalland, T.G., *The Church and the Papacy*, SPCK 1944.

Jewel, John, *An Apology of the Church of England*, Ed. by J.E. Booty, Cornell University Press 1963.

Lietzmann, Hans, *A History of the Early Church*, Trans. by Bertram Lee Woolf: Vol. I, *The Beginnings of the Christian Church*, Lutterworth Press 1962, Vol. II, *The Founding of the Church Universal*, Lutterworth Press 1960: Vol. III, *From Constantine to Julian*, Lutterworth Press 1963, Vol. IV, *The Era of the Church Fathers*, Lutterworth Press 1960.

Lightfoot J.B., (Edited and completed by J.R. Harmer), *The Apostolic Fathers*, Macmillan 1926.

Lipset, S.M., *The First New Nation*, Heinemann 1964.

McAdoo, H.R., *The Spirit of Anglicanism*, A. & C. Black 1965.

Marshall, John S., *Hooker and the Anglican Tradition*, A. & C. Black 1963.

Maurice, F.D., *The Kingdom of Christ*, SCM Press 1958, 2 vols.

More, P.E. and Cross F.L. (Editors), *Anglicanism: The Thought and Practice of the Church of England Illustrated from the Religious Literature of the Seventeenth Century*, SPCK 1962.

Munby, D.L., *The Idea of a Secular Society*, OUP 1963.

Nicholls, Aidan, *The Panther and the Hind: A Theological History of Anglicanism*, T. & T. Clark, 1993.

Nicholls, David, *Church and State in Britain Since 1820*, Routledge, Kegan Paul 1967.

Niebuhr, H. Richard, *Christ and Culture*, Faber and Faber 1952.

Niebuhr, H. Richard, *The Social Sources of Denominationalism*, Meridian Books: The World Publishing Company 1971.

Norman, E.R., *Church and Society in England 1770–1970*, Clarendon Press 1976.

Norman, E.R., *Christianity and the World Order*, BBC Reith Lectures 1978, OUP 1979.

Norris, Richard A., *God and World in Early Christian Theology*, A. & C. Black 1966.

Pollock, Bertram, *Church and State: A Review of the Report of the Commission on Church and State*, Eyre and Spottiswoode 1936.

Preston, Ronald H., *Church and Society in the Late Twentieth Century: The Economic and Political Task*, SCM Press 1983.

Ramsey, Michael, *The Anglican Spirit*, Ed. by Duke Coleman, Cowley Publications 1991.

Rawlinson, A.E.J., *Theology in the Church of England*. Article published in *The Genius of the Church of England*, Two Lectures given at the Archbishop of York's Clergy School, July 1945, SPCK 1947.

Rowell, Geoffrey (Editor), *The English Religious Tradition and the Genius of Anglicanism*, Ikon Productions 1992.

Rowlands, J.H.L., *Church, State and Society: The Attitudes of John Keble, Richard Hurrell Froude and John Henry Newman, 1827–1845*, Churchman Publishing 1989.

Reeves, Donald (Editor), *The Church and the State*, Hodder and Stoughton 1984.

Russell Anthony (Editor). *Groups and Team Ministries in the Countryside*, SPCK 1975.

Sabine, George H., *A History of Political Theory*, George G. Harrap 1957.

Sayers, Dorothy L., *The Church's Responsibility*. Paper published in *Malvern 1941: The Life of the Church and the Order of Society: Being the Proceedings of the Archbishop of York's Conference*, Longman, Green & Co. 1941.

Smyth, Charles, *The Church of England in History and Today*. Articles published in *The Genius of the Church of England*, Two Lectures given at the Archbishop's of York's Clergy School, July 1945. SPCK 1947.

Southern, R.W., *Western Society and the Church in the Middle Ages*, Penguin Books 1988.

Sykes, Norman, *The English Religious Tradition*, SCM Press 1961.

Sykes, Stephen, *The Integrity of Anglicanism*, Mowbrays 1978.

Sykes, Stephen W., *Anglicanism and the Anglican Doctrine of the Church*, Anglican Theological Review, Supplementary Series, Number 10. March 1988.

Stykes, Stephen and Booty, John (Editors) *The Study of Anglicanism*, SPCK 1988.

Temple, William, *Christianity and the State*, Macmillan 1928.

Temple, William, *Christianity and Social Order*, Penguin Books 1942.

Troeltsch, Ernst, *The Social Teaching of the Christian Churches*, Trans. by Olive Wyon, 2 Vols., George Allen & Unwin 1931.

Vidler, Alec R., *The Orb and the Cross*, SPCK 1946.

Vidler, Alex R., *Religion and the National Church*. Essay published in Alec R. Vidler (Editor), *Soundings*, CUP 1963.

Walsh, John; Haydon, Colin; and Taylor, Stephen (Editors), *The Church of England, c.1689–c.1833: From Toleration to Tractarianism*, CUP 1993.

Warren, Allen (Editor), *A Church for the Nation: Essays on the Future of Anglicanism*, Gracewing Fowler Wright Books 1992.

Wickham, E.R., *Church and People in an Industrial City*, Lutterworth Press 1962.

Wilkinson, Alan, *The Church of England and the First World War*, SPCK 1978.

Wilkinson, Alan, *Dissent or Conform? War, Peace and the English Churches*, 1900–1945, SCM 1986.

Index

The Index is comprehensive with regard to names but necessarily selective with regard to subjects. The chapter headings indicate the sections of the book where appropriate material might be found relating to the history of the Christian Church in the ancient and medieval periods, and to the Church of England.

Alexander, III, Pope 55, 58
Alternative and Other Services
    Measure (1965) 198–9
Ambrose, Bishop of Milan 33,
    40–42, 43, 45, 47
Andrewes, Lancelot, Bishop of
    Winchester 84, 96–98, 101
Anglican Communion 211, 239,
    244
Anselm, Archbishop of
    Canterbury 68
Apologists, The 21–22, 87
Apologia Ecclesiae Angelicanae
    (Jewel) 85
Arnold, Thomas 115–116,
    117–118
Articles of Religion, The Thirty-
    Nine (1571) 76, 84, 123
Aquinas, Thomas 56, 86, 240
Arianism 27, 44
Augustine, Bishop of Hippo 29,
    38, 40, 42–43, 45, 47, 53, 87,
    209
Augustine, Archbishop of
    Canterbury 67
Ausculta Fili, Papal Bull (1301)
    60
Avignon 61

Babylonish Captivity 61
Barnabas, Epistle of 36
Basel, Council of 61
Baxter, Richard 116
Bede 67
Benson, Edward White,
    Archbishop of Canterbury
    118
Bologna, Concordat of (1516)
    136, 137
Boniface VIII, Pope 58, 59, 60,
    62
Books of Common Prayer 78,
    84, 85, 86, 123, 198, 199, 201,
    222
Butler, Joseph, Bishop of Durham
    98

Calvin, John 70, 240
Calvinism 88, 95, 99, 240
Cambridge Platonists 98
Catherine the Great, Empress of
    Russia 157
Catholic Emancipation 100,
    110
Catholic Recusancy 81, 107,
    229
Chalcedon, Council of (451) 27

Charlemagne, Emperor   46,
50–52, 53, 55, 68, 75, 94, 135,
136
Charles I, King of England   108,
234
Church in –
  Africa   244
  Asia   244
  Austria   136
  France   136–7
  Eastern Europe   215
  Kenya   141, 174–189
  Latin America   215, 244
  North Africa   42, 50
  Poland   137–8, 167
  Russia   135–6, 141,
  156–172
  Scotland   139–140
  South Africa   215
  Spain   136
  Sweden   138–9
  United States of America   141,
  143–154
  Wales   118, 119
Church, R.W., Dean of St Paul's
122, 196–7
Church and State, Report of
Archbishops' Commission (1916)
197
Church and State, Report of
Archbishops' Commission (1970)
140, 199–200, 209
Church Assembly   127, 198
Clapham Sect   99
Clement of Rome, Pope   17
Clement, First Epistle of   36
Clement VII, Pope   72
Cluny   56
Codex Juri Canonici (1918)   62
Coleridge, Samuel Taylor   114
Colonna, Egidius   58
Concordat   136–8
Constance, Council of (1414–18)
61
Constantine, Roman Emperor
xi, 4, 25–30, 39, 49, 55, 75, 77,
94, 135, 236

Constantinople, Council of (381)
27
Convocations   108, 197, 202
Cranmer, Thomas, Archbishop of
Canterbury   94
Cromwell, Oliver   108
Cromwell, Richard   108
Cromwell, Thomas   73
Crown Appointments
Commission   111, 200

Dante   61
Davidson, Randall, Archbishop of
Canterbury   118–9
De Civitate Dei (Augustine of
Hippo)   42, 50
Decretum Gratiani   58
Deists   98
Didache   17, 36
Diognetus, Epistle to   23, 24
Donation of Constantine   58
Donatism   27, 42
Donne, John   96, 98

Ecclesiastial History (Bede)   67
Ecclesiastical Jurisdiction Measure
(1963)   198
Edward VI, King of England   79
Eliot, T.S.   232–4
Elizabeth I, Queen of England
74, 75, 84, 85, 94, 107, 193
Enabling Act (1919)   111, 127,
198, 200
Erasmus, Desiderius   73
Ephesus, Council of (431)   27
Erastianaism   75
Essays and Reviews (1860)   101
Eusebius, Bishop of Caesarea
24, 135
Evangelicalism   99–100

False Decretals   58
Ferrar, Nicholas   96, 98
Feudalism   52–3
Fisher, John, Bishop of Rochester
75
Forsyth, P.T.   243

Gardiner, Stephen, Bishop of
Winchester 75, 76
Gelasius I, Pope 29, 40, 43–5,
53
Gitari, David, Bishop 178, 182,
183, 185, 186–7, 189
Gladstone, W.E. 115, 124, 218
Gorham Case 111, 196
Gregory VII, Pope 54, 56–7, 61,
62
Gregory IX, Pope 58
Great Schism 61

Henry VIII, King of England 71,
72, 73, 75, 78
Henson, Hensley, Bishop of
Durham 116
Herbert, George 96, 98
Hippolytus 19, 23
Hobbes, Thomas 62
Holy Roman Empire 46, 50, 52,
53, 56, 68
Hooker, Richard 81, 84,
86–95, 101, 107, 108, 115,
196

Ignatius, Bishop of Antioch 17
Innocent III, Pope 55, 58, 59,
62
Innocent IV, Pope 55, 58, 62
Investiture Controversy 54, 56,
136
Irenaeus, Bishop of Lyons 17,
20, 87
Islam 50, 244

James I, King of England 107,
234
James II, King of England 108
Jerusalem, Council of (c.49) 16
Jewel, John, Bishop of Salisbury
84, 85
John XXII, Pope 55, 60
John of Paris 61
John of Salisbury 57
Judaism 10, 15, 16, 38
Justinian, Code of 46

Justinian, Roman Emperor 30,
40, 45–7, 50, 55, 75, 94, 135

Keble, John 196

Lang, Cosmo Gordon,
Archbishop of Canterbury
118
Latitudinarians 98
Laud, William, Archbishop of
Canterbury 97
Laws of Ecclesiastical Polity
(Hooker) 81, 86–94, 108,
202
Leo III, Pope 50
Lollards 72, 99
Luther, Martin 70, 72–3, 240
Lutheranism 70, 88, 99
Lux Mundi (1889) 101

Magna Carta 68
Manichaeism 42, 44
Marsilio of Padua 61
Mary Tudor, Queen of England
79
Maurice, Frederick Denison 117
Methodism 99, 109, 140, 229
Milan, Edict of (313) 22, 25
Monasticism 37
Montanism 37
More, Thomas 75
Muge, Alexander, Bishop 178,
182, 183, 186
Mysticism 37

Newman, John Henry 100
Nicaea, Council of (325) 27, 28
Niebuhr, Richard 5, 146
Njoya, Timothy, Presbyterian
Pastor 182
Non-Jurors 108

Okullu, Henry, Bishop 182–3,
186
Orchard, Dr W.E. 126
Origen 21, 87
Oxford Movement 100

Parker, Matthew, Archbishop of
   Canterbury   84, 95
Paul, Apostle   7, 10, 16, 17, 18,
   19, 34, 87
Pelagianism   42, 44
Peter, Apostle   26, 28
Peter the Great, Emperor of
   Russia   136, 156, 157
Pole, Reginald, Archbishop of
   Canterbury   75
Powell, Enoch   126
Principles of Church Reform
   (1883)   115
Public Worship Regulation Act
   (1874)   111
Puritanism   81, 85, 86, 88, 95,
   107, 145, 150, 229

Ritual, Royal Commission on
   (Reports 1867–70)   111
Rome, Primacy of Bishop of   11,
   26, 28–9, 43–4, 50, 54–60,
   62

Settlement, Act of (1701)   234
Shepherd of Hermas   36
Shaftesbury, Lord   99
Simeon, Charles   99
Stanley, A.P., Dean of
   Westminster   116
Stephen, Martyr   7, 16
Summa Theologica (Aquinas)
   86
Supremacy, Act of (1559)   73,
   80
Synodical Government Measure
   (1969)   111, 199

Taylor, Jeremy   96, 98
Temple, William, Archbishop of
   Canterbury   118, 209
Tertullian   22–3
Test and Corporation Acts   100,
   110

Theodosius I, Roman Emperor
   26, 29, 41
Toleration Act (1689)   108, 109
Tome of Gelasius   44, 45
Tractarianism   99, 100–101,
   122
Trent, Council of (1545–63)   62,
   85
Troeltsch, Ernst   5, 232
Two Powers (or Two Swords)
   44, 53, 55, 58, 60, 61, 69, 134,
   136

Unam Sanctam, Papal Bull (1302)
   60
Uniformity, Act of (1559)   73,
   80
Urban Priority Areas, Report of
   Archbishops' Commission
   (1985)   228

Vatican Council, First (1869–70)
   62
Venerabilem, Papal Bull (1202)
   59

Warburton, William, Bishop of
   Gloucester   109
Weber, Max   5
Whitefield, George   99
Whitgift, John, Archbishop of
   Canterbury   84
Wilberforce, William   99
William of Ockham   61
Winnington-Ingram, A.F., Bishop
   of London   113
Worms, Concordat of (1122)   54
Worship and Doctrine Measure
   (1974)   111, 199
Wycliffe, John   72–3

York Anonymous   60–1

Zwingli, Ulrich   71